Norman A. Graebner, Ph.D., University of Chicago, is Professor of History at the University of Illinois. He previously taught at Iowa State University. Dr. Graebner has written widely on American politics and diplomacy of the 1840's and on contemporary foreign policy. His articles appear in such journals as *Current History* and *World Affairs Quarterly,* and he is the author of *The New Isolationism,* published by The Ronald Press Company.

EMPIRE
on the PACIFIC

A STUDY IN
AMERICAN CONTINENTAL EXPANSION

by

NORMAN A. GRAEBNER
UNIVERSITY OF ILLINOIS

THE RONALD PRESS COMPANY · NEW YORK

Library of Congress Catalog Card Number: 55-10664

PRINTED IN THE UNITED STATES OF AMERICA

To
Harriet and Brooks

PREFACE

This volume is an attempt to isolate and explore one particular facet of American expansion to the Pacific: the essential motivation that underlay the acquisition by the United States in the 1840's of a continental domain of specific contour whose western ocean frontage remains unchanged to the present. It is a study of the general expansive forces and the political considerations which determined the course and direction of the extension of the United States across the North American continent.

When James K. Polk entered the presidency in 1845, the United States had uncontested claims along the Pacific to only the relatively useless coast between 42° and the Columbia River. During his administration that frontage was broadened to include 1300 miles of shoreline encompassing Juan de Fuca Strait on the north and San Diego Bay to the south. National expansion in the 1840's was in essence not westward at all. It was a northward and southward movement along a coastline, and it is to be understood primarily in terms of specific objectives on that coastline.

Perhaps it is the previous emphasis on pioneers, the spirit of manifest destiny, or the power exerted by war on a reluctant Mexico that has clouded the role of the coast in creating the precise goals of American expansion. Yet none of these widely recognized forces suggests any inherent objectives except in the most general terms. American pioneers west of the Rockies occupied far less territory than the United States acquired. The aims of manifest destiny, to the extent that they were defined at all, went far beyond what the nation acquired. And the military victories of the Mexican War can be seen to have purpose only in that they exerted the diplomatic pressure which permitted the Polk administration to achieve what it alone regarded as the objects of the war.

What these traditional approaches overlook is the essential fact that the expansion of the United States was a unified, purposeful, precise movement that was ever limited to specific maritime objectives. It was the Pacific Ocean that determined the territorial goals of all American presidents from John Quincy Adams to Polk. From the beginning, travelers, traders, and officials who concerned themselves with the coastal regions had their eyes trained on ports. The goal of American policy was to control the great harbors of San Francisco, San Diego, and Juan de Fuca Strait. With their acquisition, expansion on the coastline ceased.

Previous historians, it is true, have detected a persistent commercial motivation in United States interests along the western coasts. Foster Rhea Dulles, for example, has developed the theme that Oregon and California were not ends in themselves, but rather a "point of departure" for an Asiatic commercial empire. Richard Van Alstyne has held that American expansion can be only partly explained in terms of a continental domain. Frederick Jackson Turner also took the broader view of American acquisitions on the Pacific Ocean, the mastery of which, he declared, "was to determine the future relations of Asiatic and European civilization."

But mercantile interests in the Pacific provided more than a contributing motive to American expansionism. They determined the course of empire. Maritime calculations first defined the objectives of American statesmen on the distant shore. Next, they augmented the strong inclination of British and American officials to seek a peaceful solution of the Oregon controversy. And, finally, they fused Oregon and California into one irreducible issue and created a vision of empire that encompassed both regions. The sea made the settlement of the Oregon question contingent upon the acquisition of California in the fulfillment of American purpose.

Historians have agreed generally that foreign policy has

played a relatively unimportant role in American presidential elections, especially in the nineteenth century. The successful employment of a foreign policy issue to appeal to the voter in a national campaign, however, can have serious repercussions for any executive who later must resolve that issue. Nowhere in American history is this more evident than in Polk's embarrassment over the 54-40 question during the Oregon crisis. California also became involved in domestic politics. Again the partisan ambitions which it generated threatened to undermine the purposes of the administration. England saved the president in the Oregon crisis; Nicholas P. Trist performed that function in the acquisition of California. In both episodes particularism triumphed over unrestrained nationalism.

Since the writing of history is a cooperative enterprise, it has become customary, and properly so, to thank those whose courtesies and whose contributions to the finished work have carried them beyond the call of duty. My indebtedness to librarians who have helped to make my research both efficient and pleasant is beyond measure. I am especially grateful to the staffs of the Library of Congress, the National Archives, the Pennsylvania Historical Society, the New York Public Library, the William L. Clements Library at Ann Arbor, the University of Chicago Library, the Chicago Historical Society, the Newberry Library, the Stanford University Library, and the Bancroft Library of the University of California. For permission to use his typescripts of several important manuscripts located at the Massachusetts Historical Society, I extend my appreciation also to Richard Van Alstyne.

Editors of the *Pacific Historical Review,* the *Journal of Southern History,* and the East Tennessee Historical Society's *Publications* have kindly extended permission to use materials which have appeared in their journals. Earle Ross, Paul Sharp, and Walter Johnson read all or portions of the manuscript and gave me the benefit of their knowledge and insight. My wife, Laura, has added her skillful editorial help, her ready suggestions, and the understanding of one who knows the problems of writing. Betty Lemley typed the entire manuscript with her customary efficiency and care. Many have left their impression on the completed work, but I alone assume responsibility for matters of interpretation and fact.

NORMAN A. GRAEBNER

Ames, Iowa
  May, 1955

CONTENTS

CONTENTS

EMPIRE
ON THE PACIFIC

Chapter 1

THE EXPANSIONIST SETTING: 1844

§ 1

On Saturday evening, February 19, 1848, there occurred in the city of Washington a simple drama with few characters, but of huge portent to the nation. Shortly after dark a tired, though lithe and vigorous, man of frontier qualities reached the capital. Scarcely two weeks before, he had left Mexico City and had moved quickly downward through mountain passes to Vera Cruz. Ten days later his ship, the *Iris,* discharged him at Mobile. From there James Freaner, the noted "Mustang" of the New Orleans *Delta,* hastened northward to his destination. He delivered two letters at the Washington home of Mrs. Nicholas P. Trist and then sought out the residence of the Secretary of State, James Buchanan.[1] In his baggage was the recently negotiated Treaty of Guadalupe Hidalgo.

This memorable document would shortly convey to the United States the Mexican provinces of California and New Mexico. It would, therefore, complete the process of American expansion to the Pacific which two years earlier had achieved its first notable triumph in the Oregon Treaty. This dual diplomatic success of the James K. Polk administration effected the consummation of but a single purpose. Together these two treaties carried the American title to a 1,300-mile frontage on the western sea, which included the harbors of Puget Sound, San Francisco, and San Diego.

That generation which elected Polk to the presidency built an empire to the Pacific. Whatever its immediate impulse, this conquest of the continent had foundations sturdily formed through half a century. War and diplomacy filled only the final stage. Earlier Americans had given that policy purpose as well as substance—rugged frontiersmen who had penetrated the most awesome wilderness of North America and sweaty pioneers pushing out along deepening trails, bringing American ways to the valleys of the Willamette and the Sacramento. These men, like transgressors, had found the way hard. More remote in space and time were dour Yankee seamen who cruised across the Atlantic horizon in a vast pincers movement of ten thousand miles in search of markets, sea lanes, and ports of call in the north Pacific. These men called to mind spacious harbors along Pacific shores and markets a hemisphere away—Java, Manila, Singapore, Canton, and Shanghai. Subjugation of the continent was a common endeavor, belonging neither to section nor party.

Thomas Jefferson's purchase of Louisiana, to Henry Adams "an event so portentous as to defy measurement," had implied that the United States would become a great continental power. Thereafter geographical predestination alone convinced numerous British and American writers that the nation would one day reach the Pacific. Some, indeed, had regarded the prospect with considerable pleasure.[2] Not until the forties, however, did the Americans approach the high point of their expansive power when they would propel the course of empire to its long-expected fulfillment.

The stage was well set. Polk's America was as restless as a caged leopard and as charged with latent energy. In twenty years the American people had broken tens of thousands of new acres to the plow. They had created new cities where a wilderness had held sway. From New England to Pennsylvania and reaching on into the Ohio Valley an industrial revolution was multiplying the productive resources of the United States. Previous uncertainty over the nation's future was rapidly crumbling before an unprecedented vigor and self-confidence. The forties were a spacious decade. From the radiating power of American industry and commerce and the strength of a pioneering movement the distant Pacific shores would not escape.

Individual enterprise created the first centripetal force. Afterward came group ambitions and national effort, terminating in the final triumphant progression of American arms from Monterey and Buena Vista to Contreras, Churubusco, and Molino del Rey. Many streams of adventure, political maneuvering, and administrative policy played a role in the growth of the republic. But the determining factor that charted the course of the American nation across the continent to the Pacific was the pursuit of commercial empire. Through every stage of this westward extension blew the west wind and resounded the crash of heavy surf on a bold and distant shore.

It was a forbidding coast that stretched and twisted from Juan de Fuca Strait to San Diego Bay. Through most of this length offshore mountain ranges crowded the narrow coastal plains or pushed them completely into the sea, leaving thread-like beaches hemmed by jutting cliffs. Only one river, the Columbia, reached deeply enough into the interior to become a maritime port. Nature had confined her lavishness in the creation of harbors along this shore line to three locations. At the Strait of Fuca she had severed the mountains completely, permitting the sea to inundate the vast reaches of Puget Sound with its myriad of islands, inlets, bays, and harbors.

Eight hundred miles to the south was the second cut, the Golden Gate. Here she had formed a harbor of hundreds of square miles behind the lofty outer ranges and created an access to the large inland valleys of the Sacramento and San Joaquin. Far to the south where the coastal range recedes from the shore, nature provided the third major port of the Pacific coast, San Diego Bay, formed by a long, low limb of land extending westward and northward to enclose the harbor's land-locked waters. Empire-building in the forties se-

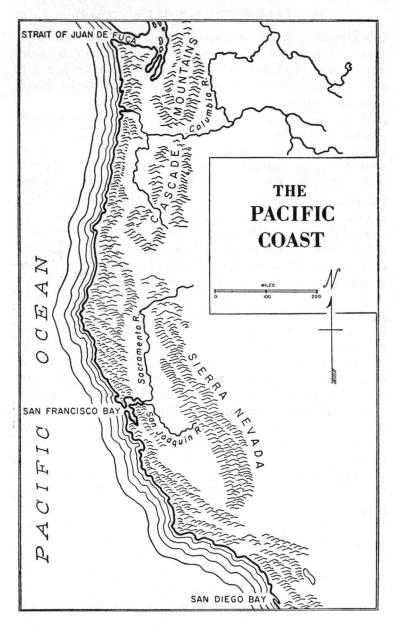

STRAIT OF JUAN DE FUCA

MOUNTAINS

Columbia R.

CASCADE

PACIFIC OCEAN

Sacramento R.

SIERRA NEVADA

SAN FRANCISCO BAY

San Joaquin R.

SAN DIEGO BAY

THE
PACIFIC
COAST

MILES

0   100   200

N

cured frontage on the western sea that encompassed precisely these three harbors, suggesting at the outset a large measure of commercial particularism in the underlying American purpose.

As late as 1844 only the sea gave real significance to regions bordering the Pacific. Over its trackless routes had passed Spanish, British, and American seamen who in a span of two centuries had carefully charted the coast's inlets and harbors. From that astonishing array of mariners loom such names as Juan de la Fuca, whose name appears gratuitously on a strait he never sailed, Sir Francis Drake, Pedro de Unamuno, Sebastian Vizcaino, James Cook, Robert Gray, and George Vancouver. Countless seamen had known this coast and had known it well before Meriwether Lewis and William Clark traversed the continent and stood breathless at the mouth of the Columbia. Yankee merchants had plied the coastal waters in search of sea otter and hides decades before American pioneers appeared in neighboring valleys. First love of Oregon and California was the broad Pacific; for New England seamen it was the tiny strip of coast hugging the sea.

Through fifty years Yankee mariners had anchored that strip to the larger world of the Pacific. Like the Spaniards who had sailed the famed Manila galleon, they had demonstrated the profitable and natural relationship that existed between the Pacific coast of North America and the great markets of the Orient. In the forties New England was invading the distant ocean with renewed vigor, but the transoceanic ties of the Pacific lay even heavier on the minds of commercial expansionists. What mattered was not the reality of that commerce in the mid-forties, but its unlimited future for that nation which could control the sea lanes of the north Pacific.

§ 2

Boston in 1844 was entering a new era of commercial greatness. Her teeming population, now surpassing the hundred thousand mark, still supported a volume of shipping second only to New York. Never before had her wharves been so congested, her harbor so crowded. During the thirties Boston had averaged fifteen hundred vessels a year; throughout 1844 her average reached fifteen a day. Few major markets of the world were excluded from her vast trading empire, but her contacts with the Far East still loomed high in her prosperity.[3] East-India merchants continued to enjoy a special prestige in New England seaport towns, and an office on Boston's India Wharf still conferred more distinction than ownership of a cotton textile mill.

Boston merchants had successfully invaded all key ports of Southeast Asia. At Canton the New England firm of Russell & Company conducted the bulk of America's share of the China trade. British goods pouring into the Orient after 1835 increased the competition for markets and reduced American sales. Thereafter United States imports of silks, teas, and coffee tended to create enormous trade balances against New England and New York merchants. The heavy British sale of Indian opium created a demand at Canton for bills of credit on London; these the American traders supplied.

China itself was assuming new commercial significance. After the First Opium War of 1842 the British forced China to open four additional ports to British vessels. Quickly President John Tyler dispatched Caleb Cushing, a Newburyport, Massachusetts, lawyer closely identified with the Canton trade, to China to secure like concessions for the United States. In the Treaty of Wanghia, which Cushing negotiated in 1844, American merchantmen gained admission to five Chinese ports, including Canton and Shanghai. This treaty broke the monopoly of the Hong merchants of China, a privileged class who held licenses to conduct that nation's foreign trade and serve as keepers of Canton's foreign community.[4] For years this group had harassed foreign merchants with annoying exactions and heavy port charges. This treaty marked the first time in six decades that United States trade with China had the benefit of American diplomacy. Suddenly to merchants, travelers, and politicians the markets of the Orient seemed staggering in their potentialities.[5]

Hawaii was a piece of New England in mid-Pacific. Boston merchants had linked the trade of these islands with California, Canton, and the south Pacific. "Honolulu," writes Samuel E. Morison, "with whalemen and merchant sailors rolling through its streets, shops fitted with Lowell shirtings, New England rum and Yankee notions, orthodox missionaries living in frame houses brought around the Horn, and a neo-classic meeting-house built out of coral blocks, was becoming as Yankee as New Bedford."[6]

New England merchants had brought Oregon into the China trade as early as 1787, when they commissioned Captain Robert Gray and the *Columbia* to visit the Oregon coast in search of sea-otter skins. From that moment the trade grew to impressive proportions almost purely by Boston enterprise. Looming large in Boston's success was the tough shipmaster William Sturgis, who entered the trade early. With John Bryant of Boston he formed the firm of Bryant & Sturgis, which revived and dominated the Northwest fur trade after the War of 1812. Until the thirties this high road of Boston commerce offered profits and adventure—rounding the Horn, bartering for fur in Oregon, trading for tea and silk in Canton.

This trade bound that stretch of coast from the Columbia to the Strait of Fuca to the hearts of Yankee seamen. By the forties the traffic had disappeared.[7] Hudson's Bay, the Northwest Fur Company, St. Louis fur traders, and Russians moving southward from Alaska created too much competition and drove fur prices too high. After 1837 only occasional New England ships skirted the coast in search of the disappearing skins. Boston's old Northwest trade was history, but its impact on the New England conscience persisted.

California likewise had captured the Yankee imagination. Long before the Mexican Republic opened these ports to world shipping, Boston vessels had frequented these coasts in search of sea otter. With the news of Mexican independence in 1822, Boston mercantile houses dispatched their ships to acquire California hides. Thereafter hides for the New England boot and shoe industry jammed the holds of returning Boston merchantmen.

Bryant & Sturgis entered the hide trade with their *Sachem* in 1822 and dominated it for the next twenty years. When Alfred Robinson, later to represent the company at Santa Barbara, arrived aboard their *Brookline* in 1829, the trade was firmly established. For another decade this house did a thriving business, keeping one or more ships active along the California coast at all times. In the twenty-year period Bryant & Sturgis exported about a half million hides, or about four fifths of the total.[8] The Bay State's exciting commerce with California, which quickly surpassed the dying Northwest fur trade in importance, stands commemorated in the pages of Richard Henry Dana's *Two Years Before the Mast.*

Whalers from New Bedford, Nantucket, and Martha's Vineyard, in pursuit of right whale oil, entered the north Pacific for the first time in the late thirties. Soon hundreds of vessels each year combed the area from the Oregon coast westward toward Kamchatka and the coasts of Asia and northward into the fog-bound seas beyond 60°. Their need for repairs, provisions, and fresh vegetables for scurvy-stricken crews sent them periodically into Hawaii or to the harbors along the Oregon and California coasts. These rough and oily "spouters," manned by hardy and enterprising New England whalemen, brought added importance to California's ports. Thomas O. Larkin, Yankee merchant of Monterey, predicted in 1844 that six hundred vessels would soon inhabit the whaling areas of the north Pacific and that "California from its proximity, salubrity of climate for sick seamen and other advantages, will be visited by many of these vessels. . . ."[9]

New England activities in the Pacific, covering fully five decades, had defined accurately a strip of coast still 150 days sailing time from Boston and New York. Yet that shore line

by the accident of geography lay opposite the cities and expanding population of the Mississippi Valley. In course of
time this hinterland would reach the Pacific and transmute
the coastal inlets and harbors into seats of great commercial
cities. In the mid-forties, however, that westward-moving seat
of enterprise and internal commerce still lay three months'
journey to the east.

§ 3

St. Louis in the forties was a pulsating river metropolis, a
mart on the Mississippi second only to New Orleans. Commercial activity along its levee filled travelers with wonder.
There in 1847 Philip Hone, the New York merchant, found
fifty large steamboats butted against the wharves, taking on
and discharging cargo over their bows. As far as the eye could
see, he recalled, the docks were piled high with barrels of flour,
bags of corn, hogsheads of tobacco, and the products of American industry soon to be lodged in the stores and warehouses of
the growing city. Along Front Street facing the river was a
range of limestone warehouses four stories high, and beyond
them several streets of wholesale and retail establishments,
shops of artisans and tradesmen, and new, elegant houses of
brick and stone. Although its thickly-settled portions were
confined to narrow limits, already the sprawling city stretched
five miles along the Mississippi and extended inland almost
three.[10]

St. Louis had a cosmopolitan air. On its crowded waterfront mingled a strange assortment of people—nattily dressed
businessmen, boatmen, draymen, laborers (white and black,
Irish and German), picturesque Spanish merchants bedecked
in gold-embroidered velvet, missionaries and priests, fringed
trappers, hunters, and French *voyageurs*. St. Louis had long
been the outpost of the trans-Mississippi frontier. Its lack of
refinement suggested the continuing nearness of the wilderness. For visitors in search of French cuisine the taverns were

a keen disappointment. One highly recommended establishment, recalled George W. Featherstonhaugh, the British geologist, in the early forties "was filled with vagabond idle-looking fellows, drinking, smoking, and swearing in *American*: everything looked as if we had reached the terminus of civilization; it seemed to be next door to the Rocky Mountains, and only one state from where we should find Nature in a perfect undress, and in the habit of eating her dinner without a knife and fork. . . ."[11]

This city stood at the apex of a vast triangle that opened westward, encompassing the area between the Missouri River reaching into Montana and the northern Rockies and the famed Santa Fe Trail stretching across the plains almost a thousand miles to the southwest. This was the great metropolitan center that called forth the enterprise, provided the resources, and reaped the profits from its great inland empire of trade and fur. It sent forth and recalled periodically to its dusty streets and crowded shops as hardy a group as any that ever invaded the West. Among them were men who had penetrated the most secret haunts of the distant mountains, who carried scars inflicted by Blackfeet and Crow Indians. Generally modest and unpretentious, they were scarcely conscious of the excitement they created. The colorful men who headquartered at St. Louis entered the councils of Thomas Hart Benton, feeding his expansionist ambitions, making him the United States Senate's leading authority on affairs west of the Mississippi.[12]

By the forties countless trappers, pushing out along the Arkansas, Platte, and Missouri, had pierced the successive ranges of the Rockies, crossed the deserts beyond, blazed trails through the Sierras (narrower than the Rockies but even more perverse), wintered at Monterey, and viewed the bay of San Francisco.

Such achievements came slowly. In 1826 Jedediah Smith, trapper extraordinary, had followed the Colorado River southward and westward around the Great Bend to the Mojave

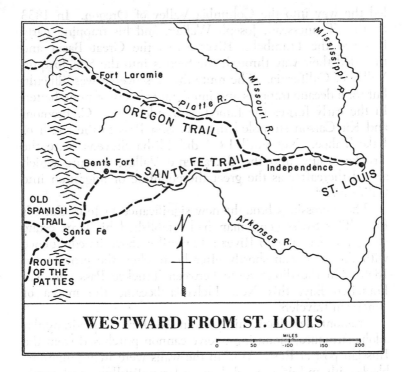

WESTWARD FROM ST. LOUIS

MILES

0   50   100   150   200

villages, and from there traversed the Mojave Desert into
southern California. Soon came the Kentuckians Sylvester
Pattie and his son, James O., across the southern deserts from
New Mexico, trapping along the Gila, tediously winding their
way to Santa Catalina Mission in Lower California, and reaching San Diego in the spring of 1828. Two years later another
resourceful frontiersman, Ewing Young of Tennessee, led a
party from Santa Fe to Los Angeles, opening the Old Spanish
Trail, which became the standard caravan route for the New
Mexico–California trade.

More significant for the future were new trails that entered
southern Oregon and northern California. During the decade
of the thirties, pioneers—trappers, missionaries, adventurers—

led the way into the Columbia Valley of Oregon. In 1833 another Tennessean, Joseph Walker, and his trapping party followed the Humboldt River across the Great Basin and threaded their way through the Sierras into the San Joaquin Valley of California. The route they discovered was difficult, but for a decade trappers and immigrants knew of none better. In the early forties the famed pathfinders John C. Fremont and Kit Carson stumbled upon Carson Pass to the south of Lake Tahoe. Not until 1844 did Elisha Stevens blaze the Truckee route into the Sacramento Valley, a route which served thereafter as the great thoroughfare of migration into California.[13]

These crossings brought new significance to John Sutter's fort. This Swiss gentleman had established his large estate along the Sacramento River a few miles above its confluence with the American shortly after he reached the province in 1839. On the direct route between Truckee Pass and San Francisco Bay, this New Helvetia became the mecca of American travelers.

Fremont described this post in 1844 as a quadrangular adobe structure, mounting twelve cannon purchased from the Russian post at Ross. Within the walls were living quarters, blacksmith and other workshops, a large distillery, and ample storehouses. Economic life at the post was intense and varied, for Sutter had forty Indians as well as thirty American, French, and German settlers in his employ. About the fort were thousands of horses, cattle, and sheep, "all in a thriving condition."[14] A schooner and a large two-masted lighter anchored below the fort attested to the wide range of Sutter's commercial activities, which reached as far as Fort Vancouver on the Columbia.

Each year growing numbers of Americans pushed into the coastal valleys never to return. In the vanguard were trappers who no longer found the fur trade profitable. Accustomed to life in the wilderness, they had no taste for the settled existence of the Mississippi Valley. Instead, many of these famed mountain men disappeared "in the direction of the setting sun, expending their remaining energies and final services in lighting the way and guiding the footsteps of the emigrant and the settler to the home they are seeking in Oregon and California."[15]

Hard on the heels of the trappers came the pioneers. After 1841 party after party ventured from the Mississippi Valley to regions beyond the mountains. By the mid-forties the tide of emigration formed a steady current across the plains. Pioneers arriving by river boat swarmed over the St. Louis waterfront, purchased supplies and equipment, and headed for staging areas to the west to organize for the long overland trek to regions near the Pacific. From Sutter's fort American settlers spread out along the lower Sacramento, converting it into an American valley. Diminutive settlements along the Columbia and Willamette in Oregon suggested also that Americans had come to stay. These settlers, like those who had ventured into Texas, could not move far beyond the focus of expansionist interest.

§ 4

The nation's mood was expansive. But in 1844 its continental ambitions were limited largely to the immediate frontier of Texas. For two decades pioneers from Missouri, Arkansas, Tennessee, and Louisiana, in creaking wagons or on horseback, had been streaming into that former Mexican province. As early as 1836 they had secured its independence from Mexico. Yet the Texas issue was not inherent in the American scene of 1844. The Lone Star Republic faced neither internal nor external crises, and many Texans appeared willing to continue their experiment in democracy. Texas became the central issue in the United States during the canvass of 1844 because of political scheming and ambition. The Democratic Party, in quest of victory, developed a remarkable affinity for the annexation question and dragged it into the political arena.

Texas fused within the party of Andrew Jackson two powerful streams of agrarian expansionism. Politicians around President Tyler, such as Duff Green, R. M. T. Hunter, and Thomas W. Gilmer, introduced the Texas question in 1843 and promoted it to the end. For them Texas was a new national interest which could be exploited to insure their hold on the South and to strengthen their political future. Annexationism remained for many Southerners a sectional issue—a program to expand the plantation system with its slave labor into the Southwest.

Texas would not long escape the attention of the great South Carolinian John C. Calhoun. At 62 he was approaching the end of a long, brilliant career. He was tall and erect, but appeared more gaunt, with large bushy eyebrows overshadowing his gleaming blue eyes. His long, coarse hair, brushed back from his high forehead, had turned snow white. Still the great master of comprehension and logic, Calhoun continued to spin out his extreme Southern doctrines on slavery and states rights.[16]

As Secretary of State in 1844 Calhoun began to promote Texas annexation with the sectional fervor expected of him. "I only ask the south to stand by me," he wrote while negotiating the Texas treaty in May. "Now is the time to vindicate and save our institutions." Everywhere Southerners shared Calhoun's ambitions. Texas was a question, wrote James Gadsden of South Carolina, upon which hinged "the very existence of Southern institutions." If Southerners proved recreant on this issue, he warned, they would remain "Hewers of wood and Drawers of water" for the North.[17] At Ashley, South Carolina, an aroused assemblage resolved that Congress admit Texas immediately or "proceed peaceable and calmly to arrange the terms of dissolution of the Union."

Southern Democrats hoped that Texas might even upset the old Van Burenite hegemony over their party and perhaps secure Calhoun's nomination in 1844. Virgil Maxcy admitted that the tariff issue alone was hopeless and that the annexation of Texas was "the only matter that [would] take sufficient hold of the feelings of the South."[18]

Texas soon slipped beyond the exclusive control of Southern politicians. Agrarian Democrats centering in the Lower Midwest, with allies in the Southwest and the East, gradually captured the issue, nationalized it, carried expansionism to its highest pitch of the decade, and rode into power on its emotional impact. These men cared nothing for the extension of slavery. They favored annexation, one was to observe later, "upon broad national grounds, elevated far above, and totally disconnected from the question of slavery."[19] In this struggle for power these nationalists added to Texas their own peculiar expansionist cause, the "whole of Oregon" issue, then sweeping the Old Northwest.

No single leader engineered this coup; it was a machine victory. Lewis Cass of Michigan, dark-faced and corpulent, a passionate advocate of expansion, stood near the head of the group. Far younger was the engaging Stephen A. Douglas of Illinois. Popularly called "The Little Giant," Douglas was herculean except for his lower limbs. He had broad shoulders, a deep chest, and a large and finely chiseled head set on a massive neck. More than any man of his generation Douglas was identified with Western causes. Others of the Old Northwest such as John McClernand of Illinois, Edward Hannegan and Jesse Bright of Indiana, and William Allen of Ohio gave this bloc distinction and power.[20]

Southwestern Democrats added force to this nationalistic crusade. Robert J. Walker of Mississippi contributed an effective pen and a small but active frame to the Texas cause. Tennessee's expansionists included the aged Jackson (who made Texas annexation his last national concern), Andrew Johnson, Lucien Chase, and James K. Polk. Ambrose Sevier of Arkansas joined Cass and Allen in the management of the expansionist program in the Senate.

Pennsylvania contributed her favorite son, the grave and dignified James Buchanan, to the movement. Daniel Dickinson and ex-Governor William L. Marcy of New York helped to round out the clique. The astute political management of these Democrats forced the Texas and Oregon issues upon the Baltimore convention of 1844, forestalled the ambitions of Martin Van Buren, and eventually secured the nomination of one of their own group, Polk of Tennessee.

Polk was no novice in public life. He had served fourteen consecutive years in Congress and two years as governor of Tennessee. He had long been a respected member of his party. Polk was slight in appearance, with small head, a full, angular brow, piercing gray eyes, a firm mouth, with hair worn long and brushed back behind his ears. He was a man of incorruptible personal honesty, an uncompromising Presbyterian, thoughtful and meditative, slow and measured in speech, methodical and industrious.[21] Although he was a dark horse candidate, his orthodox Jacksonianism made him acceptable to all factions of the Democratic Party. But with his election the new expansionist element rose to dominance over both the Democratic Party and the nation. Under Polk all reached new heights of power and influence, either in Congress or in the cabinet.

In 1844, under the compulsion of Democratic oratory and newspaper editorials, expansionism became fused with a "spiritual exaltation" (which E. D. Adams once attributed to America's conviction of the perfection of her institutions) from which evolved the new ideal called "manifest destiny."[22]

Jacksonian democracy had cast a spell over the land. Americans in the early forties viewed their political system with a Messianic consciousness, convinced that they held the future of republican government in their hands. Andrew Jackson in his Farewell Message asserted that Providence had selected the American people to be "the guardians of freedom to preserve it for the benefit of the human race."[23] Soon John L. O'Sullivan attached this democratic faith to the ideal of national expansion. "We are the nation of human progress," he charged in 1839, "and who will, what can, set limits to our onward march?" Americans possessed a mandate to spread throughout the world their four freedoms—"freedom of conscience, freedom of person, freedom of trade and business pursuits, universality of freedom and equality." To the Philadelphia *Democrat* the Anglo-Saxon race was "rich in the gifts of heaven," and destined to transmit to posterity its capacity for self-government.[24]

America's mission of humanity was not new, but the generation of the forties was the first to tie it to territorial extension. Early fears that expansion would subvert American institutions had been dispelled. New states had been added from the Louisiana Purchase without destroying the federal system of government. Robert J. Walker in 1844 perceived no visible limit to the safe expansion of American jurisdiction. "Our system of government," he wrote, "is one which, rightly administered,—administered on the principle of the States-Rights theory—will bear indefinite extension."[25] Similarly Douglas asserted in January, 1845, that "our federal system is admirably adapted to the whole continent." Indeed, to states-rights Democrats there was no better guarantee against federal consolidation than the addition of new states.

Agrarian expansionism was in part a defensive maneuver. Danger from abroad helped to focus both the Southern and Western drives for land on the region of Texas in 1844. In the reported efforts of Britain to thwart annexation, Western Democrats feared the establishment of monarchical tyranny on the American continent. Jackson in his famous letter to Aaron V. Brown in 1843 advocated extending "the area of freedom" into Texas to destroy British ambition and intrigue.[26] For the South, British abolitionism, once established in Texas, would comprise a special danger to Southern security and institutions. Gadsden believed annexation the most momentous question since the American Revolution. British policy, he wrote in May, 1844, "is enough not only to alarm us, but to awaken all our energies to stand firm to southern rights; & to resist at every peril all attempts to interfere with the institutions of the South. . . ."[27]

§ 5

Commercial America looked on, bewildered. As Whigs they possessed no dread of British encroachment; as conservatives they had no interest in the democratic emotionalism of the Texas issue. They recalled bitterly four futile years in power that produced little but the tariff of 1842, for Tyler had ruined their program. At last in 1844 they had anticipated a thoroughly Whig regime under their popular nominee and perennial leader, Henry Clay, but the appeal of the agrarians haunted them. Whig editors accused Democratic leaders of burying away the great domestic issues. Texas, they knew, was placing the Whig program in jeopardy, but as a party they stood firmly against the immediate acquisition of additional territory in the Southwest. To Southern Whigs the issue at stake was party unity; for Northern Whigs it was a question of sectional power.

For twenty years the most ardent opposition to the American system of tariffs and internal improvement had come from Southern Democratic leadership. Jeffersonian laissez-faireism was still the official program of the party, but Northern abolitionists and Whigs resented its Southern flavor. These two elements, both increasingly responsive to demands of Northern commercial and industrial interests, combined to oppose annexation on two counts: the expansion of slavery and the extension of Democratic power. The absorbing contest of the future was already clear. Would the agrarianism of the South and West or the industrialism of the East dominate national policy? Philip Hone saw clearly why the Texas issue was rocking the republic to its foundations. Southern demagogues, he wrote, were promoting their personal objects and those of the South by solidifying their power through the addition of four or five slave states.[28]

Joshua Giddings, the determined Ohio abolitionist, voiced in Congress and out the dual nature of the expansionist struggle: "Our tariff is as much an antislavery measure as the rejection of Texas. So is the subject of internal improvements and the distribution of the proceeds of the public lands. The advocates of perpetual slavery oppose all of them. . . ."[29] He demanded of New England and Pennsylvania Democrats why they would support annexation to see Texans in Congress destroy their tariff system. Would Western Democrats, he cried, willingly give up "their harbor improvements, and the improvement of our river navigation, for the purpose of improving the southern slave trade, and of perpetuating slavery in Texas?"[30] Giddings would force the parties to accept his doctrines or he would destroy them, building on their ashes a new political organization in tune with his America.

Southerners detected this incipient alliance between abolition and Whiggery. They recognized that Giddings was employing a highly emotional and moral question to bolster an economic program. Here was the combination of political appeals which might eventually destroy Southern power and bring the federal government under the control of Northern business. Ex-President John Quincy Adams, whose agitated voice in the House still cried out against the South, likewise represented this new threat. One Southerner believed the New Englander as dangerous to the South as "a mad incendiary in a powder house."[31]

In Texas and slavery, conservative Whigs detected an inescapable challenge to the permanence of the Union and their party. Frail but brilliant Alexander Stephens, the Georgia Whig, termed the entire annexation policy a "miserable political humbug" mounted as a ruse "to divide and distract the Whig party at the South."[32] Party division was merely the prelude to disruption of the nation. The *American Review* declared that no true American would calculate the value of Texas lands when the nation was in danger of destruction. Joseph Story, conservative Supreme Court justice, voiced his apprehensions for the future. Perhaps the present crisis would "soon be forgotten and forgiven by the people," he wrote to his son, "and we shall go on as we may, until by some convulsion we come to a full stop. When that will be I pretend not to prophesy; you may live to be a victim of it."[33]

At Lebanon, Ohio, Thomas Corwin speeded the time for his departure to the Senate in Washington. Few Whigs felt such devotion to their party and its program as did Corwin. Eloquent and learned, this stout, dark-complexioned, jovial conservative was one of the nation's most beloved politicians. Disheartened over Clay's defeat, he wrote to his close friend, John Crittenden of Kentucky: "What is to happen? What will the charlatans do next? Will they repeal the tariff and wage war on Mexico?"[34] Two prospects were distressing— a divided country and the demise of Whig ascendency. He wrote a note to his intimate friend and adviser, Oran Follett: "This terrible apprehension of consequences . . . disturbs me day and night, and I have resolved to hasten to Washington sooner than I otherwise would. . . . I shall endeavor to inform myself of the exact state of affairs touching this vital question as soon as I arrive at the Capital." The passage of the Joint Resolution did not absolutely insure annexation. A combination of Whigs and Northern Democrats, he wrote to Follett, might still "keep *in* the Tariff and keep *out* Texas."[35]

Texas had upset the conservative calculations. Dixon H. Lewis caught the new spirit of agrarian nationalism. "It is the greatest question of the *age*," he wrote, "& I predict will agitate the country more than all the other public questions ever have. Public opinion will boil and effervesce . . . more like a volcano than a cider barrel—but at last it will settle down with *unanimity* for annexation in the South & West & a large majority in the North." To Andrew Davezac, the New York Democrat, the issue was equally productive of change. "It has been the entering wedge," he admitted in July, 1844, "that has opened, both the ears and throats of my auditors every-where—from Baltimore to Buffalo."[36]

National expansionism in 1844 had drowned the fears of disunion, brought victory to the Democrats, and assured the annexation of Texas. But already the expansionist horizon was moving beyond Texas. Another parcel of pioneers had pointed to new regions beyond the mountains.

Where the Pacific swell broke along the western shores, two streams of expansion collided. Here the enterprise of Boston joined that of St. Louis, for both were cities of empire. From the configuration of that coast one element looked eastward toward the inland valleys for new lands to settle. The other scanned the western horizon beyond which lay new sources of wealth in the Orient.

In the United States, men of affairs contemplated the significance of American activity in those distant regions. For the Democratic agrarians such far-flung enterprise perpetuated the national outlook which had its inception in the Texas issue. When it encompassed regions beyond the Rockies, this agrarian nationalism produced the 54-40 crusade on the Oregon question and the "all of Mexico" movement of the Mexican War years. For the commercial Whigs, American objectives in the Far West remained particularistic. Geography had defined their goals precisely. The eventual shape of the American Republic would soon be hammered out in the conflict between these two expansionist forces.

Chapter 2

NORTH FROM THE COLUMBIA

§ 1

When James K. Polk entered the White House in March, 1845, the United States had no clear title, guaranteed by treaty, to frontage on the Pacific Ocean. Even its uncontested claims were limited to a wild fringe of land stretching southward three hundred miles from the Columbia River to the California border. Despite the rugged beauty of this coast, it was hardly inspiring to American commercial interests. It comprised a variety of rocky beaches strewn with half-hidden boulders hulking out of the surf, impermeable sand dunes, and trees twisted and deformed by the winds of centuries. Forested headlands, rising in the coastal range to the east, terminated frequently in forbidding cliffs which jutted precipitously from the sea. Nowhere along this shore was there a port accessible to even the smallest sea-going vessels. Few coves furnished anchorage even under the most favorable conditions of weather and season. The mouth of the Umpqua, its entrance hemmed by encroaching sand, was rendered useless by hidden dangers and a relentless surf.[1] After decades of maritime activity in Oregon, this coastal strip was almost as untouched as the day Lewis and Clark first sighted the Pacific.

This frontage alone had been conceded to the United States in 1845, and that by unwritten agreement. Jefferson's purchase of Louisiana had bridged the immense gap between the

Mississippi and the Pacific shores, but it left United States claims to a corridor west of the Rockies uncertain and inconclusive. By the Spanish treaty of 1819, which defined the Louisiana boundary, that nation conceded to the United States all claims above the forty-second parallel west of the Rockies. In 1818 the United States and Great Britain had negotiated the northern boundary of Louisiana along the forty-ninth parallel westward from the Lake of the Woods to the "Stony Mountains." Beyond the Rockies, however, the United States found itself in conflict with the expanding British Empire then pushing southward from western Canada with the Hudson's Bay Company in the vanguard. In the convention of 1818 the two contending powers agreed to leave the region equally and freely accessible for a period of ten years to the vessels and citizens of either nation without prejudice to their respective claims. In lieu of a territorial settlement, the negotiations of 1826–27 extended the principal of joint occupancy indefinitely, each nation obtaining the privilege of terminating the arrangement upon a twelve-month notice of such intention. As late as the forties Oregon was still held in this state of equilibrium by two empires struggling for mastery of the Northwest coast.

Early in the contest for Oregon both the United States and Great Britain put forth their claims to the region in vigorous terms, confident in the strength of their contentions. Through two decades of negotiation these respective claims changed imperceptibly. American diplomats assumed the position that Captain Robert Gray's discovery of the Columbia, the Northwest fur trade, the Lewis and Clark expedition, and the American Fur Company post at Astoria gave the United States prerogatives not only to the entire valley of the Columbia but also to the regions northward at least to the traditional boundary line of the forty-ninth parallel. Even the famed British explorer George Vancouver, they noted, readily admitted that Gray had discovered the mouth of the Columbia. Its course, without question, had been explored first by Lewis and Clark.

The waters of Juan de Fuca Strait and Puget Sound, conceded the Americans, had been explored gradually by Spanish, British, and United States navigators, but even in this region American diplomats claimed the Spanish rights and the pre-rogatives accruing from the fur trade. Astoria at the mouth of the Columbia merely added the right of prior settlement. Lastly, American negotiators insisted that the territory between the forty-second and forty-ninth parallels west of the moun-tains was a natural extension of United States possessions to the Pacific Ocean.

The British were far less sanguine, but hoped that by neutralizing the American claims of prior discovery, explora-tion, and settlement they could reduce the contest to a matter of actual occupation. The British, therefore, emphasized the early British explorations of the Columbia and the Strait of Fuca. They insisted, further, that the Spaniards had termi-nated their claims to the Oregon country in the Nootka settle-ment of 1790—that for the United States the Spanish rights were no rights at all. It was the British thesis that preten-sions based on discovery and exploration were at best confused and controversial and that Oregon should be divided on the basis of possession.[2]

For twenty years and as late as 1845 this remained a strong British position, for the entire region north of the Columbia had been continuously in the possession of the Hudson's Bay Company. Except for a few American trappers who ventured into the region during the 1820's, the British company, partner of the crown in the building of a North American empire, was the sole occupant of the entire area held in contention. Travelers in the forties estimated the number of Hudson's Bay employees at three thousand and described their situation as far stronger commercially and agriculturally than that of the American pioneers then in Oregon.[3] Hudson's Bay controlled a series of posts extending from Fort Hall and Fort Boise on the Snake River in eastern Oregon to Fort Walla Walla on the south bank of the Columbia, and along that river to Fort

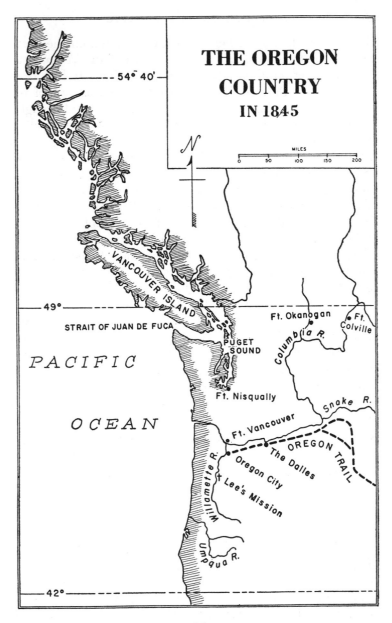

THE OREGON
COUNTRY
IN 1845

MILES

0   50   100   150   200

54° 40'

N

49°

STRAIT OF JUAN DE FUCA

VANCOUVER ISLAND

PUGET
SOUND

Ft. Okanogan

Ft.
Colville

Columbia R.

PACIFIC

OCEAN

Ft. Nisqually

Snake R.

Ft. Vancouver

OREGON TRAIL

The Dalles

Willamette R.

Oregon City

Lee's Mission

Umpqua R.

42°

George near its mouth. Fort Vancouver, located on the north bank of the Columbia opposite the mouth of the Willamette, was the chief Hudson's Bay post in Oregon. It had been established in 1825 by Dr. John McLoughlin as part of the process of overhauling the Columbia Department and strengthening the hold of the British on the entire Columbia Valley. Northward into Canada, Hudson's Bay was unchallenged. To Sir George Simpson, long-time company official and after 1839 Governor-in-Chief of American Operations, continued possession of the Columbia was essential for the maintenance of the British fur trade in Oregon. And the demands of the fur trade determined the objectives of British diplomacy.

While adamant on the Columbia line, the British gave up all pretensions south of that line even though the Hudson's Bay Company continued to maintain scattered posts in that region. George Canning, British Foreign Minister during the twenties, and other British officials pursued the principle that the concession of territory south of the Columbia would strengthen British claims to territory north of that river. Thus it was that United States claims to Oregon were unchallenged in that broad strip of land between the Columbia and the forty-second parallel. The American title to this region was not official for the sole reason that no American official would affix his signature to such an agreement. For the United States, such a division of the Oregon country was unacceptable because a settlement along the Columbia would not achieve the essential American objectives in the Pacific Northwest.

§ 2

Diplomacy could dispose of rival claims to Oregon only after it had resolved the deeper struggle for commercial position on the Pacific Coast. Behind the façade of diplomatic maneuvering on the basis of the prior rights of discovery, exploration, and settlement was the crucial drive for ocean front-

age—for a window on the sea as a "point of departure" for an
Asiatic mercantile empire. It was the struggle for commercial
supremacy in the Pacific that rendered the British proposal of
the Columbia unacceptable. Of those factors in American expansion which sought solution in the Oregon negotiations,
none appeared of greater concern to the people of the United
States than the disposition of Asiatic trade. From the beginning of the Northwest fur trade and commercial relations with
the Far East, American goals in Oregon had been fashioned
by the sea.

Since the days of Jefferson the common ambition of
American politicians and merchants in the Far Northwest had
been to find outlets for the exploitation of the rich commerce
of the Pacific. Jefferson's initial task was that of opening a
commercial route across the continent. What he asked of
André Michaux in conducting his western explorations was
that he "seek for and pursue that route which shall form the
shortest and most convenient communication between the
high parts of the Missouri and the Pacific Ocean." Again his
instructions to Meriwether Lewis in 1803 revealed his commercial purposes in unmistakable terms. "The object of your
mission," he charged the young frontiersman, "is to explore
the Missouri River, and such principal streams of it, as by its
course and communication with the waters of the Pacific
Ocean, may offer the most direct and practicable water communication across the continent for the purposes of commerce."[4] For Jefferson, as for those who followed him, the
great objective in continental expansion was the acquisition
of a passage through Oregon to the potential wealth of the
Orient. With the United States in possession of good ports
on the Pacific, predicted Francis Baylies in 1823, "the commercial wealth of the world is ours, and imagination can
hardly conceive the greatness, the grandeur, and the power
that await us."

To later travelers Oregon was likewise a key to the Pacific.
"Commercially," wrote John C. Fremont in 1844, "the value

of the Oregon country must be great, washed as it is by the north Pacific ocean—fronting Asia—producing many of the elements of commerce—mild and healthy in its climate—and becoming, as it naturally will, a thoroughfare for the East India and China trade."[5] John C. Calhoun, who accepted this conclusion uncritically, scarcely dared to estimate the magnitude of Oregon's future commerce. Opportunities in China, he prophesied, will "be followed in Japan, and all the eastern portions of the continent. These ports, like the Chinese, will be opened; and the whole of that portion of Asia, containing nearly half the population and wealth of the globe, will be thrown open to the commerce of the world and be placed within the pales of European and American intercourse and civilization."[6] Oregon, in short, offered strategic position on the shores of the Pacific.

But commercial expansionism did more than merely define American interests in Oregon. Its focus on ports guided American territorial objectives relentlessly northward from the Columbia. With increasing insistence, the writings of such leading authorities on the Pacific Northwest as Robert Greenhow, Thomas J. Farnham, Charles Wilkes, and Eugène Duflot de Mofras had convinced the representatives of commerce that the Columbia, although traditionally associated with the Northwest trade, was of questionable value as an ocean port. Their writings made axiomatic the dangers of the sand bar between Cape Disappointment and Point Adams, created by the vast quantities of sand carried down the Columbia and hurled back by the surf. "Mere description," wrote Wilkes, "can give little idea of the terrors of the bar of the Columbia: all who have seen it have spoken of the wildness of the scene, and the incessant roar of the waters, representing it as one of the most fearful sights that can possibly meet the eye of the sailor." Mofras, the noted French traveler, recalled the "hideous spectacle" of the bar, "with the foam cloaking the horizon far out at sea as if to form an insurmountable barrier to ships entering or leaving the river."[7]

During the winter months violent storms rendered the entrance all but impassable. These travelers reported that vessels often stood off the coast or inside the entrance for as long as two months awaiting a favorable opportunity for running the bar. Mofras's ship, for example, lay off the Cape for nineteen days secured by three anchors, unable either to ascend the river or beat out to sea because of the violence of the wind and current. Among the harbor's victims were several Hudson's Bay ships and cargoes and the United States warship *Peacock*. This record of destruction led critics of the Columbia to conclude that a greater proportion of men and ships had been lost entering this port than any other in the world.

In sharp contrast was their description of the Fuca Strait and the sea arms to the east of it. "No part of the world," wrote Farnham, "affords finer inland sounds or a greater number of harbours than can be found here...." Wilkes's description was equally glowing: "Nothing can exceed the beauty of these waters, and their safety: not a shoal exists within the Straits of Juan de Fuca, Admiralty Inlet, Puget Sound, or Hood's Canal, that can in any way interrupt their navigation by a seventy-four gun ship. I venture nothing in saying, there is no country in the world that possesses waters equal to these."[8] Here were the only harbors in Oregon that could be entered or left under any wind during any season of the year. This was the only region on the entire Northwest Coast that could control the waters of the north Pacific. Herein lay the primary objectives in Oregon of commercial America.

What was obvious to American expansionists in the forties had been accepted in principle by President John Quincy Adams as early as his Oregon negotiations of 1826. Adams, in search of a good naval base on the Pacific, had been convinced, perhaps by the letters of "Bill" Sturgis to the Boston *Daily Advertiser,* that Port Discovery was preferable to the Columbia for a United States naval base. That Adams clung to the forty-ninth parallel despite the pressure of Albert Gallatin, his negotiator, to concede to the British the drainage basin of the Strait is evidence of the value he placed on those waters. Yankee that he was, he viewed the controversy in the Pacific Northwest as primarily a struggle for ocean frontage. He vastly preferred to prolong the diplomatic stalemate rather than to allow Britain to endanger permanently American maritime interests in the Pacific. In his policy of containment toward England, Adams formulated the chief diplomatic tradition of the United States toward Oregon. As late as the mid-forties the demands of commercial America coincided with this historic position of United States diplomacy.

For the British two important streams of trade met in Oregon waters—commerce with the Orient and the fur trade of the Hudson's Bay Company. To British officials and traders, therefore, the Columbia River presented a watercourse of peculiar significance, furnishing both an ocean port and an access to the interior fur-bearing regions. Pressure from the Hudson's Bay Company held British officials to the Columbia boundary during the early Oregon negotiations, but increasingly British interests were shifting from the fur trade to the commerce of the Pacific.

Canning as early as 1826 was restive at the expansion of United States trade in the Far East, for British enterprise in that area was limited until the mid-thirties by the British East India Company monopoly. The British Minister anticipated keenly the day when Britain would compete on equal terms for the commerce of Asia. "Its fabled wealth," he wrote, "its teeming millions, its stores of teas, silks, and spices—all the elements that had once fired the mind of Marco Polo—were an invitation still held out to the West. The East was a golden market to which Britain would send, once the fetters of the East India Company had been broken, her surplus for exchange."[9] The real value of Oregon would become apparent, he predicted, when the China trade would be opened to British as well as to American commerce.

Giving evidence of this commercial motivation during the 1826 negotiations, Canning wrote that he would not care to have his "name affixed to an instrument by which England would have foregone the advantage of our immense direct intercourse between China and what may be, if we resolve not to yield them up, her boundless establishments on the N. W. Coast of America."[10] Keenly aware of the underlying competition for ports between the two powers in Oregon, he attempted unsuccessfully to quiet the American demand for 49° by offering a frontage of isolated territory on the Strait. Canning and Adams had defined the real issue in Oregon—the quest for ocean frontage.

Alphonse Pageot, French minister in Washington, also recognized clearly the maritime factor in the conflict. His writings reflect the concern of a neutral commercial power which viewed as momentous the struggle between England and the United States for control of the Oregon coast. "The commerce of the whole world in the Pacific Ocean," he wrote in November, 1843, "is going to acquire a development that will give to all places on its shores, susceptible of being used for ports of repair or of commerce, a considerable importance."[11]

With the gradual shift of British interests from the fur trade to Asiatic commerce, a new British policy toward the Northwest Coast was dawning. The Columbia as key to the fur trade was losing its importance, and its inadequacies as an ocean port were driving British maritime interests northward as it had those of the United States. Simpson complained in 1841 that the uncertainty in crossing the bar was "deranging the best laid plans, burdening the different branches of the business with very heavy shipping charges, and depriving us of the means of embarking in other branches of commerce, which might be carried on with great advantage, had we a depot eligibly situated on the coast."[12] Fort Vancouver, he warned, was no longer a satisfactory station for the West Coast trade. He recommended that it be replaced with an advantageous site on the southern tip of Vancouver Island.

Simpson's conversion to the requirement of a more northerly post was the one crucial alteration in British thought toward Oregon prior to 1845. Only a British surrender of the Columbia would make a peaceful settlement possible. And Wilkes's close examination of the Strait, Puget Sound, Hood's Canal, and the Gulf of Georgia in 1841 had convinced Simpson that the United States would never consent to any settlement which would bar the United States from these harbors.[13] At that moment the British position still appeared secure, for Hudson's Bay dominated the area in dispute. Until the United States could counterbalance British occupation, it lacked the force required to challenge the demands of Britain for the Columbia River boundary.

§ 3

Albert Gallatin anticipated the time when American pioneers would resolve the Oregon question. With remarkable foresight he had favored the postponement of a settlement in 1827 "until the the citizens of the United States shall have acquired a respectable footing in the country."[14] Throughout the thirties interest in Oregon dragged, however, and as late as 1842 American settlers in no way challenged Hudson's Bay for possession of the Northwest country. Yet Oregon never completely escaped the consciousness of the American people. During a dozen lean years the ground had been well prepared for the great migrations of 1843 and 1844 and a new burst of interest and enthusiasm.

Many factors after 1842 pointed the attention of a restless, energetic, pioneering people, recovering from years of depression, toward this distant land of promise. The early efforts of such Oregon promoters as Hall Jackson Kelley and Nathaniel Wyeth of New England, the often heroic response of such missionaries as Jason and Daniel Lee, Samuel Parker, Marcus Whitman, and Father Pierre de Smet to the call of the Northwest—these endeavors had brought only a few settlers to Oregon. As late as 1840, settlement in the Willamette Valley comprised just sixty families of missionaries, trappers, and

Canadians who had been employed by the Hudson's Bay Company. If the letters, editorials, addresses, and pamphlets of these enthusiasts had secured few settlers for Oregon, they had advertised the region fully.

Several other sources of information after the middle thirties fed knowledge of Oregon to the American people. Between 1837 and 1839 Congress received and published a series of reports on the region by William A. Slacum, a purser in the Navy, Caleb Cushing, and Dr. Lewis F. Linn of Missouri.[15] Secondly, a number of travelers' accounts published after 1835 helped to supply the growing demand for facts regarding the Pacific Northwest. Washington Irving's *Astoria* and his *Rocky Mountains* were followed in rapid succession by Zenas Leonard's *Narratives* (1838), C. A. Murray's *Travels in North America* (1838), Farnham's *Travels* (1839), and Greenhow's *Memoir . . . on the Northwest Coast of North America* (1840).

These accounts pointed to the general agricultural attractiveness of certain portions of Oregon, especially that of the Willamette Valley, which opened southward from Fort Vancouver on the Columbia. This valley, travelers agreed, was the most desirable portion of Oregon. It possessed the soil, climate, and the happy combination of timber and prairie to invite agricultural enterprise with the promise of easy and ample returns. In the Willamette, moreover, were rich markets, made accessible by the nearby Pacific. For many years, prophesied these writers, the home market created by persistent immigration would consume the staples of grain, pork and beef, hides and tallow, fish, wool, and lumber produced there in surplus. Thereafter China and the islands of the Pacific would afford permanent marts for all commodities of export. Already Oregonians boasted prices in excess of those in the Mississippi Valley.[16] In the Willamette, furthermore, settlement could be made peacefully and under the aegis of the United States, for it lay in territory not claimed by the Hudson's Bay Company.

After 1843 the tendency of the Midwest to swarm periodically had its repercussions on the Pacific. Farmers of the settled regions of Ohio, Indiana, and Illinois were swelling the tide into the newer lands of Michigan, Wisconsin, and Iowa. Between the Lakes and the Ohio were now three million cultivators of the soil where a half century earlier existed only a few scattered French settlements. In the half-formed villages of the Mississippi Valley were restless, adventurous souls to whom locomotion was still the ruling principal—men and women who were ready to undertake any movement that would perpetuate the pioneering exploits of previous generations of Americans.[17] Now the attractiveness of Oregon, as revealed by the reports of a decade, propelled a thousand emigrants from the Midwest into Oregon in 1843 and a like number in 1844.

This migration sealed the fate of Oregon. It revealed for the first time the practicability of hauling wagons to Oregon over the Oregon Trail and thereby laid the foundation for almost limitless migration in future years. Yet this new threat to Hudson's Bay dominion was still limited as late as 1845 almost entirely to regions south of the Columbia. Most American settlement was still concentrated in the Willamette Valley. Unlike the numerous tiny mission stations scattered along the Columbia Valley, that of Jason Lee fifty miles above the falls of the Willamette had grown into a sizable agricultural community. Oregon City, located at the falls, however, was the chief center of American occupation. Joel Palmer described this bustling village in 1845:

There were already erected . . . about one hundred houses, most of them not only commodious, but neat. Among the public buildings, the most conspicuous were the neat Methodist church, which is located near the upper part of the town, and a splendid Catholic chapel, which stands near the river and the bluff bank at the lower part of the town site. There are two grist mills . . . also saw mills, which cut a great deal of plank for the use of emigrants. There are four stores, two taverns, one hatter, one tannery, three tailor shops, two cabinet-makers, two silversmiths, one cooper, two blacksmiths, one physician, three lawyers, one printing office (at which the Oregon Spectator is printed, semimonthly, at five dollars per annum), one lath machine, and a good brick yard in active operation. . . . The population is computed at about 600 white inhabitants, exclusive of a few lodges of Indians.[18]

Although American pioneers had not challenged Hudson's Bay for control of those regions north of the Columbia, the migrations of 1843 and 1844 inflamed the expansionist mind of the Mississippi Valley beyond what Gallatin and the commercial interests had anticipated. The rapid strengthening of the American position in Oregon, added to the concern of friends and acquaintances for those who had recently made the overland journey, produced a determination among agrarian Democrats of the Old Northwest to challenge the entire British claim to the Oregon country. They demanded prompt action by the national government to strengthen the American position in Oregon. Senator Linn's unsuccessful fight for the creation of a United States territorial government in Oregon served as a stimulus for the calling of public meetings from Ohio to Illinois. One convention at Cincinnati in July, 1843, declared the rights of the United States along the Pacific unquestionable from California to Alaska.[19]

President Tyler in his annual message to Congress that year adopted this freshly enunciated demand for the whole of Oregon. "After the most rigid, and, as far as practicable, unbiased examination of the subject," he agreed, "the United States have always contended that their rights appertain to the entire region of country lying on the Pacific, and embraced within 42° and 54° 40' of north latitude." Throughout the Midwest the "whole of Oregon" suddenly became a popular cry. "Let the whole West rouse up as one man, and her voice will not be unheeded," cried one Indiana editor.[20]

In the campaign of 1844 the Oregon issue, from its inception a diplomatic and therefore an executive problem, became a weapon in a struggle for domestic political power. Western Democrats were determined to exploit the new Midwestern nationalism in the hope of achieving a Democratic victory and solidifying their power within the party. At the Baltimore convention the Democratic Party accepted these Western demands and adopted a resolution affirming "that our title to the whole of the territory of Oregon is clear and unquestionable; that no portion of the same should be ceded to England or to any other power. . . ." This merging of the Oregon and Texas issues probably resulted from no formal bargain between the South and West, but it illustrated the mounting political influence of the Mississippi Valley. Unfortunately, the Democratic campaign slogan of "Fifty-four forty or fight" was untenable diplomatically and divisive politically. A. F. Pollard, the British historian, has characterized it aptly as "possibly the crudest as well as the crispest expression of international relations to which democracy ever gave utterance."[21]

§ 4

Throughout 1844 Congress was locked in a vigorous struggle for control of Oregon policy. Congressmen from the Midwest claimed Oregon as their issue and one of vital concern to the people of the Western states. It was a question, declared John C. McClernand of Illinois, "of border safety, of territorial limits, and of relative political . . . influence, wealth, and power." Westerners cried out in speech after speech that Britain's influence over the tribes of the Western frontier endangered the safety of the Mississippi Valley just as her strategic location in Oregon threatened the very strength and independence of the United States. Issues of such magnitude could not be compromised. John Wentworth of Illinois admonished the House to remove the peril: "I think it our duty to speak freely and candidly, and let England know she can never have an inch of Oregon. . . ." Agrarian spokesmen such as Andrew Kennedy of Indiana pointed confidently to the citizens of the great valley who refused to be frightened by British power. Such American qualities, he declared, sprang from the "spontaneous feeling of patriotism which burns in

the bosoms of the whole western people, whigs and democrats. . . ."[22]

Diplomacy with Britain would not succeed, charged these
Democrats, until American pioneers had revolutionized the
power balance in Oregon. "Let either England or the United
States settle the Oregon Territory with a population of ten or
fifteen thousand arm-bearing men," observed David R. Atchison of Missouri, "and it will be a most difficult matter to dispossess them." Benton likewise placed his hopes on well-
armed emigrants. "Thirty thousand rifles on Oregon," he
shouted, "will annihilate the Hudson's Bay Company. . . ."[23]

Congress' obligation, believed the Western bloc, was merely
that of accelerating the westward movement of pioneers
through the immediate termination of joint occupancy (to
destroy the equal rights of British subjects in Oregon) and the
extension of military posts and American laws into regions beyond the mountains. Scores in the Midwest were awaiting
only the encouragement of the federal government. "Let
Congress only take some step towards the occupation of Oregon," wrote one Oregon farmer, "and the prairies of the West
will present the scene of the crusade of Peter the Hermit; our
wagons and people will be strung along the road in one un-
broken column, from the frontiers of Missouri to the Rocky
Mountains. . . ." Even such inducement might be unnecessary, predicted the confident Atchison, for soon the pioneers
would scale the Rockies and inundate the Pacific slope like a
mighty flood. "The march of empire is westward," he shouted
with finality, "nothing will, nothing can check it."[24]

Eastern Whigs challenged the West for control of Oregon
policy. Robert C. Winthrop of Massachusetts pointedly denied that it was a Western question. It was, he insisted, a
commercial question, national in scope, one in which the East
had an equal right to be heard. He reminded Western
Democrats,

I cannot forget that the American claim to Oregon, so far as it rests
upon discovery, dates back to Massachusetts adventure and Boston

enterprise. It was a Boston ship which gave its name to the Columbia River. It was Captain Robert Gray, of Boston, who first discovered that river. It was the Hancock and the Adams of Massachusetts—the proscribed patriots of the revolution—whose names were inscribed on those remote capes. And if we turn from the early history of Oregon to its present importance, and to the immediate interests which are involved in its possession, the North will be found no less prominently concerned in the question. The great present value of this Territory has relation to the commerce and navigation of the Pacific Ocean. . . . A mere western interest! Sir, I doubt whether the West has a particle of real interest in the possession of Oregon. . . .[25]

Winthrop's appeal to the maritime tradition of Oregon could not be ignored by the "ultras," a designation given the Western bloc by its Eastern critics. In debate Douglas, Wentworth, and other Democrats agreed with Eastern Whigs that the matter of ocean frontage was at issue in Oregon. Alexander Duncan of Ohio, a leading Midwestern expansionist, declared that "the nation that possesses Oregon will not only control the navigation of the Pacific, the trade of the Pacific and Sandwich Islands, but the trade of China itself on the Pacific. . . ." To C. J. Ingersoll of Pennsylvania, Oregon was a question of national moment because its possession by the United States would complete on the American continent one of nature's great monopolies. From its Atlantic ports it could grasp the commerce of the Atlantic; from those on the Pacific, the trade of the Orient. "Seat the United States firmly in Oregon," he predicted, "and the commercial enterprise and wealth of the world will centralize within our limits."[26] No Westerner could remain unstirred at the magnitude of such prophecy.

Winthrop could force an agreement on the commercial value of Oregon, but he could not establish bipartisanship in Congress on the question of the Far Northwest. Maritime considerations alone set too many limits to the political horizon. Publicly Democrats of the Mississippi Valley were in vigorous pursuit of land and security; privately they were in quest of votes. The broad avenue of nationalism that led to

54° 40′ could not be closed. The Whigs wanted the Strait of Fuca and Puget Sound, and they were confident that these limited, but essential, objects could be secured peacefully. For them time alone would liquidate the issue. They condemned as provocative, therefore, the use of pioneers to force the issue on Britain. Notice to terminate joint occupancy they believed equivalent to declaring war. "If you execute your threat and she executes hers, you certainly are in collision," warned Rufus Choate, the Massachusetts Whig. Choate demanded to know what precise Hudson's Bay policy was limiting the growth of American agricultural enterprise in Oregon. He pointed to the gradual disappearance of the hunter and predicted that with the continued destruction of the game, Hudson's Bay would retreat northward peacefully.[27] He spoke the convictions of a party.

Whigs detected a traditional Anglophobia in the Democratic position and chided them for it. Suggested the perturbed Winthrop, "There is always a lion in the path of the self-styled democratic party of the United States; a British lion, red with the blood of cruelty and oppression, which is their peculiar mission to slay. . . ." One Whig quoted George Washington's Farewell Address effectively to remind the Democrats of the danger of hating another country, for hatred often impelled nations into policies contrary to true national interests. This enmity and fear of Britain appeared to the Whigs to be unreasonable and to stem from political motivation alone.

§ 5

At issue finally in the quarrel over Oregon was the executive control of foreign policy. No element in Congress was sanguine enough to believe that diplomacy alone would secure the whole of Oregon. Negotiation implies concession, and the United States had neither the power nor the claims to negotiate a decision at the line of 54° 40′. Western Democrats

who could not tolerate such a settlement were forced, therefore, to demand a cessation of all further diplomacy. Atchison
rebuked the Whigs for wanting to maintain the question in
further suspension. "We are assured," he charged them, "that
if we stand still with our arms folded—if we will but wait a
little longer, it will be settled by negotiation. This we have
been told for the last twenty years, time and again. We have
been deceived; we are tired of this kind of diplomacy."[28]
Diplomacy, he charged the Whigs, was both dangerous and
unnecessary because Britain had no legitimate rights to Oregon. Diplomacy—a presidential agreement—had thrown open
the gates to Oregon for the Hudson's Bay Company. It was
diplomacy that now made necessary a policy of extreme vigor
and perhaps a resort to arms.

Westerners sought to keep the issue alive by challenging
the right of the President to exercise his initiative in the realm
of foreign affairs. They vigorously proclaimed the right of
Congress to debate and influence such policies. William Allen
of Ohio gave weight to the Western position by attacking the
concept of executive primacy as a dangerous departure from
the letter and spirit of the Constitution. His argumentation
moved logically. The treaty-making power in the Constitution provided for the advice and consent of the Senate and
made the two branches co-equal and co-ordinate in the exercise
of the foreign relations power. In practice, moreover, executive decisions were often destructive to an adequate foreign
policy for the reason that they often committed the United
States to a policy from which not even the Senate could re-
trieve it. Oregon, according to Allen, called for vigorous Congressional action, not the continued meddling of the executive.

Nor did the "ultras" fear the destruction of diplomacy.
Edward Hannegan of Indiana boldly proclaimed his contempt
for the wrath of England. "If declaring our own to be our
own," he shouted, "brings England, beak, talons, and all, on
Oregon, let her come." War would be the most effective
method of settling the issue permanently. It would drive

Britain from the continent, and, added Atchison, "like all other nations which have gone before her, grasping at envious domination, in the midst of her pride and her power she must speedily fall."[29] This Missourian would meet the challenge and shear England of all her power in North America.

Whigs who believed the forty-ninth parallel the basis of a possible compromise demanded with equal vigor that negotiations with Britain continue undisturbed by domestic pressures. They attacked the Democratic analysis as wrong historically as well as constitutionally. They reminded the Democrats that Oregon had been an open issue for thirty years and was still a fit subject for conversation. William Dayton, the New Jersey Whig, demanded of the opposition by what revelation they suddenly claimed the right to halt all further diplomacy. "I call upon senators," he cried, "to say what are the new lights which thus brighten their paths."[30] It was necessary, declared Dayton, to distinguish between the essential rights of the nation, upon which hinged its security and welfare, and demands of secondary importance which were always proper questions for negotiation and compromise. Oregon, he continued, fitted the latter category, for the British possession of western Canada was no threat to American security. The national interest, in short, required that the United States not refuse further negotiation.

Whigs accused the Western nationalists of flirting with war to achieve their political ambitions, for without future diplomatic probing there could be no genuine solution. In the crisis Senator William S. Archer of Virginia questioned the very liberty of the Senate to debate Oregon policy when further negotiations with Britain were pending. He denounced it as an infringement on the Constitutional treaty-making powers of the executive as well as destructive of American policy in Oregon. The exasperated Winthrop cried that the Secretary of State, whom they insisted on hobbling, was no longer a Whig but a statesman of their own party—John C. Calhoun. The Democratic attacks on diplomacy, added the Massachusetts Senator, indicated that they actually be-lieved that the United States had "some unprincipled or in-competent British whig at the head of our foreign affairs, ready to mart our territory for gold. . . ."[31] This Congressional in-terference with the conduct of diplomatic policy for political ends Choate described as a menace to peace, and he concluded that only his "sincere respect and regard for senators who pro-pose and urge it prevents my saying, still further, that it is the most indecent, indecorous, unintelligible proceeding the world of civilization ever witnessed."[32]

James K. Polk would not escape the enfilading fire of this debate. As candidate for the presidency in 1844 he rallied, and it appeared with impunity, to the Democratic cry for the whole of Oregon. As President, however, whatever the avowed stand of his party, he would of necessity assume the responsibility for the further conduct of Oregon negotiations. Unfortunately, those who opposed him in 1844 approved this presidential role, whereas the powerful bloc of his own party, the Western wing, condemned it. One thing was certain—the United States would move northward, either to the forty-ninth parallel or to the Alaska boundary, and either by war or diplomacy. If it went peacefully, negotiation would be its handmaid and the campaign pledge would be rejected. Com-promise might secure the national welfare, but it might injure the party. Such was the dilemma to which the partisan de-bates on Oregon policy had consigned the victorious Tennes-sean.

Chapter 3

SOUTH OF FORTY-TWO

§ 1

California in the forties was a vast slumbering Mexican province, stretching from the Rocky Mountains to the Pacific Coast. In 1769 the intrepid Franciscan Junipero Serra had brought the promise of Spanish civilization to the region; seven decades later California under Mexican rule remained a remote and exposed wilderness. Its less than ten thousand citizens were almost lost in a narrow strip touching the sea. The Mexican capital lay fifteen hundred formidable miles to the southeast. Endless stretches of the Mojave and Sonora deserts, rendered treacherous by marauding Apache and other desert tribes, separated the California settlements from the nearest centers of Mexican authority. Land communication was impractical and all but impossible. An occasional ship moved up the coast from Mazatlán, bearing official communiqués from the central government. But California from the beginning had lived by her own resources.

Franciscan missions—a score of them, nestled snugly in well-chosen valleys along the coastal ranges and thoughtfully spaced about a day's travel apart—bore evidence of better days. All were built on a quadrangular plan, their immense inner patios lined with the private cells of priests, kitchens and dining rooms, guest rooms, storerooms, and handicraft workshops. Viewed at a distance, their white walls, red-tiled roofs, and chapel bell towers lent immense charm to the countryside. Surrounding the mission buildings were always the gardens, vineyards, and orchards; and beyond, the sprawling pastures. Patterns of organization and design were similar; yet each mission had a quality of its own, given it by its wealth, location, architectural refinements, and the ingenuity of its leadership.

At the height of their prosperity in the 1820's, these missions counted by the hundreds and thousands the Indians who answered the call of vesper bells. Their cattle they numbered in the ten thousands. And pasturage alone limited the herds of their famed Spanish horses. For the weary traveler, a decanter of wine from the mission press, provisions of boiled tongue, chicken, bread, or boiled eggs, a proffered mount from the mission herds were marks of hospitality—and evidence of wealth.[1] For years the missions were the soul of California life, the source of her prosperity.

By the forties these venerated establishments were rapidly crumbling. Stripped of their landed possessions in the previous decade by the Mexican government, their priestly commission superseded by civil authority, they suffered a decline that was inevitable. Padres now lived in solitude or deserted the missions entirely. Indians without guidance succumbed to quick and hopeless degeneration. Soon a mere five thousand remained of the former thirty or forty thousand. Thoughtless citizens rifled the buildings of wood and tile. Walls exposed to the relentless thrusts of sun, wind, and rain quickly disintegrated into heaps of clay. In another century imagination and research would reconstruct them.

Travelers had recorded this decay. Perhaps at famed San Carlos Mission at the mouth of the Carmel River foreign visitors could best follow the course of ruination. Captain Benjamin Morrell reported in the mid-twenties that its beautiful valley responded to human endeavor, with "fine pasture lands, interspersed with pine, oak, and birch trees, with very little underwood." Yet already in 1827 a noted French traveler described the mission as "poor and almost depopulated of Indians. . . ." A decade later, W. S. W. Ruschenberger, on his voyage around the world, found the mission dilapidated and almost abandoned, the gates falling off the hinges, the tiles adorning the houses of Monterey across the shaded ridges of Cypress Point, the padre living at the Monterey presidio. Soon Thomas J. Farnham would find the establishment in total decay, thistles overrunning the fields, the buildings crumbling into dust, the Indians gone, the vineyards choked with weeds, grass growing in the courts, the cells of the friars empty, mules running wild in the hills. "With the exception of the church," wrote Sir George Simpson in 1842, "the immense ranges of buildings were all a heap of ruins."[2] The record of San Carlos was clear. Decay had set in before the secularization of the missions; ten years after that decision the ruin was complete.

Everywhere by 1845 this story had been repeated. Santa Cruz Mission, its crumbling walls contrasting strikingly with the thick forests behind it, was in the normal "state of decay and dilapidation." Once-beautiful San Juan Bautista was a picture of desolation, its wealth gone, its neophytes scattered to the four winds. At San Luis Obispo the Franciscan padre was reduced to sleeping on a hide, drinking from a horn, and eating meager strips of jerked beef. A few Indian families lived near the mission ruins. Charming San Juan Capistrano, overlooking the sea like a block of "white plaster," as well as lofty, elegantly architectured San Luis Rey to the south, showed marked signs of neglect. The courtyard of the mission of San Diego was described as oppressive with the stillness of death. Travelers reported its gardens destroyed, its Indians scattered, its great herds gone, its remaining wealth commanded by private rancheros.[3] Simpson thought the ruin at Mission Dolores on San Francisco Bay would have done credit to the "wind and weather of centuries." Only the chapel with its prodigality of ornamentation remained in a state of perfect preservation. At strategic Santa Clara Mission, Charles

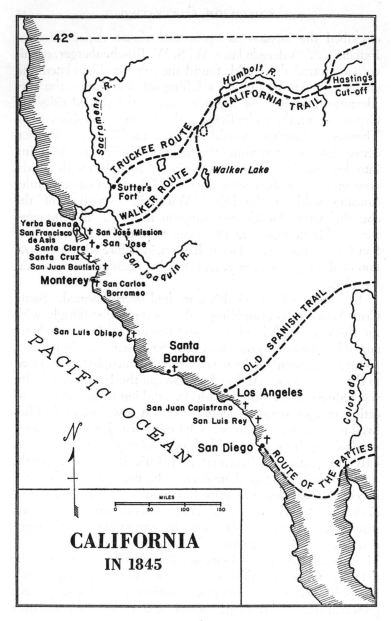

42°

Humbolt R.

Hasting's
Cut-off

CALIFORNIA TRAIL

Sacramento R.

TRUCKEE ROUTE

WALKER ROUTE

Walker Lake

•Sutter's
Fort

Yerba Buena
San Francisco
de Asis
Santa Clara
Santa Cruz
San Juan Bautista

† San José Mission
†• San Jose

San Joaquin R.

Monterey † San Carlos
Borromeo

San Luis Obispo †

Santa
Barbara
†

OLD SPANISH TRAIL

PACIFIC OCEAN

Los Angeles
†

San Juan Capistrano †
San Luis Rey †

Colorado R.

San Diego †

ROUTE OF THE PATTIES

N

MILES
0   50   100   150

CALIFORNIA
IN 1845

Wilkes reported the Indian huts destroyed, the church and mission-house dilapidated, but the padre still dispensing the establishment's traditional hospitality.[4]

Ruination of the missions precipitated the general economic decline of California. The vast herds of cattle, horses, and sheep dwindled at astonishing speed. Grain and wine production in this American Spain rapidly fell to insignificance as fields reverted to nature. Economically, the California of the early forties was not golden. It presented a picture of desolation.

§ 2

Tiny villages scattered along the coast—Yerba Buena, Santa Cruz, Monterey, Santa Barbara, Los Angeles, and San Diego— had replaced the missions as the dynamic element in California's existence. These pueblos by nature looked to the sea, for the Pacific Ocean furnished their only avenue of travel which made them part of a larger world. Along the coast sailed ships from Mexico. Over the southern horizon first appeared the topsails of the Boston hide ships that brought markets and whatever prosperity remained to the province.

New England traders and hide droghers had long tied California's economy to the sea. By the thirties their methods had become routine. Agents, momentarily deserting their ships, traveled inland on horseback parallel to the coast, arranging the purchase of hides (termed California bank notes) at two dollars apiece, but worth twice that much in Boston. In more prosperous days the missions had produced the bulk of hides for the market, some, it is said, producing ten thousand each year. The bleaching bones of slaughtered cattle around the missions bore mute testimony that for many years even their prosperity had been tied to the hide trade. While riding at night near San José in 1841, Titian Ramsey Peale, the naturalist, reported that "the continuous rattling and breaking of bones under our horses feet, had a most singular and unpoetic effect." Only California horses, he concluded, would have tolerated the sound.[5] Yankee traders regretted the destruction of the missions, for with them declined the profits of Boston. After 1835 the ranchos became the chief source of hides.

Following the *matanzas*, or slaughterings, the hides, after being staked and dried in the sun, were slowly drawn in crude native oxcarts down to the beach, or else pitched over the cliff at San Juan Capistrano. There sailors, waist-deep in the churning surf, carried the hides on padded heads from beach to longboat, "tossing the hides" in true California style, pulling loaded boats three miles to the ship. Hard, wet work it was for these men, but profitable for the owners.

Yankee ships, swaying at anchor in the long Pacific swell, were the principal mercantile establishments along the coast. Sales were often made in the ship's trade room, where for days a bustling crowd, conveyed from shore in the ship's boats, jostled one another to examine the goods and scrutinize the vessel, if only to purchase a paper of pins.[6] Ship cargo "consisted of everything under the sun"—New England hardware, cutlery, clothing, boots and shoes from Lynn (probably made from California hides), furniture, and "everything that can be imagined, from Chinese fireworks to English cart-wheels." Profits were huge, for the market was insatiable and the Californians manufactured nothing. Average prices on board were three hundred per cent above costs in Boston.

What goods did not change hands on shipboard did so at enormous profit in the establishments of New Englanders who inhabited the port towns and absorbed the inland commerce. Yankee traders, by their energy, intelligence, and resourcefulness, had gained a monopoly of the traffic and had become men of affairs in California. At the center of American activity was Thomas O. Larkin of Boston, since 1832 the merchant prince of Monterey. These Yankees spoke Spanish, avoided legal restrictions against Protestants by joining the

Catholic Church, and parried the jealousy of the Californians by marrying provincial heiresses.[7]

Competition was keen as Boston ships plied the coast in search of hides. As early as 1832 one sea captain observed gloomily, "There are several vessels on the coast and it is sharp with everyone looking out for himself. This place is like all others. Trade is almost done by so many entering into it." To the first ship in port after the slaughter went the riches. Each year the story was the same. "Hides are plenty in the Pueblo, and no goods in the market, if you get there before any vessel, you can sell your cargo off immediately. Calicoes and cottons will bring any price asked."[8] Competition became keener with the decline of the missions. During the mid-thirties six to eight ships were in the scramble for hides; by 1842 there were sixteen with a predicted export of scarcely two full cargoes.

Twelve to eighteen months were then required by a Boston firm, employing two vessels on the coast, to fill one ship to capacity for the return voyage to New England. Bryant & Sturgis' *Alert* had sailed the coast for eighteen months when Simpson viewed her in the early forties, and still she lacked over ten thousand hides for a full cargo. One Boston trader recorded a three-year voyage beginning in 1840 in which his ship dropped anchor at San Francisco Bay seven times, at Monterey thirteen times, at Santa Cruz three times, four times at San Luis Rey, seventeen at Santa Barbara, seventeen at San Pedro, and five at Refugio. During this journey he returned to the depot ten times, and frequently cast anchor at minor inlets along the shore. The crew handled each hide twenty-two times.[9]

When Richard Henry Dana sailed the California coast for Bryant & Sturgis in 1836, the trade was nearing its height; ten years later it was dead. Exports of hides to Boston reached 200,000 in 1838 and then rapidly declined under the disintegration of the mission economy and the onerous exactions, regulations, duties, and prohibitions of the provincial government. With the decrease in the *matanzas,* hides became increasingly scarce. William S. Hinckley of Yerba Buena observed the fruitless search in 1841: "All the supercargoes are in Sta Clara in chace of hides and I believe a stray hide has a poor chance. Everything in that line very scarce here." Again he wrote: "We have seven vessels in port and about 7 hides each I expect."[10] An increasing sophistication in California tastes made it difficult during the forties to sell anything but the latest fashions. Wilkes still estimated the export of 1842 at 150,000 hides, whereas Simpson suggested the more conservative figure of 60,000. What little trade remained was transferred from the lower ports to San Francisco Bay. There, Wilkes noted, "a few hulks may be seen lying, furnished with every needful article; these keep up an illicit intercourse by the connivance of the officers of the customs, by whose cupidity the revenue laws are openly infringed. . . ."

In 1843 hides still sold on the Boston market at eleven to thirteen cents per pound. During the following year three cargoes from California, plus those brought in from Havana, broke the market. Within the next two years they were disposed of at prices between nine and ten cents—less than $2.50 per hide. This was not sufficient income to maintain a ship and crew in California for two or three years. During 1845 and 1846 the three firms of Appleton and Company (successor to Bryant & Sturgis), Eaton & Company, and B. T. Reed deserted the trade. During the latter year uncertain conditions with Mexico confirmed the decision. Reed informed Larkin in June: "In the present unsettled state of our relations with Mexico it is out of the question to send a ship and cargo to your part of the world."[11] Thereafter the colorful and profitable Boston hide trade ceased to exist.

After 1840 there were reduced profits and declining trade, but new interests in the Pacific and increased knowledge of the California Coast. On the minds of New England seamen every mile of twisting beach, every roadstead and harbor had been indelibly engraved. Dana's *Two Years Before the Mast* records that impression. Travelers of the thirties and forties merely confirmed the hide drogherman's vision.

§ 3

Not along the Boston waterfront alone were there seamen who knew the coast by heart. At New Bedford and Martha's Vineyard were whalemen who had put in at Monterey and San Francisco for provisions and repairs. Occasionally a California resident, such as J. J. Warner or Alfred Robinson, came East imbued with native California enthusiasm. Henry A. Peirce, owner and master of the *Maryland*, reportedly shared his impressions with Daniel Webster and other officials in Washington.[12] Knowledge follows hard on the wings of commerce, especially when trade is profitable. Details might be lost in a maze of contradictions, but the broad outlines were clear. The political and commercial implications of life in provincial California could not be missed.

Accounts of American travelers and the occasional press notices gradually increased the measure of acquaintance with California. In 1839 Congress published Hall Jackson Kelley's observations. A year later came Dana's popular *Two Years Before the Mast*. Thereafter the volumes on California multiplied rapidly. In 1842 appeared Richard J. Cleveland's *Narrative of Voyages and Commercial Enterprises,* published, the author admitted, in response to the growing interest in the Pacific Coast. Commodore Thomas Ap Catesby Jones's capture of Monterey in October, 1842, not only focused the attention of the press momentarily on California, but also prompted Larkin to begin his correspondence with the New York *Herald*.

In his first letter of 1843 Larkin described the quality of life at Monterey: "During the time the Vessels laid at anchor here, the officers spent their leisure time ashore hunting wild Deer and dancing with tame Dear, both being plenty in and about Monterey." Larkin soon became a one-man chamber of commerce for California with his periodic letters not only to the *Herald*, but also to the New York *Journal of Commerce* and the Boston *Daily Advertiser*.[13] By 1845 the numerous letters of a California correspondent who signed his name "Paisano" engendered visions of California life for the readers of the New York *Herald*.

The years 1844–46 were peak years for the publication of books on Mexican California. First appeared the fascinating account of Thomas J. Farnham's journey along the California coast. Robinson informed Larkin that the "style of writing is very pleasing and cannot but give satisfaction to whoever reads the work."[14] Lieutenant John C. Fremont's *Narrative* went through several large printings in 1845. Requests for Congressional copies flooded the desks of Senators and Representatives. Also in 1845, although portions had appeared earlier, was published the complete five volumes of Charles Wilkes's *Narrative of the United States Exploring Expedition*. Robert Greenhow's *History of Oregon and California*, published in 1844 and 1845, and Lansford W. Hastings' *Emigrant's Guide to Oregon and California*, published in 1845, enjoyed comparative popularity. In that year Josiah Gregg's *Commerce of the Prairies* entered its second printing.

Books published in the following year continued to exploit the popular interest. Thomas J. Farnham's *Life and Adventures in California*, Alfred Robinson's *Life in California*, and Waddy Thompson's *Recollections of Mexico*, like the earlier volumes, received wide and favorable reviews in the daily press and in magazines.[15] This was also true of Disturnell's new map of Mexico and Mitchell's map of Oregon, Texas, and California, published that year. These works of the mid-forties recalled the earlier accounts of Dana, Farnham, and Wilkes.

The picture of California these writings created became more vivid and distinct, but the bold pattern never changed. Together they revealed a California in its last stages of economic decline, but one that had an infectious quality that few travelers could resist. "Solomon, in all his glory, was not more happy than a Californian," reported one Monterey correspondent in 1844. Life in this mild clime revealed the almost pure Spanish strain of its inhabitants. No self-respecting man worked if his immediate wants were supplied. Simpson observed that "time is a perfect glut with a community of loungers; and, under the plea of having no means of catching fish, the faithful enjoy, by a standing dispensation, the comfortable privilege of fasting at meagre times on their hecatombs of beef." California life was quiet, carefree, unhurried, peaceful, simple, gay, and pleasant. The Californians boasted that they had none of those "punctual men of business hurrying to their appointments, blowing like steam-engines, elbowing every body, and capsizing the apple-stalls."[16] In this land of *poco a poco* the grasping foreigner was an unending puzzle. This spirit of ease prompted historian Hubert Howe Bancroft to term the Mexican period, despite its economic decline, the real "golden age" of California history.

Only in their pleasures did the Californians move at an accelerated pace. They faced each celebration with the intensity that they might exhibit if it were to be their last day of pleasure upon earth. The Spanish habit of gambling always enlivened their games of cards and dice, as well as their amusements of cockfighting, bull- and bearbaiting, and horse racing. Their parties, often breaking up after three days of dancing and excessive drinking, usually terminated in violence and sometimes in sudden death. Such festivities would have tested the endurance of the Anglo-Americans.[17] The Californian was a man of contrasts. He was equally at home handling the guitar or the lasso, treading the steps of a fandango or trailing the herds of wild cattle over the endless plains on his spirited steed.

For the Californian the horse was the major factor of his existence. "It is a proverb here, and I find it a pretty true one," wrote John Bidwell, the early California immigrant and author, "that a Spaniard will not do anything which he cannot do on horseback." Travelers found the horsemanship of the Californians almost unrivaled on the American continent, but they were usually as much attracted to the mount as to the rider, for the California horse was famed for its matchless head and neck, fiery eyes, broad chest, and clean, slender limbs.[18] A fully caparisoned animal with its brightly bedecked rider left an impression seldom to be forgotten. Wilkes has preserved the impression of one horseman who rode up to him at a furious gallop in 1841:

He was mounted on the best horse I had seen in the country, and dressed after the California fashion, in a dark brown cloth jacket, thickly braided, both before and behind, with slashed sleeves, showing his shirt elegantly embroidered, both on the breast and sleeves; velvet breeches of bright blue, secured around his waist with a red sash, and open at the sides, ornamented with braid and brass bells, in abundance; below the knee he wore leather leggins, fastened with garters, worked in silver, and below these, shoes, over which were fastened large silver spurs, with the heavy rowels of the country; on his head was tied a red bandana handkerchief, and over that a huge broad-brimmed sombrero. . . . His horse was equally well caparisoned, the bridle being decked with silver, as were the tips of his large wooden stirrups; with pillions and saddlecloths in abundance. Few riders had so gay an air, or seemed to have so perfect a command of the animal he rode. . . .[19]

An extreme hospitality enhanced the quality of California's unhurried life; perhaps the entertainment of guests served to ease the procrastination in business affairs. At any rate, the generosity of the light-hearted and easy-going Californians knew no bounds. Simpson recorded that they literally vied with each other "in devoting their time, their homes, and their means, to the entertainment of a stranger."[20] It is not strange that California tempted some members of every ship's crew to remain.

Travelers agreed that California was an Arcadian paradise. They reported that it could produce almost every important crop in the world—not only grains, flax, and hemp, fruits of all kinds (including grapes, limes, oranges, figs, and olives), walnuts and almonds, but also coffee, sugar, indigo, tobacco, and cotton. Fremont found the Sacramento Valley "unequaled by anything we have ever seen," admirably suited to cultivation, and "covered with groves of oak-trees, principally the evergreen oak." The San Joaquin Valley he described as "beautiful with open groves of oak, and a grassy sward beneath, with many plants in bloom . . . crowded with bands of elk and wild horses . . . so beautiful that it is considered a paradise."[21] Farnham even exceeded this in his glowing tribute to the province's countryside. "California is an incomparable wilderness," he wrote, "—a wilderness of groves and lawns, broken by deep and rich ravines. Along the ocean is a world of vegetable beauty, on the sides of the mountains are the mightiest trees of the earth, on the hights are the eternal snows lighted by volcanic fires." The valley of the San Joaquin, with its herds of wild horses, elk, deer, and antelope was "a noble and valuable vale," a full "six hundred miles of prairie covered with grass and wild oats, cut by streams, shaded by lofty forests." The Sacramento was a valley "of exceeding beauty and excellence."[22]

It is significant that only Fremont of these early writers approached the province by land. All others were oriented to the sea. They were always more concerned with the shores and bays, always more speculative on commercial than on agricultural development. Their lasting contribution to expansionist thought in the United States was not their descriptions of California's civilization and soil, but their graphic and critical evaluations of the California coast from San Francisco Bay to San Diego.

§ 4

Monterey's four public buildings, unfinished or prematurely decaying, scarcely concealed the village's distinction as the leading port and capital of California. Off her beach every vessel that entered provincial waters dropped anchor to enter incoming cargoes at the customhouse. Behind these white walls hovered the provincial officials, imposing duties of eighty to one hundred per cent plus other vexatious regulations, for the customhouse alone provided the revenue of government. Only their reluctance to destroy the commerce limited their official greed as they exacted sums of five to twenty-five thousand dollars from well-laden Boston vessels. Officials lacked the power to enforce the rule that all goods be entered at Monterey. Yankee ship owners followed the simple expedient of loading more goods than listed on the manifests and peddling them off before they came under the scrutiny of the law. But revenue was required and officials were wary. One Yankee was warned: ". . . be careful you do not oversell your manifest this side of Santa Barbara, all eyes will be upon [you], do not do anything contrary to the law or the least slip will be jumped at."[23] Enough duties were collected to maintain the government; enough were avoided to keep the trade alive and profitable.

Dana thought Monterey "decidedly the pleasantest and most civilized-looking place in California." From the bay the village presented an interesting collection of several dozen scattered white adobe houses, with their contrasting red-tile roofs, clustered indiscriminately near the glistening beach. The dwellings lay on a gently undulating plain, interspersed here and there with pines and oaks. Beyond the town rose an amphitheater of rounded hills with towering evergreens extending westward until lost in the sea at Point Pinos.[24] Across the ridges several miles to the south lay crumbling San Carlos Mission.

Monterey Bay was far safer than twenty miles of open sandy roadstead warranted, for its depth provided anchorage near the shore for most of its entire width. At Monterey ships lying at anchor in ten fathoms off the beach received the protection of Point Pinos, which warded off storms from the south and southwest. Even the fierce northers could not drive a well-anchored ship ashore. Carelessness alone, believed Dana, would prevent a ship from riding out any gale in Monterey harbor. Near the bay's northern extremity was tiny Santa Cruz where sailors braved the heavy surf to acquire fresh provisions unavailable at Monterey. Here Josiah Belden cut lumber for profit from the huge trees that crowded the shore. Monterey Bay's unique position resulted not from her anchorage or the security of her harbor, however, but from the peculiar advantage that derived from her customhouse and the seat of the provincial government.

South of Monterey stretched a rugged coast, without harbors or notable roadsteads. Between Point Pinos and the rocky bay of Carmel was beautiful Cypress Point where the low pine-clad interior sloped gently toward a rocky shore line which was broken occasionally by broad sandy inundations or ended abruptly in rocky cliffs. Here gnarled, wind-swept cypress contrasted with the brilliant whiteness of the shore and the deep blue shades of the Pacific, which crashed against the boulders or glided silently in broad sheets of foam over sandy and pebbled beaches.[25]

Beyond Carmel Bay the horizon rose sharply to the rugged, treeless ridges of the Santa Lucia Mountains which towered over the sea to Point Conception. At their base stretched a flat, grassy plain that terminated in a vertical wall of rock. This sheer wall was separated from the surf by a narrow beach. At almost equal intervals the cliff was cut by narrow valleys, thickly covered with oak, that rendered access to the plains above. Mariners found this coast forbidding. Edward Vischer, who touched it in 1842, reported that "we found ourselves facing here between Santa Barbara and Monterey a high cliff wall, projecting right down to the shore line and covered with stately fir trees."

Point Conception divided the two faces of the California coast. To the south, where the coast assumed a more easterly direction, it became more naked and level. The point itself appeared to the sailor as a huge ridge rising from the sea, falling toward the interior, and then ascending again to the distant summit of the mountains.

Santa Barbara, located on the large crescent curving gently east and southeast from Point Conception, was regarded by Dana as little better than an open coast. Despite offshore islands which formed the Santa Barbara Channel, the shore was exposed to winds from the south and southwest which lashed the Pacific surf with such fury that ships dared not lie near shore between November and April. During these months captains normally anchored three miles away, with slip ropes on their cables ready to sail out to sea at a moment's warning. On one occasion Dana's vessel slipped cable before Santa Barbara and beat about four days under close sail in high seas before returning to recover the anchor.

Many early sailors and residents found Santa Barbara a dull and disagreeable village. Here Dana received his first impression of California—"the open roadstead of Santa Barbara; anchoring three miles from the shore; running out to sea before every southeaster; landing in a high surf; with a little dark-looking town, a mile from the beach; and not a sound to be heard, nor anything to be seen, but Kanakas, hides, and tallow-bags."[26] John Coffin Jones, the American merchant, wrote to Larkin in 1841: "Sta Barbara, like Monterrey, is looking miserable indeed; if I had not a wife to make me cumfortable in this disolate quarter of the globe, and ware compelled, here to anchor on shore, I should be strongly tempted to hasten my departure from this land of sorrows by the force, either, of pistol or brandy."[27]

Below Santa Barbara on a treacherous, rocky shore was the significant harbor of San Pedro. To novice seamen it had no better claim to being a harbor than any other stretch of coast. It was as exposed as Santa Barbara and the sea so shallow that the surf broke three miles off shore. As far as the eye could travel the countryside was bare of trees, shrubs, or buildings. Its slippery landing, its barrier of rocks and heavy

surf, made it the most despised of California's ports—"a regular hell for sailors."

Yet for many years desolate San Pedro beach furnished
more hides for Boston ships than any other segment of the
coast. Thirty miles to the east was a rich grazing country,
filled with ranches and large herds of cattle. In its center
was the *Pueblo de los Ángeles*—carefree, cheerful, and neat,
the largest town of California, but possessed, as one writer
complained, "of the lowest drunkards and gamblers of the
country." Over a range of hills to the east lay the once prosperous mission of San Gabriel, famed for its extensive vineyards and immense herds which in its palmier days reportedly
numbered eighty thousand head of cattle.[28] Eventually after
a ship's presence had been reported, carts and mules loaded
with hides could be seen approaching the coast over the flat
country. As the hides slowly arrived, records Dana, "we got
into the old business of rolling goods up the hill, pitching
hides down, and pulling our long league off and on."

San Diego Bay was the rendezvous of the hide trade. Here
all Boston firms maintained their coastal depots. To dry, cure,
and store hides required a warm port, free from rain, fog, and
heavy surf. San Diego alone met all these prerequisites. This
beautiful bay, so deep and placid that ships could lie a cable's
length from the smooth, hard-packed, sandy beach, become
the pivot of New England's interests on the California coast.
Protected for its entire length of fifteen miles, except for its
narrow, deep entrance, the bay was exposed to neither wind
nor surf. At one anchorage a vessel could lie within hailing
distance of the beach in twelve fathoms of water.[29] Here
were the salt vats, the storehouses where seamen and Kanakas
from the Sandwich Islands cleaned, stretched, and cured the
hides, and stored them, folded and dried, until a full cargo
of thirty to forty thousand had been collected.

Those who sailed the California coast agreed that San
Diego Bay was the only harbor of merit south of Monterey.
Dana believed it the best harbor on the coast, and Morrell

once termed it "as fine a bay for vessels under three hundred tons as was ever formed by Nature in her most friendly mood to mariners." Captain Edward Belcher, the British seaman, visiting the harbor in 1839, added, "The port of San Diego, for *shelter,* deserved all the commendation that previous navigators have bestowed on it; and with good ground-tackle a vessel may be perfectly landlocked." Another traveler called it the "finest harbor in all California."[30] Only the countryside diminished the value of the bay, for it appeared a barren waste of sand hills. The town comprised thirty or forty adobe houses scattered over a sand flat on the north side of the bay. Perhaps its greatest attraction was its one-eyed Fall River whaleman who tended bar.

§ 5

San Francisco Bay, to all who visited the coast, was the maritime wonder of California. Each decade travelers recorded again its qualities and contemplated its future in the commerce of the Pacific Ocean. No detail of the bay escaped them. They marveled at its huge arms reaching toward the interior. To the southeast was the broad expanse extending twenty to forty miles (early travelers were never sure) to the mission of Santa Clara as well as the mission and village of San José. Along the northern shore was a deep cove known as Whaler's Harbor, and beyond it another strait leading northward to San Pablo Bay, a circular basin ten miles in diameter. From the eastern end of this pool another inlet led to a bay of almost equal size which formed the receptacle for the Sacramento and San Joaquin Rivers. Through these large rivers, the harbor of San Francisco, "besides its matchless qualities as a port of refuge on this surf-beaten coast," wrote Simpson, "is the outlet of a vast breadth of fair and fertile land."[31]

Several diminutive settlements lay in the vicinity of the harbor. On its northern reaches were the missions of San

Rafael and San Francisco Solano with its village of Sonoma; across the ridge from San Pablo Bay were the former Russian posts of Bodega and Ross. Tiny Yerba Buena, nestled on the south shore of the entrance between Loma Alta and Rincon Point, was the only port town in the harbor. This site contrasted violently with the maritime promise of the bay. In 1835 it boasted one rough board shanty. The following year Jacob P. Leese, an American merchant, added a second. Wilkes in 1841 found the village still languishing. "Its buildings," he wrote, "may be counted, and consist of a large frame building, occupied by the agent of the Hudson Bay Company, a store, kept by Mr. Spears, an American, a billiard-room and bar, a poop cabin of a ship, occupied as a dwelling of Captain Hinckley, a blacksmith's shop, and some out-buildings."[32] Simpson counted eight or nine houses in addition to the Hudson's Bay Company post.

Yerba Buena's economic and social life were practically nonexistent. Hinckley reported a holiday festival to Larkin: "Nothing new here, every things as dull as can be—we had a small Christmas dinner, and smaller dance there being only 4 ladies and two little girls—so it was not great shake." Commerce was equally scarce. "This Yerba Bouna is truly a dull place," wrote an overland traveler from Monterey. "You think Mountarry is dull for trade but here business is allamost dead."[33] Despite its apparent wealth, the village had neither the provisions nor the labor to refit the numerous whaling vessels that sought shelter there. What trade flourished in San Francisco Bay centered at the village of San José.

Yet travelers viewed the harbor with wonderment. Wilkes assured the readers of his Narrative that California could boast "one of the finest, if not the very best harbor in the world." He added that it was sufficiently extensive to shelter the combined navies of Europe. Farnham called it "the glory of the Western world." To estimate fully its excellence, he wrote, "one must approach it from the sea; have a full view of the lofty shores north and south, rising at intervals into

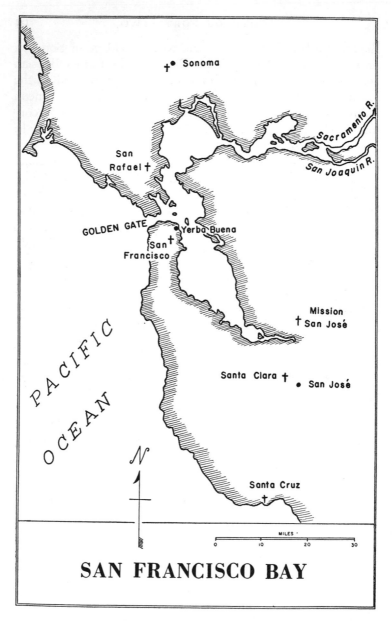

SAN FRANCISCO BAY

lofty peaks girded at their bases with primeval forests of ever-green cedars. . . ." The bay itself, he added, was "a broad sheet of water stretching off, north and south, the largest and best harbor of the earth. . . ." Morrell thought the bay the most delightful place on the western coast of America. Like Farnham, he found his attention diverted from the bay itself to the countryside—the grassy shores, the protective coves, the verdant hills, mountains, and valleys, the timber resources. It was this superiority of the adjacent country, believed many travelers, that elevated the importance of San Francisco Bay above that of other harbors. Lansford Hastings agreed that no harbor could be found "equal in all respects, to that of the bay of St. Francisco." Even Dana believed that the bay's resources of wood, climate, fertility, and facilities for naviga-tion and anchorage rendered it of greater value than San Diego and quite the best on the Pacific Coast of North America.[34]

The real importance of San Francisco Bay lay beyond the hide trade. It was American commerce with the Far East primarily that focused attention on the harbor of San Fran-cisco. This bay was regarded the unqualified answer to American hopes of commercial greatness in the Pacific area. Geographically, its location opposite Asia would give it a commanding position; its intrinsic advantage would make that position fully effective. Prevailing westerly winds had lo-cated this extraordinary harbor on the direct route of traffic between India, China, and Manila and the Pacific ports of Mexico and Central and South America. The great circle route, moreover, which established the shortest distance be-tween these two worlds passed Cape St. Lucas in Lower Cali-fornia, allowing a ship to touch at Monterey or San Francisco without venturing more than one hundred miles off course.[35] The bay appeared dedicated by nature to be the great half-way house of trade between Pacific America and the Indies, one possessing precious metals and foodstuffs; the other, tradition-ally rich and luxurious commodities.

California, noted the St. Louis *Missouri Reporter,* would stimulate this trade with the Pacific ports to the south, the Polynesian Islands, and the Orient with her products of flour, hides, tallow, butter, cheese, wines, brandy, oil, grains, fruits, hemp, flax, resin, and fur. Already her merchants shipped the products of her forests—shingles, lumber, and spars—as well as horses, to the Sandwich Islands, and beef and wheat to the Russian settlements in Alaska for bills of exchange on St. Petersburg. Her commerce would make of San Francisco the great Western depot for the silks and teas of China and India, and allow her eventually to embrace in her mighty grasp the lucrative trade of the entire Pacific world.[36]

Unlike Oregon, California was no general object of American expansionism prior to 1845. But whatever tangible goals expansive Americans might eventually seek south of 42° had already been precisely defined by New England merchants and Pacific travelers long before Polk's inauguration. As in Oregon, these future ends had been molded by the sea. Already San Francisco Bay had become the object of international rivalry among the Atlantic powers. Soon the California ports would color American expansionist views toward other portions of the coast and have a marked effect upon the entire settlement of the Oregon question.

Chapter 4

INTERNATIONAL RIVALRY FOR THE BAY

§ 1

The year was 1841. Three distinguished visitors were arousing the San Francisco Bay region from its perennial lethargy. Residents detected visible manifestations of suspicion among the three, which added to the air of excitement. In July the squadron of Charles Wilkes, the American explorer now completing his lengthy observation cruise of the Pacific, sailed proudly into the bay. Wilkes learned from Americans at Yerba Buena the disquieting news that the noted Frenchman Eugène Duflot de Mofras, then on a tour of the California and Oregon coasts, had paused there earlier on his northward journey. Mofras returned in November from the Columbia aboard the *Cowlitz,* accompanied by Sir George Simpson, who came to inspect the bay area in his capacity as governor-in-chief of the Hudson's Bay Company. After his critical examination of the harbor, Simpson would write a plague on both the French and American observers.[1] Nor was the mutual distrust of these voyagers a matter of personal rivalry alone.

California's foreign trade in the early forties was slipping away from the tiny coastal villages toward the bay of San Francisco, and with it drifted the focus of the commercial world. Ships riding at anchor off Yerba Buena still presented no "hedge of spars and rigging" as they would a decade later.

Boston hide ships and Pacific adventurers still made infrequent demands upon the bay's shelter and its surrounding resources. Along its shores were untrammeled beaches and picturesque coves behind which rose a verdant wilderness of hills and plains scarcely modified from their primeval state by human endeavor. This harbor was still separated by thousands of miles from the world's important traffic lanes, but its promise of future eminence was not lost on those seamen whose hearts quickened at first sight of her broad expanse as they sailed the Golden Gate.

Facile pens of sea captains and travelers had directed toward the harbor of San Francisco the attention not only of New England shipping interests, but also of diplomats and officials in Washington, London, and Paris. The bay was becoming the concern of the maritime powers of the Atlantic, and their desire for an inlet so remote paid a tribute to its reported magnificence. By 1841 many British, French, and American spokesmen were determined that the region's future benefits would accrue to the commerce of their own nations or to no other, for they did not underestimate its importance as a key to the trade of Asia. As the fine thread that held the province to Mexico weakened, the international rivalry for the port mounted in intensity. By 1845 both Britain and France had turned jaundiced eyes toward the United States, for American expansionism threatened to encompass the bay and destroy the balance of Pacific commerce.

§ 2

Behind the French interest which prompted Mofras's mission to the West Coast were the occasional visits of French sea captains endowed with persuasive literary talents. In January, 1827, Auguste Bernard Duhault-Cilly, captain of the French merchantman *Le Heros,* cast anchor in San Francisco harbor on a trading voyage around the world. His venture was a failure economically, but for months his educated mind recorded all that mattered in the sleepy province. No navigator before him had seen as much of its missions and villages, nor had analyzed more closely the inherent qualities of its institutions. His pungent and fascinating description of California, soon to be published in France, filled almost three hundred pages.[2] Perhaps of even greater impact on the French official mind were the memoirs of M. P. de Morineau, *Notice sur la Nouvelle Californie*, which appeared in 1834. Whether the writer ever traveled to California is uncertain, but his writings contributed to a growing anxiety of Orleanist France toward the Pacific and the re-establishment of a lost empire.

Into the bay of Monterey sailed another keen French observer in October, 1837—Captain Abel du Petit-Thouars, commander of the frigate *Venus,* then on a world tour. The captain was chiefly concerned with the Pacific whaling industry, but his ship carried also a scientific corps equipped to make hydrographic observations. Before he left the coast, he managed to survey the harbor of San Francisco. In August, 1839, the French commander, Cyrille Pierre Laplace, sailing eastward from Honolulu, anchored off Bodega. After a brief visit at the Russian post of Fort Ross, he drifted southward past San Francisco Bay, where he found only "fogs, fleas, winds, and sterility," and cast anchor off Monterey. Laplace assured the governor that he was conducting a scientific tour of the world by order of the French king, but observant Californians interpreted his voyage as pointing to French colonial ambitions in the Pacific. The narratives of both Thouars and Laplace were published by order of Louis Philippe.

French interests in the distant Mexican province became more obvious when the government instructed the suave, intelligent, and literary Mofras, attaché of the French embassy in Madrid, to report to the Pacific Coast of North America. During his two-year journey Mofras visited every important mission and pueblo in California, observing with infinite care the bay of San Francisco and its surrounding territory. His memoir, published in 1844, became the most ambitious contemporary account of the province. The only assurance of ultimate French success in acquiring California, noted Mofras, lay in the similarity of religion and temperament between the French people and the Californians.[3] At the urging of French residents in California and French officials in Mexico, the French Foreign Office in 1843 appointed M. Gasquet as Consul at Monterey.

It was harbors, primarily, that attracted the French to California. Mofras anticipated the expansion of agriculture with the advance in population, but only to supply commodities for trade. He stated clearly what he believed French objectives should be. "Two commodious ports lie at the far extremes of the province," he wrote, "San Diego on the south, and, on the north, San Francisco, which may be considered the key to the Northwest Coast and the northern part of the Pacific Ocean." Gasquet, who knew the province well, pictured it as a magnificent country "with a vast extent of shorelines, and on its coasts, bays, gulfs, anchorages, and ports which offer shelter and sure retreat to the ships sailing in these seas, dominating, by their position, the northern part of the Pacific Ocean."[4] With such advantages, he predicted, California in half a century would become a powerful auxiliary to any nation that possessed it.

Britain, like France, followed the sea to California. At no time after the voyages of Vancouver could British seamen, travelers, and officials forget the bay of San Francisco. Captain F. W. Beechey of the Royal Navy, who surveyed the harbor for the British government in 1827, spelled out its future significance. In his *Narrative* (1831) he informed the British that San Francisco Bay "possesses almost all the requisites for a great naval establishment, and is so advantageously situated with regard to North America, and China, and the Pacific in general, that it will, no doubt, at some future time, be of great importance."[5] The British government revealed its continuing interest when in 1839 it dispatched Sir Edward Belcher to survey the California coast and the port of San Francisco. His observations were published in London four years later.

Simpson was England's most remarkable visitor in California during the early forties. Upon viewing San Francisco harbor, he became a spokesman for the empire, sending a note to the British Foreign Office: "The country from its natural advantage, possessing, as it does, the finest harbor in the North Pacific, in the Bay of San Francisco, and capable, as it is, of maintaining a population of some millions of agriculturists, might become invaluable to Great Britain as an outlet to her surplus population, as a stronghold and protection to her commerce, and interests in these seas, and as a market for her manufactures. . . ." Simpson was likewise attracted to San Diego harbor, next to San Francisco "the safest and best harbour in the province, being land-locked, with deep water and a good bottom."[6] This observant Britisher concluded that California possessed two ports that rivaled the Juan de Fuca Strait.

British officials in Mexico reflected the views of British voyagers who sailed the California coast. Alexander Forbes, British merchant in the Mexican cotton-milling town of Tepic, declared the shores of California more advantageous for trade than the coasts of western Europe, possessing an unbounded future in the hands of either Britain or the United States. Richard Pakenham, then British Minister to Mexico and a leading proponent of the British acquisition of California, assured his government that no part of the world offered "greater natural advantages for the establishment of an English colony than the Province of Upper California; while its commanding position on the Pacific, its fine harbours, its forests of excellent timber for ship-building . . . render it by all means desirable, in a political point of view, that California, once ceasing to belong to Mexico, should not fall into the hands of any Power but England. . . ."[7]

§ 3

American officials from Andrew Jackson to John C. Calhoun followed only one dream of western empire—ports for the mastery of the Pacific Ocean—in their quest for Upper California. Jackson's interests were focused on San Francisco Bay by Anthony Butler, United States Minister to Mexico, and by William A. Slacum who, John Quincy Adams later recalled, kindled his passion "for the thirty-seventh line of latitude from the river Arkansas to the South Sea. . . ." Their influence on Jackson became apparent when he instructed Butler to purchase the region of San Francisco, including Monterey, as "a most desirable place of resort of our numerous vessels engaged in the whaling business in the Pacific, far preferable to any to which they now have access. . . ."[8] Powhatan Ellis, who replaced Butler, continued to urge the importance of the bay on the Jackson administration. "Its acquisition," he wrote in 1836, "would be of immense importance to the United States, not only in a national point of view, but also in reference to the comfort and protection it would undoubtedly afford our great and growing commercial marine in those seas."

Martin Van Buren made no effort to purchase San Francisco, but it was his administration that in August, 1838, dispatched Charles Wilkes from Hampden Roads to the Pacific as commander of the United States exploring expedition. This fleet, commissioned by the United States government at a cost of over a million dollars, spent several years gathering impressions of the entire Pacific area. New England commercial and whaling interests pressed J. K. Paulding, Secretary of the Navy, to instruct Wilkes specifically to examine the harbors along the Pacific coast of North America from the Strait of Juan de Fuca to San Francisco.[9]

John Tyler's administration revealed a keener acquisitiveness toward California than either of the two that preceded it.

Daniel Webster, as Secretary of State, had the typical New England attitude toward the region. To Waddy Thompson, the United States Minister in Mexico, he admitted in 1842 that without doubt "the acquisition of so good a port on the Pacific as St. Francisco is a subject well deserving of consideration. It would be useful to the numerous Whale Ships and trading vessels of the United States, which navigate the Pacific, & along the Western Coast of America." Thompson himself held as exalted an opinion of the bay as any other American official. To him Texas had little value by comparison. Not only could San Francisco harbor hold all the navies of the world, but the live oak in the vicinity could build them. The possession of San Francisco and Monterey, he wrote to Webster, "would secure the only places of refuge & rest for our numerous fishing vessels, and would no doubt . . . secure the trade of India & the whole Pacific Ocean."[10]

Webster struck out boldly to acquire the Pacific port. And he sought to secure British aid and approval by ceding to England all Oregon territory north of the Columbia. To Edward Everett he confided, "If I could see a strong probability of effecting *both* objects—California and Oregon, I should not decline the undertaking."[11] Mexico, however, refused to consider Webster's proposed arrangement.

Calhoun, Tyler's last Secretary of State and a Southerner, was no less concerned over the future of San Francisco Bay than was Webster. During 1844 Larkin urged him to employ every legal means to secure the California coast from Monterey northward to Oregon, acquiring thereby "one of the finest countries in the world, and the best and most magnificent harbours known." It would be a Yankee bargain, continued Larkin, outstripping all that the American nation had ever achieved. Calhoun himself required little incentive to negotiate for the port, for he had long recognized its significance. A city nestling on its shores, he predicted, would some day be "the New York of the Pacific Coast, but more supreme, as it would have no such rivals as Boston, Philadelphia, and Baltimore."[12] The Secretary instructed Duff Green to propose again to Mexico the sale of California. "If you succeed in this negotiation," he remarked, "our commerce in the Pacific will, in a few years, be greatly more valuable than that in the Atlantic."

§ 4

San Francisco Bay offered a heady combination of incentives in the early forties to stir the jealousy of the maritime nations. Had Mexico held the province firmly in her grasp, the Atlantic powers might have viewed the harbor with detachment or merely sought commercial concessions. But Mexico's hold was becoming increasingly tenuous. It was obvious even before 1840 that the Mexican Republic was too weak internally to maintain her sway over a province so remote.

Local revolutions in California had destroyed all but a slight semblance of government. News from Monterey often reached Mexico City but twice a year (the last deputy of the California government, residing at the national capital, received but two letters from the province in two years). Officials in California were strangers from Mexico, usually men, as Dana described them, of "desperate fortunes—broken-down politicians and soldiers—whose only object is to relieve their condition in as short a time as possible." The revolutions, he observed, were commenced by men in search of "loaves and fishes," but instead of "caucusing, paragraphing, libelling, feasting, promising, and lying, as with us, they take muskets and bayonets, and seizing upon the presidio and custom-house, divide the spoils, and declare a new dynasty."[13]

By 1841 authority in California had almost vanished. "Although I was prepared for anarchy and confusion," wrote Wilkes, "I was surprised when I found a total absence of all government in California, and even its forms and ceremonies thrown aside." California had no defense against potential enemies. The presidio at Monterey had been demolished. It still boasted three cannon in working order, but no two had the same caliber. Ammunition was scarce, and one shot sufficed as a salute if, indeed, there was a salute at all. The lone vessel of the naval force mounted no guns, and was so unskillfully manned that it could make no progress in beating against the wind. Its stores were often so badly depleted that the mate was known to have starved for three days within sight of cattle.[14]

San Francisco's presidio was in ruins; no flag floated from its flagstaff. Two of its four walls had crumbled; strewn over the piles of mud and brick were the bones of cattle that had been consumed by earlier personnel. Wilkes found the garrison reduced to one officer and one soldier. The officer was absent, and scarcely a soul in the vicinity knew him. Dogs, jackals, and vultures manned the post, recalled Farnham, but heaven help them in case of a siege! "The neglect of the government to its establishments," Beechey observed, "could not be more thoroughly evinced than in the dilapidated condition of the buildings in question." During the thirties the presidio at San Diego had only two guns, one spiked and the other without a carriage, plus twelve half-starved soldiers without a musket apiece. Sonoma's garrison had thirteen troopers, several field pieces, but no ammunition.[15]

Travelers agreed that California was drifting beyond the grasp of Mexico. Mofras believed it would belong to any nation that sent a corvette and two hundred men. What the Marquis of Bedmar once said of Venice's possessions on the mainland, he added, applied equally well to the status of Mexico's distant province—"that the Republic preserves them only for the want of somebody to choose to take them." The London *Times* observed that to conquer all of California would be no more difficult than occupying a desert island. British, French, and American officials regarded California's early separation from Mexico inevitable. Gasquet offered a summary of its provincial status to his government: "California is so far from Mexico, the ties which bind them are so weak, the central government so occupied with its interior dissensions, so incapable of working to develop the elements of richness which it contains, that on the first occasion separation cannot fail to result."[16]

California might offer little resistance to a conquering force, but no nation dared force her destiny. Mexico's title was as unimpeachable as her hold was weak. One day California would pass to another, and that by purchase or conquest, but only in fullness of time. As the forties ticked away, the official and commercial elements of Britain, France, and the United States viewed the pretensions of their rivals with increasing alarm.

French hopes in California faded first, if they ever existed beyond the minds of a few enthusiasts. France possessed no special claims to the region, nor did her power and interests in the Pacific equal those of Great Britain and the United States. Frenchmen recognized early the ambitions of the two Anglo-Saxon powers and their intense interest in Pacific ports. The more astute French diplomats predicted, moreover, that the final triumph in California would go to the British. Jones's attack on Monterey partially shattered that illusion. "It gives great strength to the opinion," admitted Pageot, "of those who believe that the United States have decided to obtain sooner or later, by force or concession, the possession of California, which offers in the magnificent bay of San Francisco the finest port on the Pacific Ocean."[17] But its very quality made it of highest importance to Britain also.

By 1843 the French anticipated an intense struggle between England and the United States for possession of California. They recognized the growing importance of the Pacific, especially China, to British commerce, and the need of a large naval station to command that area. French diplomats saw, moreover, that no harbor in Australia or Polynesia would satisfy those British demands as effectively as would San Francisco. No power, not even that of the United States, seemed sufficient to prevent the bay's eventual acquisition by Great Britain.

Frenchmen did not accept this conclusion with pleasure. Those who appreciated the maritime significance of the California coast dreaded the eventual acquisition of the province by another power. Some yet hoped that France might frustrate Anglo-Saxon ambition and assimilate the region by conquest or through a protectorate. "This would be Monsieur le Ministre," wrote Gasquet, "a thing worthy of the government of His Majesty who would forever honor the ministers who would conceive and execute such a plan. France would wreathe for them immortal crowns, and our descendants would glorify and bless their names."[18] Nothing, believed the Consul, would better elevate the power and prestige of France.

British pretensions to California were far stronger than those of the French. Whereas some British diplomats were reluctant to meddle in Mexican affairs, perhaps James Forbes, British Vice Consul in California, reflected well the views of the more ambitious of his countrymen when he wrote: "I feel myself in duty bound to use all my influence to prevent this fine country from falling into the hands of any other foreign power than that of England." He warned his government that it would be impolitic "to allow any other nation to avail itself of the present critical situation of California for obtaining a footing in this country."[19]

British diplomats acknowledged a threat from both the French and the Americans. Mofras's presence along the California coast, the appointment of a French consul at Monterey, and the occasional cruise of a French warship along the coast produced a ripple of dismay in some British circles. Both Pakenham and Eustace Barron, British Consul at Tepic, reminded Aberdeen of the official nature of Mofras's journey. Simpson warned the Foreign Office that the French were far more active in California than the British, and he called for the dispatching of a British man-of-war to remind the residents of California, as well as the competing powers, of British intentions.

Yet to Simpson and to most anxious British officials the chief danger to San Francisco Bay came from the United States. They conceded that California would go either to Britain or to her Anglo-Saxon rival. Pakenham's intense concern for California in 1841 was the product not only of his knowledge of California, but of his fear of foreign encroachment as well. Like Forbes, Pakenham insisted that "California, once ceasing to belong to Mexico, should not fall into the hands of any Power but England."[20] His fears and those of others, aimed particularly toward the United States, were borne out by Jones's spectacular seizure of Monterey. It was then that Pakenham, with authority granted him, quickly bestirred himself to appoint Forbes as Vice Consul in California.

The British, unlike the French, had a program for acquiring the Mexican province. Alexander Forbes in his *History of California*, published in 1839, not only drew an attractive picture of the area but also included a chapter on the prospects of foreign colonization. Quite significantly he recommended that the British possess California by an assumption of Mexican debts. His vision of a company of British investors exercising sovereignty over the region in the manner of the British East India Company was one easily conveyed to British diplomats and businessmen. In fact, as early as 1837 the Mexican government had sanctioned the consolidation of the Mexican bonds by Messrs. Lizardi and Company, a British firm, and authorized the bondholders to locate one hundred million acres within the departments of Texas, Chihuahua, Sonora, New Mexico, and California. The Mexican congress approved this policy in 1839. Soon the investors sought an assignment of Texas lands, and failing there, turned to California.

By August, 1841, Pakenham was advocating this plan and assured his government that it would ultimately secure California for Great Britain. "It is much to be regretted," he wrote to Lord Palmerston, "that advantage should not be taken of the arrangement some time since concluded by the Mexican Government with their creditors in Europe, to establish an English population in the magnificent Territory of Upper California."[21] A year later the bondholders were still exerting pressure on the British legation in Mexico to secure an assignment of land in California. British officials in London, however, had no interest in colonization projects nor in the proposal of the Irish priest, McNamara, who in 1844 presented a plan to the British legation in Mexico City to colonize California with Irish immigrants. The British minister reported the plan to Aberdeen; the Foreign Office never even acknowledged its receipt.

American officers never possessed accurate knowledge of the official British and French attitudes toward California, but what they knew of European interest in San Francisco Bay disturbed them. The American fear of British ambitions was reflected in Jones's report of 1842. He explained, ironically enough, that it was his dread of Britain that prompted his dash northward to Monterey from Peruvian waters. Thompson warned Webster concerning California in April, 1842, that "France and England both have their eyes upon it; the latter has yet." The Hudson's Bay Company was an enigma to him, and he predicted that if it ever secured a monopoly of Pacific commerce, "not an American flag will float on its coasts." England in possession of San Francisco Bay would, he feared, destroy American commerce in the Pacific.[22]

What caused Thompson and his successors in Mexico even more anxiety were the persistent rumors of a British mortgage on California. He reported the British policy for purchasing California to the State Department in July, 1842, and predicted lugubriously that England would secure a cession of the province within ten years. By 1844 Wilson Shannon, his successor, could inform Calhoun that the British were negotiating with Santa Anna for the purchase of California. Assuming that the minister was acting under official instructions, Shannon concluded that the acquisition of California was "the settled policy of the English government." Duff Green repeated this warning and urged the Secretary to obtain a copy of the deed in either Mexico or London, for he predicted that England, possessed of San Francisco, would control the entire Pacific Coast of North America.[23]

§ 5

What had started as a three-power rivalry for the bay of San Francisco had become by 1845 a bipolar struggle with British and French leaders now concerned only with the prevention of its acquisition by the United States. Imperceptibly at first, then with growing awareness, it dawned on European officials and travelers that the United States had too many advantages in this contest. British and French observers in California recognized with misgivings the increasing number of hunters and immigrants who drifted into California from the Mississippi Valley. The great barrier of mountains, deserts, and vast distances which separated the Pacific shores from St. Louis, they anxiously admitted, was slowly disintegrating under the westward encroachment of the American frontier. Pioneers penetrating the Pacific slope spelled out so that all could understand the geographical advantage which accrued to the United States in her competition for California. Sutter's post, which dominated the Sacramento Valley, noted one British traveler, was admirably situated "for fostering and maturing Brother Jonathan's ambitious views."

Emigrants were already demonstrating their expansive force. Mofras predicted logically that Texas would decide the fate of California, and added pessimistically that like New Mexico, California would be absorbed by contiguity. From Mazatlán the French representative warned his government gloomily that American pioneers would take the province by the conquest of pick and shovel. British officials evidenced this same fear for California. Sam Houston had warned Charles Elliot, British Minister to the Lone Star Republic, that Texas would become "a cantonment for the pioneer in the van of the mighty advance whose political power will not halt short of the Isthmus of Darien."[24] Simpson recognized the American superiority in "an unscrupulous choice of weapons," and if England did not act quickly, he warned, the people of the United States would "inundate the country with their own peculiar mixture of helpless bondage and lawless insubordination." The London *Times* reiterated this theme when it informed its readers that the Americans conquered provinces "as the cuckoo steals a nest." Cried one British officer at San Francisco, "D–n it! is there nothing but Yankees here?"[25] This picturesque phrase symbolized the frustration of Europe as it stood helplessly aside and contemplated the power of American pioneering as it pushed relentlessly toward the Pacific.

During 1845 the British and French press drummed a warning to their readers of American power as it reached beyond Texas. That seizure will not stand alone, warned the Liverpool *Mercury*, for California is already annexed "in purpose and intention." Texas would feed, but would not satisfy the greedy republicans, observed *Wilmer and Smith's Times*. The British press challenged not only American insatiability, but also the complete lack of regard for Mexican rights. Complained the *European Times:* "California and Santa Fe are tempting baits, and Jonathan, by an instinctive love of interest, would stand pardoned, by his own reading of the moral code, in laying violent hands on them."[26] Members of the British and French press feared the vast increase in power that would come to the United States through the acquisition of California. The conquest of Mexico, warned the semiofficial Paris *Journal des Debats,* would be a wide step toward the enslavement of the world by the United States. "Between the autocracy of Russia on the East, and the democracy of America . . .

on the West," ran its prediction, "Europe may find herself more compressed than she may one day think consistent with her independence and dignity."[27]

Many British officials favored positive action in both England and Mexico to prevent the impending conquest of California by the United States. Pakenham in 1845 continued to warn the Foreign Office of the consequences which might result from the American possession of the California coast. He pressed his government to enter a policy of joint action with France for the purpose of preventing the dismemberment of Mexico. Lord Aberdeen, the British Foreign Secretary, in turn assured British officials in Mexico that the London government would view with extreme dissatisfaction the establishment of authority over California by any other foreign nation. In October, 1845, he urged the Mexican government, as a final resort, to protect its interests in that distant province by adopting such "prudent & vigorous administrative measures" as would preserve that splendid region from American expansionists. "Were California to fall into the hands of the enemy," ran his warning, "Mexico would thenceforward look in vain for external peace and security."[28]

French officials were equally perturbed as American expansion threatened to reach the Pacific. Like the British, French diplomats to the end were reluctant to see San Francisco Bay pass to a rival nation. They regretted deeply, as did Aberdeen, the incapacity of Mexico to advance her rich province. French officials in Mexico followed uneasily the progress of American emigration and agreed that it would, if not prevented, soon make the United States master of the region. "One fine day," wrote the dejected Gasquet in October, 1845, "the Mexican flag will be hauled down, and in its place the Union flag will be hoisted, and all will be over. It is an almost inevitable result, and, in my opinion, quite deplorable."[29]

Pageot begged for action from his government against American arrogance which threatened the "balance of forces in this hemisphere." He was convinced that the American spirit of usurpation could "endanger the peace of the world," if not "restrained in time by serious warnings presented with an accord that would overawe its presumptuous heedlessness." In July he clamored for a European declaration that would destroy the strange illusion of aggrandizement under which the United States was laboring. François Guizot, the French Premier, declared his views publicly before the Chamber of Deputies: "It behooves France to preserve the balance of power in the Western Hemisphere."[30] Guizot's statement made a singular impression on members of the American press.

British and French diplomacy, which became so grand in its pretensions and so disillusioning in its eventual failure, ended finally as little more than a tribute of commercially minded powers to the grandeur of the California coast and the growing importance of the Pacific Ocean. It is true that the ambition of many leading British and French diplomats toward San Francisco Bay were sufficient to produce mutual antagonisms, but neither government ever revealed any true imperialism toward the Mexican province.

Frenchmen who knew California coveted it to the end, but they never inaugurated any policy toward Mexico that might have acquired it. And if they directed any attention toward California at all, it was because it appeared so desirable on the one hand and so easily obtainable on the other. Nor did the British government have any real design on the province. British bondholders contrived to lobby extensively for a mortgage on California, and British officials in Mexico never ceased to inform the Foreign Office of the value of the province and the weakness of Mexican control. Yet as late as 1845 neither group had succeeded in achieving its purpose. The Mexican government would execute no mortgage, and the British Prime Minister, Sir Robert Peel, did not reflect the enthusiasm of many British officials for another colony. He feared that any British move to acquire California would be tantamount to declaring war on the United States, and that England might erroneously assume an indefensible position against American pioneers pushing out from the Midwest.

British admirals stationed near the California coast never revealed any interest in California, and Admiral Thomas thought Commander Jones's contention of British ambitions absurd.[31] Throughout 1845 the British government continued its policy of noninterference in American affairs. But British editorials, quoted widely in the American press, went far beyond the official position. The London *Times,* for example, insisted that "England must think of her own interests, and secure the Bay of Francisco and Monterey . . . to prevent those noble ports from becoming ports of exportation for brother Jonathan for the Chinese market."[32]

Such editorials misled the American public. In the United States the official British and French positions were unknown, but such was not the case for the views of British diplomats in the New World. American expansionists were convinced that England was the chief barrier to the American acquisition of the Mexican province. This fear set the stage for the growth of American acquisitiveness which, in 1845, finally reached the California shores. Herein lay the ultimate significance of British and French concern for the bay of San Francisco.

Chapter 5

"WESTWARD THE COURSE OF EMPIRE"

§ 1

During the early spring of 1845, American destiny was reaching toward the Pacific with new insistence. For some months prior to Polk's inauguration on March 4, Texas had commanded the stage of American expansionism. The Texas issue had dominated the campaign of 1844 and was one of the factors that swept Polk into office. Three days before President Tyler transferred his duties to his successor, however, he signed the famed Joint Resolution which invited Texas to join the Union. During March this juncture was yet far from complete, but already the expansionist gaze was shifting from Texas toward the summit of the Rockies and beyond where Oregon still beckoned. Nor did annexation itself satiate the American appetite for Mexican lands. Instead, by destroying the respect which many citizens of the United States still held for Mexico's territorial integrity, it actually pointed the way toward new acquisitions in the Southwest. "The Rio Grande has no more efficacy as a permanent barrier against the extension of Anglo-Saxon power than the Sabine possessed," predicted the Baltimore *American*. "The process by which Texas was acquired may be repeated over and over again. . . ."[1]

California for the first time was becoming fused with Oregon in the American consciousness. For Polk, that fusion was already complete. George Bancroft, his first Secretary of the Navy, recorded forty years later that the new President entered the White House with four great ambitions, not the least of which were the acquisition of California and the settlement of the Oregon question. If this statement of Polk's purposes is true, the new President was in the vanguard of public opinion in March, 1845. Oregon had long posed a knotty problem in the American search for empire and was still pressing for solution. For a decade American officials had viewed California with interest, and two administrations had even sought to purchase the region. California, however, had been no issue before the American people in the campaign of 1844, and one finds in the newspapers little more than the barest mention of it prior to Polk's inauguration.[2] This Mexican province had not been singled out as an immediate objective by politicians and editorial writers. Not until the summer of 1845 did the American interest in California rival in intensity that which pointed toward Oregon.

Suddenly the dream of a continental, ocean-bound republic which included both Pacific regions stimulated the nation's emotions. During the Texas debate James Belser of Alabama had declared that it was useless to talk of limiting the "area of freedom—the area of the Anglo-Saxon race." The course of America was westward, he cried. In another half century one would "hear the song of the American reaper on the shores of the Pacific." The New York *Herald* observed: "The flight of the eagle is toward the west, and there it is he spreads his wings for freedom."[3] The same popular feelings which promoted Texas annexation, voiced the editors, would soon bring California and Oregon into the Union.

§ 2

California hung low on the expansionist horizon in 1845. It required more than the logic of geography, however, to bring that region into the American expansionist crusade.

The press produced the first tangible motive early in 1845 when it publicized a new revolution in California. In 1842 the Mexican government had dispatched an army to reestablish its control over the province. For two years the revolutionary tendencies remained quiescent while impoverished Mexican troops foraged the chicken yards of Monterey.[4] Then late in 1844 revolt swept the province. By the spring of 1845 the metropolitan newspapers of the United States reported that General Manuel Micheltorena had met defeat at the hands of the Californians—that he and his *cholos* were on a ship bound for Mexico.

The ease with which the Mexican forces were defeated spoke volumes. For hours the San Fernando Valley resounded with the crash of long-range artillery, but as the smoke of battle lifted no casualties were found. The New York *Herald* observed that, contrasted with other revolutionary movements, this was a "ludicrous affair." In the final "desperate conflict," conclusive enough to prompt the General to surrender, the slain and wounded amounted to six horses. "The men were wiser," wrote Larkin, "keeping out of the way of Cannon balls & grape—they only like the latter (under the same name) when distilled."[5] The ineptness of Mexican rule was rapidly casting California adrift. Travelers had predicted it for a decade; now it became the concern of an expansive American public.

Notices from Monterey declared that the province "from Bodega to San Diego, is now once more under its own command." At Mazatlán one Californian observed that "the holy cause of liberty is triumphant, we are independent." Rumors of a new Republic of California filtered across the continent. As Mexico's final effort to control her distant and unruly child ended in fiasco, official spokesmen in Mexico City admitted that the region had slipped beyond their grasp.[6] Still, an independent California was unthinkable. Bands of thieving soldiers sent by Mexico, or General Manuel Castro's "robbers and cut throats"—the new power in California—might harass the residents. In the United States, however, existed the deeper conviction that a greater threat to the independence of California lay in the alleged ambitions of Great Britain in North America. J. Fred Rippy has noted that "manifest destiny never pointed to the acquisition of a region so unmistakably as when undemocratic, conservative Europe revealed an inclination to interfere or to absorb. . . ." As in the Texas issue, it was this danger from abroad that guided American expansionism toward California in the spring of 1845. British and French activities in Mexico and California now assumed a new significance, for they gave meaning to the rumored danger of European encroachment along the Pacific Coast. This westward migration of the alleged British threat from Texas to the San Francisco Bay region was both simple and logical.

Editors suddenly thought they recognized in the effort of Britain to prevent Texas annexation an underlying design to prevent American acquisition of more vital areas to the west. As the New York *Herald* explained, England knew full well that if Texas were annexed, California would soon follow. Andrew Jackson warned a Democratic friend in 1844 that if England successfully established her power in Texas, she would use it to prevent American emigration to the Pacific. Duff Green knew something of British policy in Texas, and he argued the same view.[7] As the debate over annexation neared its conclusion, American editors warned their readers that if British diplomacy failed in Texas, England would double her efforts to secure California. The New York *Journal of Commerce* reported in February, 1845, that Great Britain, in anticipation of the passage of the Joint Resolution, was already negotiating for a country of even greater size and value. The New York *Herald* simultaneously issued a word of warning: "Should Texas be annexed, the next movement of Great Britain will probably be to negotiate with Mexico for the purchase of California. . . . In this she will be successful unless intercepted by our government."[8]

Fear of England more than any other factor carried manifest destiny to the Pacific in 1845. Expansionist editors, confronted with another threat of British encroachment, their efforts in behalf of Texas all but completed, rushed into a new crusade for an empire on the Pacific. In the vanguard were James Gordon Bennett of the New York *Herald,* Moses Y. Beach of the New York *Sun,* and Thomas Ritchie of the semiofficial Washington *Union.* Bennett quickly became the most violently expansionist editor in America. He admitted that, as far as he was able, he would "take care of California." Beach, boasting that his press had secured the annexation of Texas, shifted attention with undiminished momentum to regions on the Pacific. Ritchie was equally clamorous, indicating the Polk administration's purpose of creating as well as reflecting opinion for expansion.[9]

Soon the enthusiasms for California of newspapers from Boston to New Orleans exemplified George Berkeley's phrase, "Westward the course of empire takes its way." By the end of the year the Whig press had also caught the fever, and when in January, 1846, the *American Review* published a long, ebullient article demanding the acquisition of California, the *Union* was up in arms. Its editor warned the Whigs of the dangers of stealing Democratic thunder with a gentle reminder of what happened to Mercury's fingers when he tried to steal Jove's potent bolts.[10]

Forbes's *History of California* served as grist for the expansionist mill. Some reaction had arisen in the United States at the time of its original publication, but this had quickly subsided. In June, 1845, however, the Washington *Semi-Weekly Union* resurrected this work as proof of British ambitions on the Pacific Coast of North America.[11] Although the writer insisted that British aspirations had not slept since the date of publication, it was not until autumn that the American public learned of British efforts to carry out the project of the author. In October, Caleb Cushing published a letter in the New York *Courier and Enquirer* on the British bondholders who had been endeavoring to secure a mortgage on California. Cushing admitted that the lobby had failed, but its very purpose and method disturbed the expansionist fraternity of the press.

Editors over the nation republished this letter and heralded its determined stand against British ambitions. They voiced the conviction that California must shortly constitute an integral portion of the American Union if only to limit the commercial and maritime power of the British Empire. San Francisco Bay was too strategically located for commanding trade between Asia and America to allow it to fall to Britain. The *American Review* warned in January, 1846: "If England got San Francisco, she would be mistress of the seas—not for a day, but for all time." In possession of California, Canada, and the West Indies, with Mexico as an ally, she would enfold the United States in her net as completely as "the bloodiest intentions of extermination could possibly desire." Waddy Thompson believed California worth a war of twenty years to prevent England from acquiring it. Even lukewarm publications, such as *DeBow's Commercial Review,* emphasized the need of acquiring California to keep reactionary Europe from extending her hold over the North American continent.[12]

These expansionists, ironically, never understood that the European inclination to interfere in American affairs resulted largely from a fear of this nation's apparent continental ambitions. The mushroom growth of American acquisitiveness toward California in 1845 was actually more alarming to European observers than the annexation of Texas. But these natural British and French reactions toward American expansionism merely aggravated the American desire to annex California. European intervention seemed to threaten the normal growth of the nation and endanger the entire concept of the Monroe Doctrine.

American writers feared the consequences of what *Blackwood's Magazine* termed the British principle of "unavoidable expansion." They recalled that European powers often applied the rule of purposely hindering the growth of "morality, freedom, trade, industry, or any thing that adds to the supposed rival's greatness." The New York *Sun* demanded emphatically that its readers consider whether the United States could permit England and France to tell her in effect "you are growing too large, you are too ambitious; we must bring you under the control of the Allied Sovereigns, or we will cripple your resources and check your rapid growth and advancement."[13] Editors warned their public not to regard lightly this European threat of maintaining a balance of power in North America.

Some who were more confident of America's future explained that European bluster would do little good. The New York *Herald*, pointing to the twenty-five million Americans possessing the resources of a mighty continent, laughed at European interference. Looking forward a century, one editor asked how Europe could "kick the beam against the simple solid weight of two hundred and fifty, or three hundred millions . . . destined to gather beneath the flutter of the stripes and stars." It would do England and France little good to grow surly, concluded the poet in the *Democratic Review*, for

We have, thank heaven! a most prolific brood;
Look at the census, if you aim to know—
And then, the foreign influx, bad and good;
All helps new lands to clear—new seeds to sow;
We must obey our destiny and blood,
Though Europe show her bill, and strike her blow![14]

§ 3

America was rushing westward. During the spring and summer of 1845 the restless Pacific-bound pioneers who crowded the streets of St. Louis and Independence, Missouri, comprised the greatest exodus yet recorded. For weeks these outposts rang with the shouts of voyagers, the soft beat of horses' hoofs, and the creaking of wagons. One writer cheered

on the prairie schooners as they filed past toward the west—
each, he recorded, "drawn by six or eight stout oxen, and such
drivers! positively sons of Ának! not one of them less than
six feet two in his stockings. Whoo ha! Go it boys! We're in a
perfect *Oregon fever*."

Migration to Oregon in 1845 totaled three thousand and
doubled the population of the Willamette Valley. At Fort
Hall in eastern Oregon, a portion of the westward flow was
diverted to California. As early as May, Jacob P. Leese wrote
from Sonoma that some "western wagons, cows, & oxen, arived
here some few Days past from a crost the Mountains." Although much of the enthusiasm for an overland passage to
California was not extensively revealed until the greater migration of the following year, Larkin reported in November
the arrival of three to four hundred Anglo-Americans in the
San Francisco vicinity.[15]

Expansionism in 1845 took strength from this steady march
of American pioneers to the Pacific. Editors observed with
elation the annexationist force which they exerted. No power
on earth, it seemed, could stem the power of American emigrants to reach their objectives. Aggressive frontiersmen
promised shortly to drive the British from the Columbia. The
Cincinnati *Enquirer* lauded the pioneers trailing into the Far
Northwest: "Theirs is the destiny to lead the way to civilization, and to lay the foundation of a new republican State on
the Pacific coast." Pioneers assured the eventual acquisition
of California as well. Members of the press could not ignore
the Texas precedent. The New Orleans *Tropic* foresaw the
day when thousands of pioneers would create a second "Lone
Star Republic" on the shores of the Pacific. "Once let the
tide of emigration flow toward California," joined Alfred
Robinson, "and the American population will soon be sufficiently numerous to play the Texas game."[16]

But the pioneer impact on expansionism sank deeper. The
significant Anglo-American population winding over the
wagon trails to the Pacific tended to remove all those factors

which had dimmed the assurance of California's eventual acquisition by the United States. Albert K. Weinberg has shown that American expansionism during the movement for Texas was marked by an "egocentricism and exclusiveness" that recoiled from the prospect of annexing assumedly inferior peoples. The presence in California of a Mexican population threatened to stifle the ambitions of Americans to acquire the region. Even the expansionist Alexander Duncan of Ohio admitted early in 1845 that American laws and institutions were peculiarly adaptable to the Anglo-Saxon race, but not to other peoples. He pointed to the decline of the French and Spanish on this continent when American laws had been extended to them.[17] It was their unfitness for "liberal and equal laws, and equal institutions," he assumed, that accounted for this inability to prosper under the United States. In the summer of 1845, however, the tide of migration to California removed this objection. Pioneers rapidly reduced the proportion of Mexican residents. In July the *Democratic Review* noted that the semblance of Mexican influence in this distant province was nearing extinction, for the Anglo-Saxon foot was on her border.

Here was a guaranty that California would never belong to Great Britain. England had certain advantages in her bid for California, such as a superior Pacific fleet, but she lacked the means of directing her population to so remote a territory. Essentially the pioneers spelled the difference in the British and American struggle for California. Editors queried, moreover, what chance British settlers would have if they happened to meet American frontiersmen "trained from their childhood to struggle and provide against the hardships and privations incident to the settlement of a new country." To these editors the question of California had been settled by men who knew no fear. "The pioneers and hunters of the West . . . have said that California is *theirs*—and the word they have said with the tongue, they will make good with the rifle."[18] If the United States government could not impede the progress of the American frontiersmen, wrote one Indianan to President Polk in June, how much less could England—"Whose threats they despise, Whose opposition they court?" He continued:

The Elements are even Now at work which will ultimately Shear Great Britain of her gigantick power, possessions, influence and wealth. She will then Stand a monument, a landmark, to other Nations, of the folly and Weakness which governs her Councils . . . of that lust of dominion, which . . . sought conquests abroad on Continents, which God and Nature never intended She Should Possess, or Possessing retain.[19]

The American pioneer was, lastly, the vehicle by which the United States might extend her laws and democratic institutions to distant portions of the continent. One writer for the *Democratic Review* enumerated in July the characteristically American appurtenances borne by the California pioneers: "Already the advance guard of the irresistible army of Anglo-Saxon emigration has begun to pour down upon it, armed with the plough and rifle, and marking its trail with schools and colleges, courts and representative halls, mills and meeting-houses." It was essentially this civilizing mission that made the march of the Anglo-Saxon race so irresistible. Actually, believed the expansionists, the American people had no choice, for they were fulfilling the destiny to which they had been appointed. In any acquisition of Mexican territory, voiced the St. Louis *Missourian,* the American people would merely be displaying "great political sagacity, and carrying out a decree of the Almighty."[20]

Since in her pioneers rested the possible fulfillment of this nation's destiny, the press followed enthusiastically their progress toward the Pacific. "WESTWARD! THE STAR OF EMPIRE TAKES ITS WAY," shouted the New York *Sun* in urging them on. Western newspapers teemed with accounts of the colorful, hardy, enterprising, energetic emigrants who were traveling westward across the plains and mountains and seeping into the Pacific regions. These stories were widely publicized in the metropolitan press of the East. Early in the spring of

1845 the St. Louis *New Era* urged the emigrants to repair to the frontier immediately. The Burlington *Hawkeye* reported that it was astonished by the tide setting out for the fertile lands of the Pacific. The St. Louis *Reporter* informed the nation that almost every steamer that arrived at St. Louis brought a large number of emigrants from older states who were seeking homes in the new. By fall the press caught the contemplated move of the Mormons to the West and urged them on to California. Observers predicted that they would cause the incorporation of that region into the United States in less than two years.[21]

During the traveling season of 1845 the press fostered this trek of pioneers in every conceivable way. It published minute instructions as to equipment needed and the best routes to the various rendezvous in Missouri and Arkansas. During the summer it kept the restless nation abreast of John C. Fremont's third exploring expedition to the Far West, and by the early spring of 1846 advertised his new route to California. It called the attention of young men to the unrivaled advantages of life in the Pacific regions, and the wonders of climate, soil, and harbors. Typical were the urgings of one Monterey correspondent in July, 1845: "The fertile plains of Oregon and California are resounding with the busy hum of industry; all around us are the germs of empire, prosperity and wealth. Those who would reap the harvest should come out early—come out young—secure their lands, and in ten years they will have fortunes."[22]

Lansford W. Hastings' *Emigrant's Guide to Oregon and California* was the most prominent example of boom advertising. Hastings worked indefatigably for California's development both by writing and by actually leading wagon trains from Salt Lake to the Sacramento. His book was a deliberate attempt to promote the settlement of the West. Published precisely at the time when America turned to the Pacific, it exerted a pronounced influence on the flow and direction of westward migration. H. H. Bancroft insisted that Hastings merely covered the same ground as John Bidwell's pamphlet, published in 1843.

Hastings characterized the Umpqua Valley of Oregon as "very beautiful and rich." The Willamette he described as "very beautiful and productive . . . well timbered, well watered, and . . . admirably suited to agricultural, and grazing purposes." With his usual embellishments and pleadings Hastings pictured California in *couleur de rose*. According to this writer there were no defects in the California environment: "The deep, rich, alluvial soil of the Nile, in Egypt, does not afford a parallel." He visualized California as a land of "genuine *Republicanism,* and unsophisticated *democracy,*" which would "stand forth as enduring monuments to the increasing wisdom of *man,* and the infinite kindness and protection, of an all wise, and ever-ruling Providence."[23]

§ 4

One thought still marred the promise of a continental nation. The fast-moving Mississippi Valley frontier, pushing out into Wisconsin, Iowa, Missouri, and Texas, still remained separated from the western coasts by almost two thousand miles. These vast distances were aggravated by rugged mountains and endless deserts. Communication at best was slow and hazardous; the reluctant trails which traversed these reaches gave little promise of becoming commercial thoroughfares. Many empire enthusiasts were not convinced in 1845 that the regions on the Pacific would become integral portions of the United States.

Asa Whitney of New York, expansionist and Pacific traveler, foresaw an independent maritime republic on the Pacific. Many in California and Oregon shared his fears. They visualized a region isolated and alone, without access to American industry which alone could give it commercial advantage and power. Larkin, on the other hand, in a widely publicized letter to the New York *Journal of Commerce* in July, 1845, predicted neither a strong nor an independent republic. He reported a Mexican province preparing for the coming of either John Bull or Uncle Sam, and he was not convinced that the derelict would complete the southwestern boundaries of the United States.[24] Whether the threat to the American expansionist purpose came from an independent Pacific republic or from British ambitions, something was required to overcome the vast distances separating the Mississippi from the western ocean.

To that generation there was an answer—a transcontinental railway. Expansionists pounced upon this solution to dispute those who insisted that the Pacific regions could not be held in the Union. Such a railroad, declared the *Democratic Review*, would bind "together in its iron clasp our fast settling Pacific regions with that of the Mississippi Valley. . . ." Charles Fletcher, a Pennsylvania railroad booster, also discounted the pessimism. "Let this railroad be finished," he informed the President, "and all their arguments will vanish. . . ." Similarly Whitney assured Secretary of State James Buchanan in June, 1845, that rail communications with Oregon would prevent that distant region from becoming a separate nation.[25] The day was soon coming, predicted the enthusiasts, when representatives from Oregon and California would reach Washington in less time than formerly was required to journey from Ohio.

Whitney was the most prominent of the transcontinental railroad promoters of 1845. Early that year he submitted a memorial to Congress asking for western lands sufficient to finance the building of a railway from Lake Michigan to Oregon. His proposed route would begin at Milwaukee, cross the Mississippi at Prairie du Chien, the Missouri at Big Bend, the Rockies at South Pass, and terminate at the mouth of the Columbia. Whitney defended this route as the most feasible on the globe, without mountains, swamps, or streams to impede its operation. "It would seem," he concluded, "that the God of nature had fixed this as the route. As the Red Sea in olden times, so here the mountains are opened for our passage. . . ." Before the year had elapsed, the expanding interest in the Pacific produced a wide variety of proposals. Stephen Douglas of Illinois published a second plan in the Chicago *Democrat* in November, 1845, to connect Chicago with San Francisco through Rock Island, Council Bluffs, and South Pass. To help finance the project and provide homesteads for settlers he proposed land grants of alternate sections extending several miles on each side of the route.[26]

James Gadsden, President of the South Carolina Railroad Company, and other railroad-minded Southerners publicized the advantages of a more southerly route. At the Memphis Convention of November, 1845, Gadsden broached a railroad from either Vicksburg, Natchez, Memphis, or New Orleans on the Mississippi, across Texas to Mazatlán on the Gulf of California. Here was a route, declared its proponents, of shorter distance, without mountain barriers, and with year-round availability and a population already present. Soon *DeBow's Commercial Review* carried the torch for a route from Memphis to El Paso on the Rio Grande, then westward through the Gila Valley to San Diego. John C. Calhoun proposed this route to Congress in the following year. Albert M. Gilliam, author, traveler, and railroad booster, pointed to the ease of travel across the plains to Santa Fe and thence westward to San Francisco Bay, a route, he claimed, without a single obstruction. Indeed, in December, 1845, Josiah Gregg, America's leading authority on the Southwest, offered his services to the President in exploring the region west of Santa Fe for a practicable wagon road to the Pacific.[27]

Slavery and the sectional struggle for power were already complicating factors in the search for a route. *DeBow's* reminded the North that Memphis as a terminus was accessible both to New England and to the South. This factor also made St. Louis an especially suitable entrepôt on a railway to the Pacific. George Wilkes, editor of the *Police Gazette*, proposed in 1845 a road from Independence, Missouri, to California, built by the federal government to avoid land speculation. Eventually routes beginning at all important cities on Lake Michigan and the Mississippi and terminating at all key Pacific ports from Mazatlán to the Fuca Strait were publicized by such newspapers as the New York *Herald,* New York *Sun,* New York *Journal of Commerce,* and Washington *Union,* as well as *DeBow's Commercial Review.*

Railroads, to the expansionists, would complement the force of pioneers. Emigrants would win the competition for possession; railroads would bring the economic and military power of the United States to bear on the western coasts. It was the latter that assured eventual American greatness on the Pacific. The moment the railway was completed, predicted the New York *Herald,* the commercial power of England in the Pacific would vanish as by the wand of an enchanter. The ceaseless flow of troops, stores, and munitions for land and naval forces would establish American dominance on that ocean and throughout the world. With her naval power in the Pacific the United States would become mistress of the seas. Fletcher boasted that England might "use her navy in the Atlantic, but the . . . commerce of America will be on the Pacific and the whole Pacific Ocean will be under the control of America. . . ." Eventually, he predicted, American power radiating from California would weaken Britain's distant commercial empire in the Orient; and eventually Britain's need of United States friendship in the Pacific would force the end of British aggression in the Western Hemisphere.[28]

Other visions were even more exhilarating. The course of trade over a railway from the Eastern industrial cities of the United States to the harbors along the Pacific actually promised to fulfill the purpose of centuries. Herein lay at last the direct passage to "Golden Cathay and the Oriental Ind!" From the day that Cortez had informed the Spanish king that a strait would reduce "the navigation from the spice countries to the kingdom of your Majesty" to "two-thirds less than the present navigation," Europe had sought that direct passage to China. Now in 1845 this route lay at the feet of the American people, reducing the distance from western Europe to the Orient by more than six thousand miles. "For the last three centuries," cried one writer in *Hunt's Merchants' Magazine,* "the civilized world has been rolling westward; and Americans of the present age will complete the circle. . . ."[29] Along that route magnificent cities rivaling New York and Boston would "rise in glory and grandeur on the Shores on the great western Ocean."

Commercially, this new passage to the Orient would produce a revolution. New marts for American produce, new vistas for American ingenuity filled the immediate future. "The riches of the most unlimited market in the world," wrote Wilkes, "would be thrown open to our enterprise, and . . . our commerce would increase till every ocean billow between us and the China seas would twinkle with a sail." Whitney predicted that the new railroad would command the trade of the more than eight hundred millions of people residing in the Pacific area. Nor was dominion over the Atlantic trade beyond the American dream. One American expansionist, whose enthusiasm was apparently limitless, predicted that through the railroad all Europe would be made tributary to the United States. A New York congressman foresaw Europe finding "her India market where she now purchases her cotton, tobacco, and corn."[30] Silas Wright thought the railroad scheme momentarily impractical, but when completed he agreed that it would become the "greatest inland thoroughfare in the world." Expansionists contemplated the final impact of this commercial route on the American future. The governor of Ohio admitted simply that it would "produce results in commercial, moral and political points of view vast beyond our limited capacity of conception at this time."[31]

Eventually speculation on a transcontinental railroad combined and clarified American expansionist views toward the Pacific as no other phase of her Western interests had. The contemplated linking of a railroad with the sea lanes of the north Pacific gave a new and special relevance to the harbors of Oregon and California in the expansion of United States power and commerce. Ports would serve as the termini of railroads as well as harbors for ships and emporia for Oriental goods. Gilliam warned that only the Strait of Fuca in all of Oregon could command the commerce of India and China, and he urged the Polk administration to stand firm at the forty-ninth parallel to protect the overland route to the Pacific Northwest.[32] Yet he admitted that the Strait was vulnerable to the British on Vancouver Island. Security required San Francisco as an American depot and naval station as well.

Everywhere by 1845 thoughtful Americans seemed to sense the commercial importance of San Francisco. Larkin described its real significance: "It must, will be, the medium stopping place from New Orleans and New York to the China Ports now open to all the world." Similarly Gilliam believed that that harbor provided for California "commercial facilities of so commanding a character, as to render it, in the hands of an enterprising people, the great depot of the Pacific. It will be to that coast, if in the possession of the Anglo-Americans, what New York is to Atlantic countries, the great emporium of commerce and civilization. . . ." Even Hastings acknowledged an unlimited confidence in California's commercial growth, for he prophesied that it would in a very few years "exceed, by far, that of any other country of the same extent and population, in any portion of the known world." Daniel Webster revealed vividly the contemplated role of San Francisco in New England's broadening horizons when he wrote in March, 1845: "You know my opinion to have been, and it now is, that the port of San Francisco would be twenty times as valuable to us as all Texas."[33]

§ 5

California's immense potential value to the United States, whether seen from the agrarian or commercial point of view, made a rationalization of American acquisitiveness almost unnecessary. Yet the apparent contrast between California's backwardness in 1845 and her future possibilities led automatically to an explanation of American interest in terms of the regeneration of California's soil. Thus the St. Louis *Daily Missourian* observed that, despite the wonders of the region, under its present government it was "doomed to desolation and a barren waste, instead of the garden of the world." In a sublime passage the editor noted the need for its acquisition by the United States:

That Mexico shall domineer over it, merely for the sake of domineering, without calling forth its resources, to contribute to the comfort and happiness of man—that enterprise shall be prevented from entering, exploring and bringing forth the fruits of that rich field—that this delightful land should only be a theatre for robbery and plunder, instead of being devoted to the uses which nature and nature's God designed it, we cannot believe. But that it can become other than it now is, we cannot see, unless settled by our countrymen—which we believe, is inevitable, as it seems to be a law of nature, as a western statesman has well remarked, 'that the children of Adam follow the sun;' or, as the poet has it,

'Westward the star of empire holds its way.'[34]

The *American Review* expanded this theme. After three centuries of Spanish and Mexican rule, California, despite its natural advantages, possessed no commerce, little agriculture, and no industry. In every respect, asserted the writer, the region was as devoid of wealth, cultivation, and power as when the Spaniards first sailed its coasts. But to him such conditions could not continue, for "No one who cherishes a faith in the wisdom of an overruling Providence, and who sees, in the national movements which convulse the world, the silent operation of an invisible but omnipotent hand, can believe it to be for the interest of humanity, for the well-being of the world, that this vast and magnificent region should continue forever in its present state. . . ."[35] California, to become that seat of wealth and power which Nature had intended, would of necessity pass to another.

Albert Gilliam agreed. He believed that within a century San Francisco would dominate a "wealthy, populous, and powerful empire" under Anglo-Saxon rule. Under Mexico, on the other hand, he foresaw a "small, unimproving, and decaying old town, and the rich country around it an undeveloped waste." Destiny, however, was on the side of the Americans, he believed, for the "all-wise Being, who created the sea, as well as the earth for the dominion of man, doubtless intended, in his own fullness of time, to render the beautiful waters of San Francisco of corresponding benefit to his intelligent creatures, and will cause them to accomplish the evident designs of nature." The progress of empire in world history, he noted, had been to the west; now the rapid emigration to the Pacific was the culmination of the historic progress of empire toward the setting sun.[36]

Few such brief periods in California's evolution have been more formative than those months between Polk's inaugural and his resumption of negotiations with Mexico in the late autumn of 1845. It was precisely then that an excitable America, having disposed of the Texas issue, adopted California as a specific object in its manifest destiny. Oregon was not the all-important issue of 1845. Nevertheless, the growing interest in California during the summer and autumn revived enthusiasm for Oregon, where, expansionists noted, hardy pioneers, British pressures, and magnificent harbors also demanded an early definitive settlement.

As American interests in the western coasts deepened, the two issues of Oregon and California became increasingly inseparable in the minds of American expansionists. If Polk was ahead of the metropolitan editors in March, 1845, his instructions to John Slidell in November revealed the strong impact of an intervening American awakening. When the President, from his dread of British encroachment and his desire for ports to accommodate America's rising trade empire in the Pacific, sought to purchase varying portions of Upper California from Mexico, he was, in a sense, merely following the precepts of that French Revolutionary leader who, peering from his window at the crowd below, shouted: "There go my followers. I must follow them. I am their leader."

Chapter 6

POLK AND THE PACIFIC

§ 1

To what extent the American dreams of empire, which encompassed varying portions of the Pacific Coast in 1845, would reach fulfillment hinged upon the wisdom and judgment of President James K. Polk. The achievement of American territorial objectives would necessitate either successful diplomacy or, with its collapse, the waging of victorious war. With his accession to office in March, the new President seemed to assure the force of executive leadership behind the expansionist purpose of the American people. His professed stand on Texas and Oregon in the campaign of 1844 indicated that he was prepared emotionally to fulfill one of the privately acknowledged purposes of his administration—that of securing ample frontage for the United States on the shores of the Pacific Ocean.

Polk quickly discovered upon accepting the responsibilities of his office, however, that regardless of its political effectiveness, his party's decision to submerge the Oregon issue in politics could eventually curtail his freedom to act in the national interest. In identifying himself completely with the "whole of Oregon" platform, he ignored both the lack of enthusiasm for that issue among many Democrats and the warning of the Whigs that the stand of 54° 40′ was incompatible with any diplomatic settlement of the Oregon question. In his inaugural, however, Polk persisted in his conviction that the American title was "clear and unquestionable." He entered the White House, it seems, with a determination to maintain the cohesiveness of his party by adhering to his campaign pledge. Nor did he vary that purpose in his subsequent negotiations with Great Britain during the summer of 1845.

Polk's inheritance went beyond the extreme demands of his party for all of Oregon to the Alaska boundary. He was the recipient also of a long diplomatic tradition that had offered compromise to England at the forty-ninth parallel. He could not long ignore this historic reality, especially when his inaugural aroused adverse public sentiment in the United States and even produced talk of war in Britain. The London *Times* answered him by declaring that the British people were "prepared to defend the claims of this country to the utmost, wherever they are seriously challenged." Warned *Wilmer and Smith's Times:* "About whatever savors even remotely of intimidation, John Bull is characteristically thin-skinned. There are certain animals that may be led, but won't be driven—John Bull is one of them. . . . The new president's peremptory style has stirred up his bile. . . ." The London *Colonial Magazine* asserted that "a war with America cannot but be productive of good."[1] What perturbed the British press was the official character of Polk's uncompromising position. For many British writers and officials the time for appeasement had vanished. The English countenance was stern. Yet behind the scenes in London moved the Foreign Minister of Sir Robert Peel's government, Lord Aberdeen, marshaling his forces for peace and eventual compromise.

Polk's offer of a settlement at the forty-ninth parallel in July, 1845, presents no enigma, for he entered those negotiations with neither hope nor expectation of success. He possibly feared war with England if he brought all previous efforts at compromise to an abrupt termination. To insist on 54° 40′ meant war, recalled Thomas Hart Benton; to recede from it was to abandon the platform. Polk met the first

danger with a half-hearted effort at negotiation, which eased
the international crisis. In his deference to domestic political
considerations he admittedly offered less to Britain than she
had demanded in preceding negotiations. James Buchanan,
Secretary of State, revealed the administration's lack of interest in a British acceptance of its proposal. "Should it be rejected," he wrote, "the president will be relieved from the
embarrassment in which he has been involved by the acts,
offers, and declarations of his predecessors."[2]

Even more significant, however, was the President's candid
admission in July, four months after he assumed office, that his
private views toward Oregon differed little from those of the
commercially minded Whigs. Ports, he admitted, were of
primary concern. He agreed, therefore, that the United
States could well settle at 49°, "since the entrance of the
Straits of Fuca, Admiralty Inlet, and Puget's Sound, with
their fine harbors and rich surrounding soil, are all south of
this parallel." Polk accepted without question the verdict of
travelers that the country to the north was unfit for agriculture and incapable of sustaining anything but the fur trade.
With his advisers he doubted "whether the judgment of the
civilized world would be in our favor in a war waged for a
comparatively worthless territory north of 49°, which his
predecessors had over and over again offered to surrender to
Great Britain, provided she would yield her pretensions to
the country south of that latitude."[3] Above all, Polk and his
Secretary of State acknowledged the importance of continuity
and realism in the maintenance of successful foreign relations.

Privately the administration admitted a genuine interest in
compromise. Yet it was determined to prevent a recurrence
of its politically imposed dilemma. Polk therefore placed the
burden of future negotiations squarely on the British with the
veiled threat that only the whole of Oregon would now be
acceptable to the United States. As the New York *Sun* suggested, the transfer of negotiations to London would exhaust
time and allow additional migration to flow into Oregon be-

fore the question would be finally settled. The President instructed Buchanan that if the British minister should call, "No intimation should be given to him of what the views or intentions of the administration were, & [but] leave him to take his own course."[4] When late in October T. W. Ward, the Boston agent of Baring Brothers, called on the President to seek his views, Polk noted the result in his diary: "He learned nothing, and after apologizing for making the inquiry he retired."

Only Buchanan of the cabinet questioned Polk's decision to adhere further to the extreme position of the Democratic platform. He warned the President repeatedly that the country would not justify a war for any territory north of 49° and that if he took such a position in his December message, he would be attacked for maintaining a warlike tone. Polk's reading of party opinion, however, convinced him that his success as party leader was still contingent upon his insistence on the whole of Oregon. His gravest danger, he assured Buchanan, lay in an attack on the administration for having yielded to the tradition of his predecessors. "I told him," Polk recorded, "that if that proposition had been accepted by the British Minister my course would have met with great opposition, and in my opinion would have gone far to overthrow the administration; that, had it been accepted, as we came in on Texas the probability was we would have gone out on Oregon."[5]

Polk's message to Congress in December, 1845, again assured the Democracy that he was thoroughly attuned to the declaration of the Baltimore Convention. He declared: "The extraordinary and wholly inadmissable demands of the British Government, and the rejection of the proposition made in deference alone to what had been done by my predecessors, and the implied obligation which their acts seemed to impose, afforded satisfactory evidence that no compromise which the United States ought to accept, can be effected."[6] Our title to

Oregon, he repeated, was maintained "by irrefragable facts and arguments."

The President appeared to promise that he would not weaken again, but he carefully avoided any phraseology that would deny him the right to submit a compromise treaty to the Senate in the future. The President also urged Congress to study the matter of protecting American citizens in Oregon, but to do nothing that would violate the stipulations of the Convention of 1827. To terminate joint occupancy required a year's notice, he reminded Congress, and without such action the United States could not assert exclusive jurisdiction to any portion of the territory. He asked that Congress authorize him by law to give the notice. Polk was prepared to exert pressure on Britain, but he still refused to assume the diplomatic initiative. Such was the doubtful status to which politics had consigned the Oregon question when Congress convened in December, 1845.

§ 2

Polk turned with greater resolution toward California, for that issue was not encumbered by politics. During 1845 the pressures that had motivated previous efforts to purchase the region, now exerted vociferously in the American press, converged in full measure on the new President. Nor had Polk any intention of ignoring them. American expansionism, however, faced in California a dilemma only partially present in Oregon. The United States had no legal claims to the area. The acquisition of this derelict necessitated bargaining with its owner. During the summer of 1845, as visions of a two-ocean empire illuminated the pages of the American press, the chances of negotiating with Mexico appeared slight indeed. The mutual antagonisms created by the Texas and claims issues had severed completely the weakening thread upon which diplomacy between the two nations had hung for a decade.

Scarcely a month had elapsed after Polk's inauguration when General Juan Almonte, Mexican Minister to the United States, boarded the packet barque *Anahuac* at New York and sailed for Vera Cruz. Calhoun in 1844 had assured Mexican officials when he sought to annex Texas that the United States was "actuated by no feelings of disrespect or indifference to the honor and dignity of Mexico, and that it would be a subject of great regret if it should be otherwise regarded by its government." But Mexico repeatedly threatened war if Texas were annexed. After the passage of the Joint Resolution, Polk sought diligently to avoid a break. James Buchanan assured Almonte that the new administration would make every effort to adjust amicably all outstanding complaints. But expressions of good will were not sufficient. To Mexico the move to annex Texas was an unbearable affront. She promptly took the preliminary step of severing diplomatic relations by recalling her minister in March. But the pressing issue of California required an immediate renewal of diplomatic relations with Mexico. Aboard the *Anahuac*, which carried Almonte to Vera Cruz in April, was William S. Parrott, long-time resident of Mexico. On his special mission to renew negotiations with Mexico rested the hopes of the President.[7]

The feeling of urgency mounted during the summer and autumn months of 1845. It began when disquieting reports from American officials in England, Mexico, and California pointed to British and French ambitions along the Pacific Coast. Robert Armstrong, Consul at Liverpool, advised the administration of such British intention in August. "England must never have California," he concluded, "and it seems to me advisable to make Oregon the bone of contention to prevent it. The whole country will sustain you on Oregon." More forceful was his warning of two months later. So outraged were the British over Texas annexation, he declared, that England was pressing Spain to attempt a reconquest of Mexico. "I suppose the crown heads would make a family affair of it and take part," he cautioned the President.[8] Parrott complained that British intrigue in Mexico City was blocking his path to the Mexican government. Such cunning, he warned Buchanan, had but one purpose, the British acquisition of California. From California the administration heard rumors that England and France had agreed to recognize the provincials of California in their independence movement, provided the new republic would never allow itself to become annexed to the United States.[9]

Even more frightening were Larkin's revelations from Monterey. He informed Buchanan that the British and French governments were maintaining consular posts in Upper California, although neither nation had any ostensible commercial interests there. The French consul at Monterey, with no apparent tasks to perform, was receiving a salary of four thousand dollars per year. The British consul, living on a ranch fifty miles from the coast where he could render no services to British merchants, remained in California, Larkin assured the Secretary, only to fulfill some sinister purpose. "Why they are in Service their Government best know and Uncle Sam will know to his cost," warned Larkin in his widely published letter to the New York *Journal of Commerce* in July. Not one British merchant ship except those of the Hudson's Bay Company had visited California in many years. But it was this giant company, Larkin reminded the administration, that had long been a source of apprehension to Boston traders.

Larkin's reports produced a wave of excitement in the administration. "The appearance of a British Vice Consul and French Consul in California at this present crisis without any apparent commercial business," Buchanan answered Larkin, "is well calculated to produce the impression that their respective governments entertained designs on that country. . . ." Buchanan similarly informed Louis McLane, United States Minister at London, of his strong suspicions that France and England were intriguing in both Mexico and California with ambitions of acquiring the latter. Wrote the Secretary: "I need not say to you what a flame would be kindled throughout the Union should Great Britain obtain a cession of California from Mexico. . . ."[10]

This rumored threat of European encroachment in North America fell heavily on the Polk administration. By the autumn of 1845 leading Democrats and newspaper editors were demanding that the President either reopen negotiations with Mexico to purchase the province quickly or reaffirm the principles of the Monroe Doctrine. In September the New York *Herald* urged Polk to assume even higher ground than had Monroe, and to "put into operation those principles and elements of power, which have been committed to the hands of the American people by the Almighty, for the purpose of regenerating, not only this continent, but the old continent of Europe, in due process of time." An imagined danger from Europe was awakening some American expansionists to the importance of their destiny. The writer, pressing the President to acquire California, continued:

American patriotism takes a wider and loftier range than heretofore. Its horizon is widening every day. No longer bounded by the limits of the confederacy, it looks abroad upon the whole earth, and into the mind of the republic daily sinks deeper and deeper the conviction that the civilization of the earth—the reform of the governments of the ancient world—the emancipation of the whole race, are dependent, in a great degree, on the United States. Let Mr. Polk ponder these things, and let his message be worthy of the nation and of the crisis.[11]

Polk officially challenged England and France in his December message. The United States, he declared, "cannot in silence permit European interference on the North American continent; and should any such interference be attempted will be ready to resist it at any and all hazards." Although he specifically mentioned only Oregon in his message, Polk was equally concerned with Mexican territory. Late in October, while his message was in preparation, he informed Benton that the United States "would not willingly permit California to pass into the possession of any new colony planted by Great Britain or any foreign monarchy." At the same time Buchanan wrote to Larkin that the President "could not view with indifference the transfer of California to Great Britain or any other European Power," and that the future destiny of California was a subject "of anxious solicitude for the Government and people of the United States."[12] This nation, the Secretary continued, would not interfere between Mexico and her province, but it would "vigorously interpose to prevent the latter from becoming a British and French Colony."

Expansionists believed that the permanent answer to the British threat lay in the immediate purchase of California by the United States. It seemed logical and proper that Polk renew the offers of Jackson and Tyler, for it was obvious that the impecunious Mexican government, torn by strife and dissension at home, could no longer maintain possession of her province. Such a purchase, observed the Norfolk *Herald*, would relieve the Mexican treasury and enable that government to re-establish its authority over the Mexican nation. And the advantages that would accrue to the United States, believed the writer, would be sufficient to merit the expenditure of ten times the millions that would be required to obtain it by war.[13] "Instead of menaces," wrote Charles J. Ingersoll, "we should have a great mission there to give them almost any price they ask for San Francisco and peace." He suggested that the President send Henry Clay to negotiate for the purchase. Larkin proposed in July an arrangement similar to Webster's of 1843 by which the United States would settle the Oregon question at the Columbia and thereby secure the approval of Britain for the purchase of eight degrees south of forty-two. He reminded his Eastern correspondents that Oregon would be rendered useless to Americans by the failure to acquire San Francisco Bay.[14]

One form of coercion was available against Mexico. The Polk administration could exert moral pressure on the Mexican government by demanding a settlement of the claims of American citizens against the Mexican government for alleged losses of property in Mexican ports. This simple device of assuming the Mexican debts to American claimants in exchange for Mexican territory was not new. As early as 1842 Webster prepared to extend such an offer to Mexico, but was forced to withdraw his proposal when Jones seized the port of Monterey. In March, 1845, Governor N. P. Tallmadge of Wisconsin urged Polk to purchase Upper California north of 37° and assume all or part of the amount due United States citizens from Mexico. A few months later Richard Coxe, Washington attorney for the claimants, asserted that fifty million was a cheap price to pay for California because of its essential importance to the whaling and commercial interests of the United States. With a generous expenditure of several millions in addition to the assumption of claims, however, Coxe believed that the United States might acquire all of Upper California peacefully.[15]

Claims against Mexico were never a legitimate cause for war, but they were far more than the "usual odds and ends that can easily be accumulated for such a purpose"—as James Truslow Adams once termed them. The claims issue had first placed a strain on United States–Mexican diplomacy a decade earlier when Andrew Jackson laid them before Congress and suggested that they be presented to Mexico from the deck of a warship. Under the convention signed in 1839, two million dollars were finally awarded American claimants, but the financial condition of the Mexican Republic never tolerated the liquidation of this assumed indebtedness.[16] Moreover, this commission disposed of only a small portion of the American demands. A second convention was negotiated by the Tyler administration in 1843, but it was never ratified by the Mexican government.

By 1845 the issue of claims had become public news in the United States and threatened to destroy whatever peaceful intentions the expansionists still held toward Mexico. The alleged perfidy of the Mexican government caused the American press to launch a bitter attack against Mexico. In May the Washington *Semi-Weekly Union* published a series of articles critically reviewing the entire history of the claims. The evidence was sufficient, declared the editor, to demonstrate that Mexico's conduct had been "marked by cruelty, faithlessness, and utter disregard to all the obligations which the laws of truth and honor impose."[17] The *Democratic Review* asserted that Mexico's actions had been characterized by "an insolence, stupidity, and folly, very little favorable to the cultivation of liberal and conciliatory dispositions on our part."

The anarchical and confused state of Mexican politics offered little hope of more candid negotiations in the future. Mexico's treasury was exhausted. Wrote Ben Green, "Any proposition to pay money at all, and particularly to foreign claimants, is extremely unpopular." Thus Mexico during the early months of Polk's administration earned the severe condemnation of American writers. Declared the New Orleans *Picayune:* "Enfeebled, humiliated, and disgraced, she plunges madly into further embarrassments; she insults and would exasperate the enemies her insolence has provoked and at whose mercy she exists; and, as if struggling with the frenzy of despair or the involuntary throes of dissolution, she appears fain to lend a suicidal hand to assist in her own dismemberment and annihilation."[18] Mexican policy promised no reparation for the past and no security for the future.

By autumn, claims had become a pawn in an expansionist game. For many they had become a *casus belli* by which the Polk administration could bring to bear on the Mexican government the threat of military force. One Western Democrat assured the President that a war with Mexico would make his administration bright and glorious, give the Mexicans the drubbing they deserved, and "acquire N. Mexico and Upper California, which has of late become indispensable to the government, to complete our defense and wants on the Pacific." The New York *Herald* predicted that a thrust at Mexico would secure California before England could possess it and perhaps do the Mexicans a favor. "The bastard republic of Mexico," argued the writer, "appears to be in the last stages of decline; it is a mere skeleton of a nation, and can only be restored to full health by the Anglo-Saxon race, given in suitable doses. . . ."[19] To the St. Louis *Missouri Reporter* a direct move into New Mexico and California would establish the American position on the Pacific and help bring pressure to bear on the British in Oregon. Aaron Leggett, the New York merchant, summarized the views of these expansionists when in October he pressed the administration for action. "If I was the President," he declared, "I would order one of our Ships of War to go and take Monterey and all California & keep it as pay for what Mexico owes us."[20]

Polk refused to accept either war or the seizure of California as a solution to the Mexican question. It was, in fact, only the recurring threats of hostility from Mexico to recover Texas that forced him to take defensive measures. In August, when he summoned the touring Buchanan to Washington, his orders had already placed General Zachary Taylor on the Texas frontier near Corpus Christi. In this maneuver the President accepted the responsibility of defending the border against any possible aggression from Mexico.

Polk believed that a show of force would prevent rather than provoke war. "I do not anticipate that Mexico will be mad enough to declare war," he wrote in July, but "I think she would have done so but for the appearance of a strong naval force in the Gulf and our army moving in the direction of her frontier on land." The *Missouri Reporter* approved this show of strength, and some Democratic leaders urged an even larger force for the Texas frontier. The President maintained, however, that his military and naval movements were strictly defensive. "We shall not be the aggressors upon Mexico," he assured one member of Congress in August. Though prepared for war, wrote Buchanan the following month, the President desired a settlement "by negotiation and not by the sword."[21]

It is not strange that the President failed to reflect the martial spirit of some Democrats. While these ardent patriots cried aloud that war would demolish both Mexican and British resistance to American destiny, cooler heads recalled the unsettled Oregon dispute with England and feared that war would ruin that negotiation. Buchanan added his warning: "We ought not in my opinion to do any thing at the present moment which might tend to make G. B. the ally of Mexico, in case of war. . . ." Conflict would end every hope of counteracting British influence in Mexico City, whereas friendship with Mexico might isolate England. Only when the United States had eased its tensions with Mexico could it talk to the European powers more explicitly about "the balance of Power, the trade of the Pacific, and *European interference in American disputes.*"[22]

§ 3

Successful policy toward California could comprise the purchase of the province from Mexico. But it might entail, rather, the eventual annexation of an independent California republic. Some Americans still predicted a new nation on the Pacific, consisting of California and portions of Oregon, with its capital on San Francisco Bay. Should California become free of Mexico, therefore, the problem facing Polk was that of hedging against any movement that might seek to perpetuate the independence of a California republic. The Washington *Semi-Weekly Union* urged the appointment of a United States commercial agent in California to counteract the British and French consuls. The editor recognized likewise the need for efficient consuls at Mazatlán, Monterey, and Acapulco.[23] To keep the British from gaining control of California, added one New Yorker, "would seem to require on the spot an active, discreet, and intelligent agent, to protect American citizens and give to our government the earliest information."

Quietly in October, 1845, the President initiated this policy. In Larkin, who had been United States Consul at Monterey since 1844, he found a trustworthy agent, thoroughly devoted to the American cause. Polk defined clearly Larkin's new duties. He was to play no role in the struggle between Mexico and her province; but if California should become fully independent, he was to render all the kind offices due a sister republic. Buchanan warned him, however, to "take care not to awaken the jealousy of the French and English governments there by assuming other than your Consular character."[24] He was to make the native residents aware of the danger of European interference to their peace and prosperity and, conversely, "to arouse in their bosoms that love of liberty and independence so natural to the American continent." Lastly, Larkin could assure the local residents that if they desired to unite their destiny with that of the United States, they would be received as soon as it could be accomplished without affording Mexico just cause for complaint.

Larkin's instructions did not anticipate war. Yet if a clash should occur, positive action would be required to seize the ports and defend California against Mexican oppression or British aggression. Polk had been warned that Britain's expanding Pacific squadron would seize and hold San Francisco in case of war. In this contingency the task of defending American interests in the Pacific would fall to the Pacific squadron under Commodore John D. Sloat. Late in June, 1845, Sloat had been instructed to possess San Francisco and blockade or occupy any other port his force would permit if he "ascertained with certainty" that Mexico had declared war on the United States. While Buchanan prepared instructions to Larkin, Bancroft repeated the earlier orders to the naval commander. He then dispatched Commodore Robert F. Stockton, commander of the *Congress,* then at Norfolk, to the Pacific to carry Larkin's instructions to Monterey and join the Pacific fleet.[25]

During November Polk initiated the second phase of his California policy—an immediate effort to purchase the province from Mexico. This maneuver followed hard on encouraging reports from Mexico. Parrott's mission to Mexico City was bearing fruit. In September this agent informed the President that Mexico would resume diplomatic relations with the United States. The cabinet immediately agreed to reopen negotiations and tender the ministry to John Slidell of New Orleans, but to keep the mission secret lest the European powers interfere. It agreed further to offer Mexico forty million dollars for a boundary from the mouth of the Rio Grande along that river to the thirty-second parallel, and thence westward to the Pacific. At the same time Buchanan requested John Black, the United States Consul at Mexico City, to approach the Mexican government officially and corroborate Parrott's story. The Mexican government formally notified Black in mid-October that it would receive any commissioner dispatched to Mexico City with full power "to settle the present dispute in a peaceful, reasonable, and honorable manner."[26] Behind this acceptance of the President's wishes lay the promptings and good advices of Charles Bankhead, the British Minister in Mexico, whose pride at maintaining peace resulted perhaps from a desire to prevent United States expansion through a conquest of Mexico.

During the early days of November the State Department worked in feverish haste. After diplomatic channels had been closed for seven months, the prospects of settling the momentous questions in dispute were cheering. There were, moreover, disquieting rumors of the impending collapse of the peacefully disposed José Joaquín Herrera regime. Within four days instructions and other documents had been prepared for Slidell, who had accepted the appointment. These orders then had been dispatched to Pensacola, where the minister awaited them for his immediate embarkation for Vera Cruz. By early December Slidell had taken up residence in Mexico City.

Slidell's instructions summarized the administration's view of Mexican relations. They revealed the dread of British and French designs on California. "You will endeavor to ascertain," ran Buchanan's injunction, "whether Mexico had any intention of ceding it to the one or the other power; and if any such design exists, you will exert all your energies to prevent an act, which, if consummated, would be so fraught with danger to the best interests of the United States."[27] His principal object, he was told, was "to restore those ancient relations of peace and good will which formerly existed between the Governments and citizens of the sister Republics"; but he was warned against accepting the mediation of any European power, since "the march of free government on this continent must not be trammeled by the intrigue and selfish interests of European powers."

In his wide variety of boundary proposals Polk was adamant only on the Rio Grande, for this appeared a natural choice. This line had been defined by United States diplomats in the Florida settlement, had been accepted by Santa Anna after his capture in 1836, and was declared by the Texas congress to be the limit of the new republic in December of that year. In June, 1845, the President had guaranteed this boundary to both Sam Houston and A. J. Donelson, his chargé in Texas. By November this line had been widely accepted in the United States, and the New York *Journal of Commerce* observed: "Public opinion seems unanimous in requiring that it shall be the Rio Grande, certainly no line East of the River."[28]

California also was beckoning Polk. Slidell was asked to negotiate for its purchase and to mention simultaneously the matter of claims in a "prudent and friendly spirit." Since Mexico was obviously in no condition to pay the latter, the Secretary proposed to guard the honor of both countries by adjusting the boundary so that the burden would be assumed by the United States. Polk would assume all American claims for the Rio Grande boundary alone. For New Mexico he would add five million dollars above the claims; for San Francisco, twenty million; and with Monterey included, twenty-five million. Privately the President believed that New Mexico and Upper California could be acquired for fifteen million, but during December, in his intense desire to secure a treaty, he authorized Slidell to increase the maximum amounts. The acquisition of some portion of California was never a *sine qua non* to any settlement, however, for Slidell was permitted to conclude a treaty if Mexico would agree to any one of the President's specific proposals.[29]

The President revealed repeatedly in the formulation of his California policy, as he had in his initial Oregon negotiations, that his interests in American expansion to the Pacific were essentially maritime. "The interests of our commerce and our whale fisheries on the Pacific ocean," he had instructed Larkin, "demand that you should exert the greatest vigilance in discovering and defeating any attempt which may be made by foreign governments to acquire a control over that country."

His boundary proposals to Slidell were defined solely in terms of California ports. These started with San Francisco and Monterey, but they included also a suggested boundary reaching westward from El Paso along the thirty-second parallel to the Pacific—this to include the harbor of San Diego. New England merchants during 1845 reminded the administration of American commercial property in that port which might require the defense of a naval vessel in event of war. "Knowing you desire to give every protection to the Commercial interest," Sturgis wrote to Bancroft hopefully, "I doubt not that orders have been given to take care of this branch of it in case of hostilities with Mexico." Bancroft's orders to the Pacific fleet, however, indicated that throughout 1845 San Francisco Bay remained the key objective of the Polk administration along the California coast. He instructed Commodore Sloat to occupy that bay in case of war, as well as "such other ports as your force may permit."[30] And Polk had admitted in conversation with Benton that in his reassertion of the Monroe Doctrine he had "California & the fine bay of San Francisco, as much in view as Oregon."

§ 4

Polk embarked upon his venture to secure peace with Mexico, the Rio Grande, and perhaps California with pardonable optimism. The Mexican government of Herrera, Black had assured him, favored the amicable adjustment of pending difficulties. It was the weakness of the Herrera regime, however, that proved the undoing of the Slidell mission. Despite its promises, the tottering administration dared not recognize the American envoy, and the Mexican foreign minister admitted the reason: "You know the opposition are calling us traitors for entering into this arrangement with you." No president of Mexico could survive that accusation in 1845. Perhaps well-intentioned, the Herrera administration was forced to reject Slidell in order to maintain itself. Since Texas was the only question open for discussion, ran the Mexican rationalization, a minister *ad hoc* to settle this question alone would be acceptable to Mexico, but not an "envoy extraordinary and minister plenipotentiary." Polk refused to change the commission and has borne a century of condemnation because of it.

Why did the President remain adamant on the matter of Slidell's commission? With considerable premonition the Washington *Union* anticipated the queries of Polk's critics: "A great many people are asking this question, and the world will ask it hereafter." Spokesmen for the Polk administration insisted not only that Texas annexation was a *fait accompli* and no longer a subject for negotiation, but also that the Mexican government was avoiding the issue of claims. They were convinced, moreover, that public opinion in Mexico would not have sustained a settlement approaching the American demands and that a new commission would merely have forced the Mexican government to seek a new explanation. The British minister in Mexico urged the Mexican government to recognize Slidell, for he feared that the Mexican attitude would render future peace impossible. "Even if the Mexican government be diplomatically right," wrote the Mexican correspondent of the London *Times*, "it is politically wrong."[31] He was perturbed that Mexico, unsure of European support and cognizant of the aggressive spirit of her neighbor, would furnish the United States an excuse to take California.

In January, 1846, the Herrera regime collapsed and the conservative forces under General Mariano Paredes, with a "grito for the integrity of Mexican soil," entered the capital. Polk quickly instructed Slidell to approach the new government, but Paredes, like his predecessor, declined the offer of negotiation.[32]

Polk realized suddenly that the chief obstacle to his peaceful acquisition of California was the lack of a government in Mexico that had the courage to negotiate with the United States. He reasoned that any Mexican regime could best be sustained by a well-fed army. By the end of March, 1846, he seriously considered submitting a request to Congress for a half million or a million dollars which might enable Paredes, upon the signing of a treaty, to maintain himself in power until the document could be ratified by the United States.[33] Polk recalled the secret service fund provided for Jefferson in 1806. The problem, the President admitted to his diary, was not only that of obtaining the Congressional appropriation but also that of shielding its true purpose from the American public and foreign governments. Benton believed the project feasible if debated first in executive session.

On Benton's advice the President called in other leading Democrats. Lewis Cass and William Allen, two vigorous expansionists, agreed readily to the plan. Calhoun, whose support was essential, recognized the importance of California and reminded the President that in 1844 he had sought to purchase San Francisco Bay. He believed the plan inexpedient, however, for he doubted that the purpose of the appropriation could be kept secret. If it became public, feared Calhoun, it might embarrass the settlement of the Oregon question.[34] Lacking this Democrat's support, Polk dropped the matter.

Polk's first year of diplomacy achieved no foothold on the Pacific, but it defined clearly the new administration's objectives and did so purely in terms of ports. His policies reflected a fundamental willingness to translate the expansionism of the American people into concrete acquisitions. The course of empire was rushing on, and the President was still in control of California policy. The province belonged to Mexico and had not, therefore, become a fit subject for political debate. When Polk placed the responsibility for further Oregon negotiations on the British government, however, he was admitting that his domestic political commitments had effectively destroyed his freedom to formulate policy on that important question.

Chapter 7

ACQUISITION OF THE STRAIT

§ 1

There was little indication when the Twenty-ninth Congress met in December, 1845, that within six months the settlement of the disturbing Oregon question would be assured. Polk's message had followed his personal conviction that the "only way to treat John Bull was to look him straight in the eye." Enthusiasm for the whole of Oregon, engendered by the President's stand, rapidly translated United States claims in the Far Northwest into what Albert K. Weinberg has termed a "defiant anti-legalism." It no longer mattered that the American title to territory north of the Columbia was far from conclusive, and above the forty-ninth parallel practically nonexistent. It had become, wrote John L. O'Sullivan of the New York *Morning News,* "our manifest destiny to occupy and to possess the whole of the Continent which Providence has given us. . . ."[1] To 54-40 proponents that seemed to settle the issue.

Early in January, 1846, Robert Winthrop called the attention of Congress to this new doctrine. The American title to Oregon, he cried, now appeared to lie in *"the right of manifest destiny to spread over the whole continent."* American expansionism was shifting its emphasis to a higher law. Edward D. Baker of Illinois informed the House that he had little regard for "musty records and the voyages of old sea captains, or the Spanish treaties," for the United States had a better title "under the law of nature and of nations."

These higher law precepts assumed that God preferred to be on the side of morality rather than on the side of law. Expansionists viewed the struggle for Oregon as one between democracy and monarchy. Morally the title went to the United States because it was a democracy. Representative Frederick P. Stanton of Tennessee provided the twist which placed American claims on the chosen side. The acquisition of Oregon by the United States was not right because it was destined. On the contrary—it was destined because it was right. The extremists carried their title even further into the realm of higher law when they added the right of "geographical predestination." The proximity of Oregon to the United States when contrasted to the vast distances which separated it from England meant obviously that nature had given the region to the American Republic. Two lines of poetry summed up the contention of the *Democratic Review:*

> The right depends on the propinquity,
> The absolute sympathy of soil and place.[2]

John Quincy Adams provided a third aspect of American higher law claims. He called upon the clerk to read from Genesis: "Be fruitful, and multiply, and replenish the earth, and subdue it. . . ." To Adams this Biblical command gave the American people better right to the region than the Hudson's Bay Company. England desired Oregon merely for navigation and hunting while the United States wished to carry out the behest of God Almighty and "to make the wilderness blossom as the rose." Finally, Baker rested his defense on the principle of security for present and future generations of Americans. He pointed out that the United States had a continent before it in which to "spread our free principles, our language, our literature, and power; and we had the present right to provide for the future progress. To do this was to secure our safety, in the widest and highest sense; and thus our destiny had become so manifest that it could not fail but by our own folly."[3]

The most uncompromising of the "ultras" in Congress were the representatives from the Midwest—Ohio, Indiana, and Illinois. It was Senator Hannegan of Indiana who proposed a toast for a meeting at Philadelphia: "Oregon—every foot or not an inch; 54 degrees and forty minutes or *delenda est Britannia.*" Similarly, George Fries of Ohio roared in the House of Representatives: "We pitched our tents, and, if God willing, they shall never be struck till the stars and stripes wave over Oregon, every inch of Oregon." Appeals for the whole of Oregon flooded the office of Senator Allen of Ohio. The declaration of one writer that "our title is clear and indisputable to 54° 40' and no less" spoke the convictions of all.[4]

Cries for the whole of Oregon, in fact, resounded from all portions of the nation. One Virginian lauded Allen for his patriotic stand: "Der Sir I have noted your cors in United States Senit Ever since you have been there and pleas to receive my sincir thanks." From Charleston, South Carolina, came the observation: "I have met with more 54° 40' men here, amongst prominent merchants, than I had any idea existed in the whole state." George D. Phillips reported late in December from Georgia: "I heard a crowd on Christmas, not one of whom knew on which side of the Rocky Mountains Oregon was, swear that they would support and fight for Polk *all over the world,* that he was right, and we would have Oregon and thrash the British into the bargain."[5] Such Southern members of Congress as Seaborn Jones of Georgia, Henry Bedinger of Virginia, and Lucien B. Chase and Andrew Johnson of Tennessee matched on occasion the expansiveness of Western Democrats.

Cullen Sawtelle, of Maine, lauded the President for his firmness and rebuked Webster: "We want no more half-English half-American secretaries to barter away any other portion of our territory." A tenseness pervaded the capital as members gathered for the opening of Congress. The "ultras" appeared to have captured the public, and others hesitated to challenge their patriotism. John C. Calhoun admitted later that when he arrived at Washington in December it was dangerous even to whisper "forty-nine."[6]

§ 2

It quickly becomes evident from a study of the great Oregon debate of 1846 that this expanding outlook was doomed from the beginning by the patent interests of American commercialism. Too many Congressional eyes were narrowly trained on ports to permit the triumph of agrarian nationalism. Oregon's waterways had not lost their peculiar significance as windows on the Pacific. The persistent attention to trappers, missionaries, and pioneers had never obscured for some members of Congress the strategic importance of Oregon to the trade of Asia. Samuel Gordon, of New York, phrased for the House in January, 1846, his district's cogent evaluation of Oregon: "It is the key to the Pacific. It will command the trade of the isles of the Pacific, of the East, and of China."[7] Similarly Washington Hunt, also of New York, voiced this repetitious theme: "Its possession will ultimately secure to us an ascendency in the trade of the Pacific, thereby making 'the uttermost parts of the earth' tributary to our enterprise, and pouring into our lap 'the wealth of Ormus and of Ind.' "

Salt spray had also conditioned New England's outlook during the Oregon debate. Early in January, 1846, Winthrop had defined clearly the objectives of commercial America. "We need ports on the Pacific," he shouted. "As to land, we have millions of acres of better land still unoccupied on this side of the mountains."[8]

During the preceding year William Sturgis, still actively a member of Boston's commercial aristocracy, had popularized such particularistic notions in the Bay State. His three decades of intense maritime activity in the Pacific had channeled his attention to ports and not to land. The expansionism of

Western agrarians he attributed to an exaggerated opinion of the Oregon countryside. In his famous lecture to the citizens of Boston in January, 1845, Sturgis admitted that the Willamette Valley was both attractive and productive, but he added that he had never seen or heard of any Oregon lands which were superior to millions of uncultivated acres east of the Rockies.

Sturgis indicated, moreover, which ports in Oregon the United States would require to assure fully her future position in Oriental trade. The Columbia, he warned, was always dangerous for large ships and almost inaccessible for a considerable portion of each year. Instead, this nation's maritime greatness in the Pacific would derive from the possession of the Strait of Juan de Fuca and its numerous branches, which were "easy of access, safe, and navigable at all seasons and in any weather."[9] This lucid analysis of American interests on the Northwest Coast, complementing the writings of other travelers and merchants, determined fully the Congressional views of commercial America toward the Oregon question.

Northeastern Congressmen were not alone in debating the Oregon question in commercial terms. Agrarian spokesmen of the Midwest readily acknowledged that Oregon held a special mercantile significance for their constituents as well. This ardent group saw that the Strait of Fuca was the future link between the Mississippi Valley, with its surplus of grain, and the teeming millions of the Orient, who in exchange for the grain could enrich the great valley with cargoes of tea, porcelain, silks and satins, velvets, sugar, and spices. Through possession of the Strait, moreover, the United States would challenge the commercial supremacy of England in the Pacific. Andrew Kennedy of Indiana sought to erase all doubts as to the tangible value of Oregon to the Midwest:

> It is the inch of ground upon which we can place a fulcrum, giving us the lever by which to overturn the world of British commerce. It will give us a cluster of manufacturing and commercial states on the Pacific corresponding with our New England States upon the Atlantic.

Then the inhabitants of the great Mississippi Valley, who have in their possession the garden of the world and the granary of the universe, will stretch out one hand to the East Indies through the Pacific chain, the other to Europe through the Atlantic channel, grasping the trade of the civilized earth, as we now hold in possession the means of subsistence of the whole human family.[10]

What alarmed these nationalists, however, was the fact that the constant reiteration of the commercial value of Oregon bespoke compromise at the forty-ninth parallel, for that boundary would give the United States access to the Strait. Representatives of commerce who wished to secure permanent title to the magnificent inlet pointed out that the United States could acquire all the excellent harbors in Oregon and still proffer an olive branch to England. Sturgis, for example, had argued that a settlement at 49°, with the granting of Vancouver Island to Great Britain, would secure the maritime objectives of the United States and still not deny to England the navigation of Fuca Strait, a right which she would not relinquish.[11] Albert Gallatin in his pamphlet, *The Oregon Question,* also insisted that ports were the primary consideration in any equitable and peaceful division of Oregon and that they pleaded for a settlement at the forty-ninth parallel.

On the other hand, Wilkes had described the Pacific Coast north of 49° as being devoid of good harbors or any extensive commercial inducements. Similarly R. R. Waldron, a naval sea captain, had informed Secretary George Bancroft in April, 1845, that the forty-ninth parallel was sufficient for American needs. "From personal observations of four months in the interior of that country," he wrote, "I think we shall get about all that is worth having. . . ." Such writings merely substantiated the view that everything of value in Oregon lay to the south of that line. Bradford Wood, of New York, assured Congress that it "knew nothing of the country north of that parallel. All that had been said of its value and beauty were mere draughts on the imagination."[12]

Uncompromising Democrats were driven by the logic of the commercial argument to assume the task not only of proving the value of Oregon north of 49°, but actually of doing so in realistic commercial terms. The acquisition of the Strait alone, they sought to illustrate, hardly touched the commercial possibilities of the Northwest Coast. They reminded Congress that a compromise would lose the islands of Vancouver and Washington with their sturdy forests for American shipbuilding, their excellent harbors, their unparalleled fisheries, and their commanding position on the sea lanes. With such a settlement would go also other valuable islands and the bays and harbors which indented the coast. They demanded to know why the United States would voluntarily grant such enormous commercial advantages to Great Britain. John McClernand, of Illinois, impressed upon the mercantile spokesmen of the House the fatal error of compromise when he declared:

Commercially, indeed, by such a concession, we voluntarily decapitate ourselves upon the Pacific seaboard; we lose that portion of Oregon which bears the same relation to the Pacific, in furnishing a commercial marine upon that ocean, which New England now bears upon the Atlantic. . . . The American or British marine, which will whiten the Pacific, and carry direct trade to Asia, Polynesia, and South to the Atlantic capes, will be built, owned, and navigated by a similar people, who shall dwell north of the 49th parallel. This must naturally come to pass, because the harbors, bays, timber, and material, to give existence to a marine, exist there in combination; and there, too, are fisheries which nurse seamen.

Similarly warned Hannegan: "Let England possess Nootka Sound, the finest harbor in the world, commanding as it does the Strait of Fuca, and consequently the access to Puget's Sound, and she has all of Oregon worth possessing in a commercial and maritime point of view." He turned his abuse on men dominated by narrow commercialism. "It is the opinion of six-sevenths of the American people," he shouted, "that Oregon is ours—perhaps I should rather say five-sevenths,

for I must leave out of the estimate the commercial and
stockjobbing population of our great cities along the seaboard,
a great portion of whom are English subjects, residing among
us for the purpose of traffic. . . ."[13]

Because of the alleged "Bargain of 1844" and the necessity
of agrarian unity in achieving the whole of Oregon, Hannegan
would not write off the South or its Democratic leadership so
easily. He castigated that region for losing interest in free
territory after it had acquired Texas. Actually, the South,
like the Northeast, revealed its inclination to compromise in
commercial terms. No American publication called the attention of its readers to the importance of Asiatic commerce
in more ebullient terms than did *DeBow's Commercial Review*
of New Orleans. In January, 1846, its editor declared:

The commerce of the East Indies has for ages been a glittering object
in the eyes of trading nations. They have sought it, and grown up to
power and influence under its support. What, for instance, were the
Italian republics, until the bounteous products of the East were thrown
into their lap; and where were Venice and Genoa and Pisa, when the
Portuguese, by a shorter passage to the Indies, had cut off these rich
resources? Britain, too, what has been her advance since she has
enjoyed an almost monopoly of this invaluable trade? If possessions
on the Pacific Ocean will facilitate such a commerce—if they be necessary to its existence—then, surely, we will not be neglectful of these
possessions.

Even those Southerners who believed that the trade of
Oregon would accrue to the benefit of other sections insisted
on the preservation of the Strait. But they would court no
conflict by demanding more than 49°. George McDuffie, of
South Carolina, agreed that the United States as a civilized
nation might claim all Oregon country fit for cultivation, but
he doubted the "right of a Christian people to drive off savages from a region fit only for savages." To Jefferson Davis,
of Mississippi, the forty-ninth parallel guaranteed American
interests in Oregon: "Possessed, as by this line we should be,
of the agricultural portion of the country, of the Straits of

Fuca, and Admiralty Inlet, to American enterprise and American institutions we can, without a fear, intrust the future."[14]

Spokesmen of all sections agreed that harbors were of real consequence in the development of commerce in the Pacific, but the northern position of the Strait of Fuca blinded many to its potential value as an ocean port. Several noted writers and travelers after 1845, rejecting the Columbia and ignoring the Fuca Strait, increasingly diverted the expansionist attention southward to the harbors of San Francisco and San Diego. Thereafter many American politicians and members of the press believed the commercial growth of the United States in the Pacific contingent largely upon the acquisition of these California ports. Albert Gilliam warned that Oregon was so devoid of harbors that if the United States did not secure ports in California it would ultimately lack sea room.[15] Similarly Waddy Thompson, seeing no hope for commercial greatness in Oregon's waterways, praised San Francisco in words reminiscent of Farnham and Wilkes. When by 1846 this ardent quest for ports had encompassed the questions of both Oregon and California, it increasingly motivated a compromise at 49° and actually determined the fate of the Pacific Coast from Lower California to Alaska.

It is not strange that many Americans were willing to trade off varying portions of Oregon for an opportunity to acquire California. That Daniel Webster had little interest in land empires but enormous enthusiasm for spacious ports of call for his Yankee constituents is well known. In 1843 he had attempted to cede all of Oregon north of the Columbia in exchange for the acquisition of San Francisco from Mexico through British intercession. During the following year Thomas O. Larkin urged this permanent arrangement on Calhoun.

By 1845 the tremendous burst of enthusiasm for California which followed the passage of the Texas resolution convinced many commercial expansionists that America's real interests lay to the south of Oregon. Larkin again found the solution to the Oregon question in the expanding maritime interest in California. In a letter to the New York *Journal of Commerce* in July he wrote: "If the Oregon dispute continues, let England take eight degrees north of the Columbia, and purchase eight degrees south of forty-two from Mexico, and exchange." The *Journal* concurred in the view that California was this nation's real objective and therefore the United States could well settle at the Columbia and still retain ten degrees of coast. John Tyler never lost the vision of Webster's tripartite proposal. He wrote to his son in December, 1845, regarding the Oregon question: "I never dreamed of conceding the country, unless for the greater equivalent of California, which I fancied Great Britain might be able to obtain for us through her influence in Mexico. . . ."[16]

Even the British press saw the impact of American interest in California on the Oregon question. Before the news of the Mexican War had reached Europe, the London *Times* insisted that "if any incident should lead to the declaration of war against Mexico, the seizure of Port St. Francis and of Upper California, would be considered all over the Union as a sufficient pretext for adjourning the discussion of the Oregon Convention."[17]

It was more than the desire for San Francisco Bay that caused the California issue to prompt compromise on Oregon. The pervading fear that England was negotiating for California had not only designated that province as an immediate objective of manifest destiny in 1845, but it now also convinced certain American observers that the United States might well compromise on Oregon to diminish British pressure in California. In urging Americans to settle the Oregon question the Richmond *Enquirer* warned: "It is clearly England which retreats. But it is too much to retreat at the same time in Oregon and California. The English annals present no example of such prudence." In one terse observation the New York *Herald* summed up the entire issue: "We must surrender a slice of Oregon, if we would secure a slice of California."[18]

§ 3

By January, 1846, the movement for compromise in the United States had effectively challenged the hold of the extremists on American thought. Quite significantly that month the *North American Review* demanded a settlement of the Oregon question on consideration other than that of shopworn titles which neither side intended to concede. "We have been arguing the question for thirty years," charged the writer, "and stand precisely where we did when the discussion commenced." The debate, he declared, sounded like a "solemn mummery" in which too many ambitious politicians were preventing the vast majority from regarding the issue with perfect indifference. Continued the writer: "Not one in ten thousand . . . would be immediately affected by the successful assertion of our claim to the whole of Oregon."

Soon even the metropolitan expansionist press was fostering compromise vigorously. Because of its addiction to California, the New York *Journal of Commerce* succumbed early to the desire for a settlement at 49°. By January, 1846, both the New York *Herald* and the New York *Sun* had joined the trend, as had also the Washington *Union* and the St. Louis and New Orleans press. These leading compromise editors stressed the maritime significance of the Pacific Coast, minimized the worth of Oregon's soil, especially as compared to that of California, and denounced members of Congress who still favored the whole of Oregon even at the cost of war.

In January, the *North American Review*, in characteristic fashion, depicted Oregon as a barren wilderness. The writer suggested that the United States and England, like the two famed Scotsmen, Daniel Dimond and his neighbor, Jock, were arguing over land "lying high and exposed," and capable of feeding but "a hog, or aiblins twa in a good year." He advised the two nations to follow the course of the Scotsmen, and rather than engage in a foolish lawsuit, they go home, "take a pint and agree." After citing Wilkes, Farnham, and Green-how to prove that Oregon (except for the Willamette Valley) was an "arid and rugged waste," inhabited only by hunters and Indians, the author concluded that "it is hardly too much to say that what Siberia is to Russia, Oregon is to the United States."[19]

Throughout the months of the great debate, editors of the South and East persisted in the policy of contrasting unfavorably the Oregon countryside with that of California. The Nashville *Union* asserted simply that "Oregon is but a bleak, barren waste, compared with California." In favoring California over Oregon, the New York *Journal of Commerce* declared that the United States would acquire "a really fine country, instead of mountains, rocks, and barren sands." The refrain was inescapable. As proof of these contentions was the steady stream of pioneers moving southward from Oregon. Members of the press predicted that most emigrants who entered Oregon would eventually move into California. As early as March, 1845, the New Orleans *Picayune* observed that Oregon settlers were thankful for the opportunity to move to "a more fruitful and congenial clime." A year later the same paper reported "a yet greater influx of disappointed pioneers to Oregon, who wander on farther south in search of better lands and happier skies." By May, 1846, the St. Louis *Republican* wondered if many pioneers would continue to venture into Oregon and "strive for a place in that *debate-able* land."[20] So marked was this theme in the American press that British publications such as the London *Illustrated News* feared that the migration to Oregon was merely a ruse to annex California.

Throughout the commercial East, writers condemned the extremists for engaging in war talk to advance their political fortunes. They accused certain Democrats of clinging to an unrealistic issue and employing it to play upon the nationalistic emotions of the American people, not to obtain Oregon, but to attain political power. To that end they were purposely keeping the Oregon question in a ferment and preventing its peaceful solution. The New York *Journal of Commerce* asserted with some bitterness that some members of Congress sounded little like sober, reflecting, and intelligent men. The verbal lash fell most repeatedly on John Quincy Adams, whom the newspaper fraternity suspected of holding tenaciously to his 54-40 views simply because Southerners were turning toward compromise.[21]

There was in 1846 a general revulsion in all sections of the United States at the thought of war with Britain. Few Americans would admit a willingness to concede more than the forty-ninth parallel to the British. Neither did more than a small portion evince any desire to fight for more than that boundary. "I do not think the territory worth a groat to the United States," wrote one Texan in urging a peaceful policy on the administration. "As to Oregon," wrote another, "it is not worth the Red flannel which would be required to envelope our cartridges." Eastern merchants who invaded the capital complained that threats of war were already hampering United States commerce over the world, for no whaler or East India merchantman would venture freely onto the high seas with a war in the offing.[22] "This will all do famously for the valley of the Mississippi, where they have all to gain by a war and nothing to lose," grumbled the New York merchant, Philip Hone. "But we on the seaboard must fight all, pay all, and suffer all."

Even from the Northwest, where anti-British feeling was strongest, came demands for peace. There were issues besides Oregon in the election of 1844, declared one Ohioan in pressing compromise on Senator Allen:

> I am much astonished to find you so eager to throw the Country in horrors of *War*, more so when I consider your pretensions to *Democracy*. . . . Sir, permit me to say that eagerness you display in pushing the question which has the least shadow of *War*, is by no means marked by the least *love* for the poor of the Country or true Democracy. . . . It was the Opposition to the U. S. Bank that the people

came forth and elected J. K. Polk and not that of fighting for
Oregon.[23]

In Congress the movement for compromise enjoyed the
leadership of two powerful Democratic factions. One comprised the old Van Buren group then led in the Senate by
Thomas Hart Benton and John A. Dix. The other was under
the leadership of John C. Calhoun. Calhoun with McDuffie
and several other members of Congress planned as early as
February to introduce a resolution to advise the President to
reopen negotiations with England for a settlement at 49°.
Calhoun regarded himself as the Senate's spokesman for a
peaceful compromise, and so the press regarded him also. His
role was well defined by a Washington correspondent of the
New York *Journal of Commerce*: "Mr. Calhoun, from the
moment of his arrival here, has exerted himself to calm the
agitated waters. He has counselled admirably, and is still
engaged in promoting a good understanding between the
British Minister and our Government. . . . To do this, he has
used his efforts both with Whigs and Democrats, in both
Houses, and has succeeded."[24]

Whig support assured the eventual triumph of Calhoun's
views in Congress. In fact, by late February it had become
obvious to the administration that a compromise on the forty-
ninth parallel would probably receive a two-thirds vote in the
Senate. In April it was increasingly clear that the strengthening voice of the Senate called for 49°, no more and no less.
Said the New York *Herald* of Congressional opinion:

> This is the line that we define,
>   The line for Oregon;
> And if this basis you decline,
>   We go the "whole or none,"
> We go the "whole or none," Lord John,
>   Up to the Russian line;
> Then, if you're wise, you'll "compromise"
>   On number forty nine.

Quite contentedly the Whigs followed the leadership of
Calhoun. Wrote Webster in January: "Most of the Whigs

in the Senate incline to remain rather quiet, and to follow the lead of Mr. Calhoun. He is at the head of a party of six or seven, and as he professes still to be an administration man, it is best to leave the work in his hands, at least for the present." The New York *Herald* described well this strange political alignment: "The chivalry of the West goes hot and strong for 54-40, while the ardent South, and the calculating East, coalesce, for once, on this point, and quietly and temperately call for 49."[25]

§ 4

American historians have analyzed thoroughly the factors which compelled Great Britain to settle the Oregon question at the forty-ninth parallel in 1846. In fact, in British rather than in American policy is to be found the key to the several well-known interpretations of the Oregon compromise. England had long since quit her claim to the regions south of the Columbia, while the United States had traditionally offered to yield all territory north of 49°. As late as July, 1845, Polk had offered to treat on that line. Viewed from diplomatic history, therefore, a compromise at 49° was a British surrender. Melvin Jacobs has stated clearly this widely accepted assumption:

Taking into consideration the indefiniteness and weakness of claims to new territory on the basis of discovery and exploration, in contrast to occupation and settlement, instead of raising the question as to the reasons why America did not secure the whole of Oregon to fifty-four degrees and forty minutes, it appears to be more appropriate to raise the question as to why England lost the territory between the Columbia River and the forty-ninth parallel after she had both occupied and, apparently, possessed it.[26]

Students of the Oregon question have attributed the British inclination to retreat from the Columbia to a variety of factors. First, such historians as Thomas P. Martin and St. George Sioussat have concluded that the harvest shortage of 1845 and the corresponding need of American grain contributed to

British pacificism. Frederick Merk, however, has questioned this interpretation by citing evidence that the scarcity of food in the British Isles was not sufficient to alter either prices or trade considerably.[27]

Secondly, historians have found the key to the Oregon settlement in the improved commercial relations between the United States and Great Britain during the spring of 1846. This popular interpretation—the free-trade analysis—rests primarily on evidence that, to several important British and American officials, commercial intercourse between the two nations was of greater interest and concern than the Oregon question. This thesis takes strength from a variety of British statements, such as one of Sir Robert Peel: "The admission of Maize will I believe go far to promote the settlement of Oregon." Lord Aberdeen, the Foreign Secretary, also wrote in December, 1845: "The access of Indian corn to our markets would go far to pacify the warriors of the Western States."[28] Apparently these British spokesmen believed that the opening of the British grain market would provide an outlet for the surplus wheat of the Old Northwest and reduce, in direct proportion, the persistent Anglophobia of the region.

There is evidence, furthermore, that low tariff advocates in the United States, such as Calhoun, wanted to compromise the Oregon issue not only to avoid war but also to facilitate the acceptance of low tariff policies on both sides of the Atlantic. The Charleston *Mercury* gave evidence of the Southern preference for free trade to the acquisition of the whole of Oregon when it declared that Southern statesmen would not maintain a clear and unquestioned title at 54° 40′ at the price of two million bales of cotton per year. Thomas P. Martin has shown that American free traders urged British officials to drop their antislavery policy and repeal the Corn Laws to conciliate the powerful Democratic elements of both the South and West behind a low tariff policy in the United States. Even President Polk agreed that markets for manufactured goods were of infinitely more value to Britain than any por-

tion of Oregon, and he predicted optimistically that a reduction of American tariffs might tempt the British to surrender
all of Oregon.[29] Whigs in Congress feared that the Democratic administration would pursue the course of soothing the
British with tariff reductions so enthusiastically that it would
destroy the budding manufacturing interests of the United
States.

Perhaps more agrarian tempers were vexed than soothed
by the repeal of the British Corn Laws, however; for it removed the advantage of easy entry into the British Empire
trade through Canada. Many Westerners, moreover, refused
to admit any relationship between the tariff and the Oregon
question. The free-trade editor of the *Ohio Statesman* wrote:
"Withered be the hand that dismembers Oregon, and palsied
the tongue that consents to an act so treasonable, foul and
unnatural." Hannegan spoke for the "ultras" in the Senate:
"Free trade I love dearly, but it will never be bought by me
by the territory of my country." Orlando Ficklin of Illinois
warned against placing reliance in the British repeal bill.
"Great Britain has a sliding scale not only in regard to her
corn laws," he cried, "but she has one also in regard to the
faith which she keeps with other nations."[30] The hope that
the British action would facilitate a settlement of the Oregon
question proved false. The South and East were highly
pleased, but the West, for whom the sedative was intended,
continued to fume with customary vehemence.

A third interpretation of the settlement of the Oregon question attributes British conciliation to the pressure of American
pioneers. There were few Americans north of the Columbia
in 1846, but it is unquestionably true that the British viewed
the growing numbers of pioneers south of the river with dismay, for they endangered the peace and threatened to disrupt
the fur trade. When in 1845 the Hudson's Bay Company
moved its main depot to Vancouver Island because of the decline of the fur traffic and American immigrant pressure, it
admitted that its perennial *sine qua non* in any treaty, the

Columbia, was no longer its vital trade route. This surrender of the Columbia, says Merk, was the key to the Oregon settlement.[31]

There was yet a fourth dimension in the British inclination to retreat—the maritime factor. Lord Aberdeen, who as Foreign Secretary led the British government toward compromise, analyzed cogently his own predisposition for compromise in terms of Pacific ports. He wrote to Sir Robert Peel in September, 1844:

> I believe that if the line of the 49th degree were extended only to the waters edge, and should leave us possession of all of Vancouver's Island, with the northern side of the entrance to Puget's Sound; and if all the harbors within the Sound, and to the Columbia, inclusive, were made free to both countries; and further, if the river Columbia from the point at which it became navigable to its mouth, were also made free to both, this would be in reality a most advantageous settlement.

A year later Aberdeen admitted that England could obtain everything worth contending for in Vancouver Island, the navigation of the Columbia, and free access to all ports between the Columbia and 49°.[32]

Aberdeen's purpose in 1845 and 1846 was to propagandize the British people into an acceptance of this view. His specific task was to convince them that British claims to Oregon were imperfect, that Oregon was not worth a dispute with the United States, that the British fur trade was dying, that the Columbia offered little security for heavy commerce, and that the United States had reasonable claims to good harbors on the Pacific.

Several major British journals spread these doctrines for him. In an anonymous article the *Edinburgh Review* of July, 1845, emphasized the unattractiveness of Oregon and the worthlessness of the ports south of the Strait. Similarly the *London Illustrated News* concluded later that year: "The value of the whole territory in fee simple would not be worth the expense of one year's war." The *Quarterly Review* termed a settlement at 49° a "subject of honorable negotiation and compromise." Convinced that the United States would concede no more, the writer accepted that line as "best for our interests and sufficient for our honor." By January, 1846, the London *Times* became the special champion of Aberdeen's foreign policy, and its conversion helped the Foreign Secretary marshal the support of many other leading British newspapers such as the London *Spectator,* the *Manchester Guardian,* the Liverpool *Times,* and the Leeds *Mercury.*[33] Thus the British willingness to compromise in 1846 was in a sense a triumph for Aberdeen's maritime views.

The real significance of the famous British Corn Law crisis in motivating compromise rested in its creation of a realignment of British parties that brought into power in England a coalition that was willing to settle the Oregon issue for an equitable distribution of ports. The essential fact is that by May, 1846, Aberdeen, upon the passage of the resolution by the United States Congress to terminate the Joint Convention of 1827, was permitted by both the British government and British public opinion to proffer to the United States an acceptable treaty.

§ 5

That President Polk without hesitation presented the British proposal to the Senate indicates that he had moved far from his public position of 1845. Historical analyses of this apparent policy shift fall basically into two categories. Julius Pratt has developed the thesis that Polk was convinced by Minister Louis McLane early in 1846 that the British would fight rather than concede more than the forty-ninth parallel, and that thereafter the President was less inclined to look John Bull in the eye. Other historians, such as Albert K. Weinberg, attribute Polk's desire to compromise to the growing threat of war with Mexico.[34]

Since Polk bore the responsibility for the conduct of American diplomacy, he became the focus of all pressures for peace with England. Politicians and the press sought vigorously to assure the administration that the overwhelming majority of the American people would sustain it in the face of the current popular outcry against England. "Six clear heads in Washington," argued one editor in an effort to stiffen the executive, "are much more likely to come to a correct conclusion of the Nation's welfare, than hundreds of popular meetings composed of tens of thousands of excited individuals."[35] Those who urged the President to assume the diplomatic initiative sensed correctly a peaceful intent in the administration.

This tremendous pressure to avoid war was only one factor motivating compromise in the President. It must be remembered that long before he forced the Oregon issue upon Congress and the British ministry in December, 1845, his vision of America's future position in the West had been fashioned by the Pacific. As early as July, 1845, he indicated a willingness to compromise the Oregon question on a fair distribution of the coastal inlets. It was largely his interest in ports that turned his attention to California in 1845 and stimulated his desire to limit British encroachment in North America. He demonstrated this interest again when he attempted to purchase San Francisco from Mexico in the Slidell mission of November, 1845. Yet at no time did the President lose sight of the Strait of Fuca. In his first message to Congress he declared that the United States could never accept a settlement in Oregon that "would leave on the British side two-thirds of the whole Oregon territory, including the free navigation of the Columbia and all valuable harbors on the Pacific."[36] Before the end of December, Polk noted in his diary that he would submit to the Senate for its previous advice any British offer that would grant to the United States the Strait of Fuca and some free ports to the north.

Again Polk's interest in Pacific ports was apparent in his vigorous resistance to arbitration during the early months of 1846. To British officials he made it clear that he would not so jeopardize the United States acquisition of harbors on Admiralty Inlet and Puget Sound. Oregon, he asserted, presented the avenue for United States commerce between Asia and the western coasts of North America. This vast region, moreover, had no safe and commodious harbors except near the forty-ninth parallel. For commercial purposes, he informed McLane that "the United States might almost as well abandon the whole territory as consent to deprive ourselves of these harbors; because south of them, within its limits, no good harbor exists."[37]

Throughout the Oregon crisis of 1846, Polk was unable to face the challenge of marshaling public opinion behind his personal acceptance of the forty-ninth parallel. The unequivocal language of his message and the pressures within his party tied his hands both diplomatically and politically. Increasingly his position became untenable, for he found himself trapped between the ultimate necessity of negotiating a settlement at 49° and the immediate necessity of supporting the "ultras" of his party.

Polk's dilemma became clear in January, when Congress, upon the recommendation of his December message, began the debate on the joint resolution to extend the twelve-month notice to England for terminating the Convention of 1827. Since this action would convey to the executive a mandate for a prompt and final settlement of the Oregon question, it made considerable difference to members of Congress how the President would use his authority. Would he negotiate a compromise, or would he maintain American rights to all of Oregon and possibly provoke a war? Week after week the quarrels in Congress revolved around efforts of conflicting Democratic factions to interpret the President's objectives.

Neither Polk nor Buchanan wished to antagonize the Western Democrats. This faction of the party had not only secured the President's nomination in 1844, but also it promised him its loyal support on tariff reduction and the re-establishment of the Independent Treasury. Buchanan reminded the President repeatedly that the 54-40 men were the true friends of the administration. John J. Crittenden, the Kentucky Whig, saw some discretion in Buchanan's valor. "The hardest swearers are for fifty-four forty," he wrote, "and he thinks, perhaps, by taking the same position he may escape more *curses* than in any other way."

Polk hoped to avoid a party split and therefore condemned the efforts of Democratic Congressmen to guess the intentions of the administration. "I told Gen'l Cass," he recorded early in March, "that I regretted such collisions between my political friends."[38] The President believed his opinions to be clearly expressed in his message, and thought therefore that the debate had "taken a strange direction; that instead of examining and discussing my views as communicated in these documents, Senators had been guessing or conjecturing what I might do hereafter, and were approving or condemning what they supposed I might or might not do."

To those who called at the White House, therefore, the President was noncommittal. When early in January James A. Black of South Carolina sought the President's views, Polk recorded: "I told him that my opinions were contained in my message, that they had been well considered, and that I had not changed them; that I had recommended the Notice and thought it ought to be given." Such an answer was hardly satisfactory when Congress could not agree on the meaning of the message, but it served to extricate Polk from an impossible political defile. When Senator Hopkins L. Turney of Tennessee sought to ascertain the intention of the administration in order better to govern his own conduct in Congress, Polk discreetly referred him to the message. The powerful and compromising voices of Calhoun and Benton could not be ignored, however, and the President assured them privately that he would submit any British proposal for a fair settlement to the Senate for its advice before rejecting it.

It was William H. Haywood, of North Carolina, who stimulated the "ultras" into action early in March when, while clamoring for a settlement at 49°, he professed to speak the views of the administration. The exasperated Hannegan prophesied that if this were true, the President "would sink so deep that the Trumpet of the Angel of Resurrection would not reach him!" The Indianan stormed into the executive office and demanded a clear-cut decision. "I answered him that I would answer no man what I would do in the future," hedged the President, "that for what I might do I would be responsible to God and my country and if I should hereafter do anything which should be disapproved by himself and others, it would be time enough to condemn me."[39] Similarly he informed the inquisitive Cass that his views on Oregon were contained in his message.

Allen presented a stronger case when he called at the White House. He argued logically that he required the authority to speak for the administration if he were to regain his position as the spokesman for foreign affairs in the Senate. He presented to Polk a prepared statement for his endorsement, but the President would not be trapped. "I told him I could give no authority to him or any one else to say anything in the Senate," replied the President, "that I had given no such authority to Mr. Haywood and I would give none such to him; that I did not wish to be involved in the matter & that what he said he must say on his own responsibility."[40]

The President gradually became embittered over his repeated embarrassments and turned his abuse on the Democratic leadership in Congress. He recalled that his party had a decided majority in both houses, and yet in four months they had not passed the notice. The nation, he feared, would hold the Democratic Party responsible for the failure of Congress to act. He was completely unable to comprehend his own or his party's role in the confusion, and attributed the party divisions rather to personal ambitions. "The truth is," he wrote in April, "that in all this Oregon discussion in the Senate, too many Democratic Senators have been more concerned about the Presidential election in '48, than they have been about settling Oregon either at 49° or 54° 40'."

§ 6

Domestic political forces in the United States forced England to assume diplomatic leadership in the crisis. In April Congress passed the resolution for notice. As the administration had anticipated, Britain responded with an acceptable proposal, which the President without hesitation forwarded to the Senate. The final treaty was ratified in June.

Undoubtedly Polk merits much of the approbation given him for pushing the Oregon question to an acceptable conclusion in 1846. Richard Rush spoke for many friends of the administration and for later historians when he wrote: "For one, I am unshaken in the belief that it was the President's opening message to the first Congress he met . . . that produced the settlement of the Oregon difficulty. It was like a great bomb-shell thrown into the British cabinet. It took them by surprise, and first roused them to the unavoidable necessity of a settlement."[41] Webster, however, argued that Polk could not have produced a settlement, because, clinging as he did to the party platform, he denied himself the right to negotiate further after August, 1845.

Webster placed the credit elsewhere: "The discussions in Congress, the discussions on the other side of the water, the general sense of the community, all protested against the iniquity of two of the greatest nations of modern times rushing into war. . . . All enforced the conviction, that it was a question to be settled by an equitable and fair consideration, and it was thus settled." Pakenham, the British Minister at Washington, agreed. To him Polk had remained attuned to 54-40 too long to exert any influence in bringing a final settlement. He attributed the treaty to either the "wisdom and integrity of the Senate, or the intelligence and good sense of the American people."[42] Even such Democratic leaders as Calhoun believed to the end that the final settlement was achieved against the influence of the President.

The ratified Oregon Treaty differed in only two minor respects from Polk's proposals of July, 1845. The President had demanded the extension of the forty-ninth parallel to the Pacific, with Britain ceding to the United States the southern tip of Vancouver Island. He omitted all reference to British navigation on the Columbia. Aberdeen countered with the British position: the forty-ninth parallel to the middle of the channel between the mainland and Vancouver Island, and then southward through King George's Sound and the Strait of Fuca to the Pacific. This line would convey all of Vancouver Island to Great Britain. In addition, Aberdeen demanded common use of the Columbia.

McLane in 1846 urged the acceptance of the British position, for he was convinced that the British would not retreat on either demand. Polk conceded the loss of Vancouver Island early, but he believed this concession sufficient to terminate all further conversation over free ports to the south of the Strait. He resisted granting the British perpetual navigation of the Columbia, fearing that some unforeseen conflict might again challenge peace between the two nations. As a compromise on the Columbia River question, McLane recommended that its use be limited to the Hudson's Bay Company.[43] These two modifications of Polk's initial position, agreed to in advance by both governments, comprised the only real diplomatic achievement on the Oregon question.

For neither Polk nor Aberdeen, who had long been in essential agreement over the equitable distribution of Oregon waterways, was the Oregon Treaty a major compromise at all. For large portions of both the British and American people, however, the final settlement was viewed as a sacrifice. The task of leadership in the crisis consisted of bringing public opinion in both nations to an acceptance of the forty-ninth parallel. Since domestic partisanship effectively tied Polk's hands, the movement for compromise in the United States had to come from Congress and the metropolitan press. For Aberdeen the task of securing support was even more difficult, since

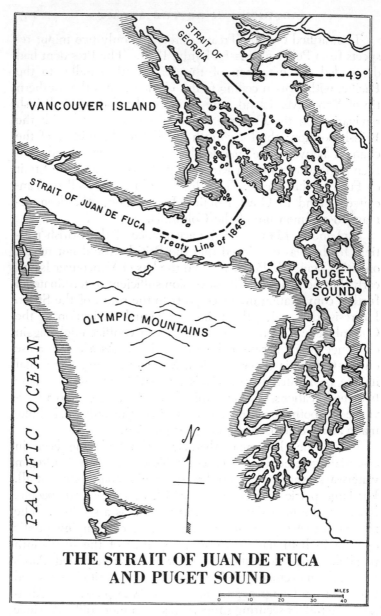

THE STRAIT OF JUAN DE FUCA
AND PUGET SOUND

Britain, unlike the United States, was forced to retreat from its traditional offer.

Both nations as a whole were content with the distribution of lands and ports. During the closing argument on the Oregon Treaty Benton passed final judgment on the forty-ninth parallel: "With that boundary comes all that we want in that quarter, namely, all the waters of Puget's Sound, and the fertile Olympian district which borders upon them." The Oregon settlement brought to the business community on both sides of the Atlantic relief from the evils of suspense and uncertainty. A brief poem of America's leading expansionist press, the New York *Herald*, summed up well the attitude of the English-speaking world:

Old Buck and Pack
Are coming back
And will soon together dine.
And drink a toast
Upon their roast
To number forty-nine.[44]

Chapter 8

WAR AIMS

§ 1

On May 14, 1846, the conservative *National Intelligencer* apprised its public of the outbreak of the Mexican War: "Our readers will learn, nine-tenths of them with well-founded alarm and dismay, that the Congress of the United States have adopted the War with the Republic of Mexico. . . ." Although months of semiobscure diplomacy with Mexico had been leading the nation toward conflict, the actual war message caught the politicians by surprise and threw the Whig Party into confusion. For a year Whig spokesmen had bitterly predicted a clash over the annexation of Texas. In a lapse of mind, however, they upheld the war when it came. Then quite as suddenly they sobered, reconsidered, took stock of the war's political capital, and shortly made it the most extensively criticized war in American history.

Zachary Taylor's presence on the Rio Grande, not regarded by the President as an act of aggression, left sufficient doubt in the minds of his opposition to elicit an unending review of the war's circumstances. Cried the noted abolitionist, Joshua Giddings: "With indecent haste, with unbecoming levity, under the gag of the previous question, our nation was plunged into a bloody war." To the query whether the United States had just cause for war, Joseph Root of Ohio retorted: "Sir, I invoke the scrutiny of the Searcher of Hearts, when I declare that I believe we had not."[1]

Gradually the abuse settled on the President. Alexander H. Stephens, of Georgia, termed it an "Executive war" resulting from Polk's "imprudence, indiscretion, and mismanagement." Giddings declared that no sophistry could disguise the fact that "the President obviously intended to involve us in a war with Mexico," while Thomas Corwin averred in a letter to William Greene in June that he would hold the guilty authors of the war to a strict account. By June the Whig press had moved into line, and when Congress adjourned in August, 1846, Robert Winthrop boasted that the Whigs in Washington were unanimous in their opposition to the administration.[2]

Although the Polk administration had erred sufficiently in its relations with Mexico to contribute some plausibility to this attack, the simple Whig incantations hardly encompassed the entire truth. From the moment of Texas annexation and the formal break in diplomatic relations, the tensions between the United States and Mexico had been driving the two nations toward war. By the autumn of 1845 an impetuous element in the United States was demanding action. "I arrived in this place this morning," wrote one administration correspondent from Philadelphia in August, "and hear nothing else talked of but war with Mexico." The New York *Herald* that same month summed up tersely the belligerent spirit of Americans: "The multitude cry aloud for war."[3] Even the *American Review* feared that the temper of the United States would drive the government into deeds of rashness. "There is a yearning for excitement," admitted the writer, "a desire for change—a restlessness—to which the prospect of war and its chances is soothing. . . ." Not long thereafter Calhoun observed the youthful vitality of the nation. "Our people are like a young man of 18," he wrote, "full of health and vigor and disposed for adventure of any description."[4]

News of Slidell's rebuff by Mexico produced an even more violent reaction in the United States. "All is excitement about Mexico," observed the New York *Herald* in January. The New York *Courier and Enquirer* believed the time for action had arrived: "We hope that our Government will promptly force our Mexican affairs to a crisis." The New Orleans *Picayune* urged that United States–Mexican relations no longer be kept "in a state of doubtful peace."[5] Although anticipating the failure of his mission with deep regret, Slidell wrote privately to Polk that "a war would probably be the best mode of settling our affairs with Mexico."

Slidell's failure to approach the new Paredes government again threw the nation into an uproar. It is no secret, warned the New York *Herald* in March, that the ruling powers of Mexico are bent on war. The editor of the Philadelphia *North American* demanded, "Where is the Executive? . . . What new dishonor is necessary to arouse our government to action?" Why, he wondered, should the United States submit to being "kicked and scuffed, wronged and dishonored" by a nation like Mexico? Even the London *Times* admitted early in May that Polk was pledged by all that was sacred in democratic sovereignty to exact exemplary satisfaction.[6]

Amid such public declarations against Mexico, Polk prepared to bring before Congress in May, 1846, the question of claims against Mexico. Meanwhile, his orders of January to place Taylor on the Rio Grande were bringing relations with the Mexican Republic to a crisis. This decision gradually took the President from a position based on Mexican procrastination to one that had all the appearance of United States aggression. After April United States troops were in a contested area where a few scattered shots could transfer the responsibility for war from the follies of Mexico to alleged goading by the administration. American policy had reached the juncture where the least contact between probing bands of United States and Mexican troops in a distant wilderness could effectively destroy the uneasy peace. With the notice of hostilities along the Rio Grande, the cabinet agreed unanimously on war. On May 13, 1846, Congress accepted the President's request for a formal declaration.

The Democratic press rushed to the defense of the President's orders. The *Democratic Review* recalled with considerable truth that for a full year the United States had attempted to settle the dispute it had inherited from Texas, but Mexico would not treat. The administration therefore had ordered the occupation of the disputed area in the hope that the presence of an American army before Matamoras might induce the Mexicans to negotiate. At least it would strengthen the American claim, and in case of actual conflict it might save American lives. Rather than provoking aggression, declared the Washington *Union*, Polk's orders illustrated the wisdom and prudence of the Democratic leadership.[7] This may have been diplomatically sound, but it led the nation to war. And it was a political blunder, for it exposed the Polk administration to unlimited partisan attack.

Nor was the clash of arms near the Rio Grande the only cause of war. General Winfield Scott assumed the popular Whig view that war was inevitable after the annexation of Texas. "Hostilities with Mexico," he recalled in his memoirs, "might, perhaps, have been avoided, but Texas lay between— or rather in the scale of war." It is true that Mexico was offended by annexation, but a year later she had not declared war. In reality Texas annexation was only the most serious in a long succession of diplomatic crises. In a sense, the causes of the Mexican War resided deeply in the web of diplomatic and commercial relations covering fully two decades. At the close of the war Lt. Robert S. Ripley wrote with remarkable insight that "the controversies in arms in which great nations of modern times have engaged have almost invariably been brought about by a long series of circumstances, so connected, that in their succession the danger of the conflict could hardly be perceived until its occurrence was inevitable."[8]

This was true for the Mexican War. It came basically because neither nation made a sincere effort to avoid it. For years Mexican politicians had been generating fear, hatred, and jealousy toward the United States by picturing her as a grasping neighbor. Abusing the republic to the north became the standard procedure of Mexican parties to gain power. By the mid-forties public opinion against the United States was uncontrollable. Those who knew better, wrote Shannon in 1844, were not bold enough to express their opinions. When Slidell arrived in Mexico, the entire nation seemed to resound with patriotic appeals to prepare for the reconquest of Texas. By March, Paredes had ordered that attack.

Still some magnanimity within the Polk administration toward Mexico might have prevented war. Mexican provocation understandably produced frustration and antagonism in Washington, but it need not have led to military conflict. American security was not endangered. Polk had the power to recall Slidell quietly and to hold Taylor at the Nueces. But in the balance against peace was the pressure of American public sentiment and a measured acquisitiveness toward California.

§ 2

Undaunted by political hostility, Polk not only assumed the burdensome task of conducting a victorious war, but he also determined to achieve his specific war aims. These objects, first formulated during the autumn of 1845, he often made known privately to his cabinet and friends in both conversation and letters. While Congress debated the war message, Polk informed the cabinet that although the war had not been undertaken "with a view to acquire either California or New Mexico or any other portion of Mexican territory," in a treaty the United States "would, if practicable, obtain California and such other portion of the Mexican territory as would be sufficient to indemnify our claimants on Mexico, and to defray the expenses of the war. . . ."[9]

Polk's military policy was calculated to achieve concrete territorial objectives. He recognized, first of all, the necessity of bringing power to bear on Mexico proper to force an acceptance of the most favorable territorial arrangements sought in the Slidell mission. To this end he quickly tendered the command of the army in Washington to General Winfield Scott, called for twenty thousand volunteers to bolster Taylor's forces, and sought legislation from Congress for a vigorous campaign into northern Mexico. Before the end of May, Polk had unfolded also the second phase of his military policy—an expedition of mounted troops to gain possession of "California, New Mexico, and perhaps some others of the Northern Provinces."[10] He followed this conviction with immediate orders to Stephen W. Kearny, Colonel of Dragoons at Fort Leavenworth, to occupy Santa Fe and proceed overland to Upper California.

Before autumn the American flag floated over all but a small portion of California. In May, John C. Fremont, on his third journey to the West, was encamped at Marysville Buttes on the Sacramento when American pioneers suddenly congregated at his camp and instituted the Bear Flag movement. They swept into Sonoma, captured General Mariano Vallejo, occupied the village, and raised their new flag. Fremont and his men now joined the movement. It seemed momentarily that American emigrants would make of California a second Texas, but the invasion of the American fleet quickly relegated the Bear Flag revolt to a secondary role in the American conquest of the Mexican province.

Commodore Sloat, commander of the Pacific fleet, was anchored off Mazatlán, well-armed with Bancroft's instructions, when news arrived from Mexico City that war had been declared. He placed his frigate, the *Savannah,* under full sail, and on July 2 reached Monterey where he found two United States sloops of war. On July 7 Sloat took possession of Monterey; two days later United States forces occupied San Francisco and Sonoma. Commodore Robert F. Stockton, who received the command from Sloat midway through July, enlisted the Bear Flag pioneers and dispatched Fremont by ship to San Diego to gain the rear of the California forces. Stockton followed in the *Congress*, raised the flag at Santa Barbara, and took possession of San Pedro. In less than one month all ports of the province were in American hands.

This rapid conquest of California did not necessarily expose the expansionist trump in the President's hand, for the Mexican province was a logical military objective. But Polk and his Secretary of War, William L. Marcy, tipped their cards in June when they commissioned Colonel Jonathan D. Stevenson of New York to recruit, organize, and train the famed New York Volunteer Regiment. This unprecedented military unit was designed to enlist mechanics, armed with the tools of their trade as well as rifles, who as settlers would agree to accept their discharges in California or in the nearest United States territory at the close of the war. From the outset, the press appraised it rightly as a colonizing rather than a military expedition. Its obvious expansionist nature made it a political liability. The administration anticipated an early sailing with a minimum of publicity. Instead, the regiment was three months in preparation and received a well-merited derision almost daily in the local partisan press.

Stevenson was Marcy's political crony who had repeatedly pressed his claims for public office from the Polk administration. After planning this expedition the President quickly dissolved his political obligation by appointing Stevenson commander of the new regiment. The New York press believed the appointment as ridiculous as the training antics taking place on Governor's Island, where the regiment was congregating. From the beginning it questioned the Colonel's ability to lead such an expedition. Before long the beleaguered Stevenson's honesty came under speculation. Marcy discovered that his appointee had been dabbling in war contracts, had engaged in a questionable scheme to provide clothing for his troops, and had superseded the Quartermaster Department to negotiate privately for transports. Then in August, 1846, General Thomas J. Sutherland of New York demanded a court of inquiry, charging Stevenson with profiteering on clothing sales and falsifying his officer rolls to obtain commissions for his favorites. Marcy admitted his embarrassment. To ignore the charges would bring public censure; to press them would delay the expedition. He mused hopefully, "I exceedingly wish he was upon the high sea."[11]

By September newsmen were betting that Sutherland would succeed in breaking up the enterprise if it did not fall apart of itself. "In either case," noted one writer, "a partisan of the government has been liberally rewarded." To escape arrest "dead or alive," Stevenson departed so hurriedly late in September on his long voyage around the Horn that he stranded several dozen volunteers in New York harbor without supplies or baggage. But the expedition was off at last, declared one critic, "shorn somewhat of its numerical force, as it has long been almost wholly of its moral." For the administration there was only relief.[12]

During the early weeks of the Mexican War the President noted repeatedly in his diary that he would accept no treaty which did not transfer New Mexico and Upper California to the United States. It was left only to hammer out the precise territorial objectives. Initially, San Francisco and Monterey were the chief California attractions to Polk and his cabinet. Bancroft assured Samuel Hooper, Marblehead merchant and son-in-law of William Sturgis, that by mid-June the United States flag would be floating over these two northern California ports. "I hope California is now in our possession, never to be given up," he added. "We were driven reluctantly to war; we must make a solid peace. . . ."[13]

With this promise Hooper would not rest. He prodded the administration to look southward along the coast. Settlement at the thirty-second parallel, he informed Bancroft, would secure both Los Angeles and the bay of San Diego. It would encompass, moreover, all the Anglo-American population in the province and remove future annoyance by leaving a barren wilderness between Upper California and the larger Mexican cities to the south. Should the United States acquire

San Diego as well as Monterey and San Francisco, he continued, "it would insure a peaceful state of things through the whole country and enable [the Americans] to continue their trade as before along the whole coast. . . ."[14] Hooper advised the capture of Mazatlán and Guaymas only as annoyances to Mexico for the war's duration.

Thereafter the administration looked to San Diego. When late in June cabinet members Robert J. Walker and Buchanan debated the relative merits of the twenty-sixth and thirty-second parallels as war objectives, the President declared his preference for the southernmost limit, but would accept the thirty-second if more feasible. At the same time Bancroft assured Hooper that the administration would accede to New England's wishes. "If Mexico makes peace this month," he wrote, "the Rio del Norte and the parallel of 35° may do as a boundary; after that 32° which will include San Diego." In private conversations with Senators Thomas H. Benton and George McDuffie in July, William S. Archer in September, and John J. Crittenden in January, Polk reaffirmed these war aims.[15]

During the summer of 1846 Bancroft had renewed his instructions to the Pacific fleet. Again he explained precisely the administration's purpose in ordering Sloat to seize the ports of California: "The object of the United States has reference to ultimate peace with Mexico; and if, at that peace, the basis of the *uti possidetis* shall be established the government expects, through your forces, to be found in actual possession of Upper California." Sloat himself had understood the significance of his maneuver. "It is not only our duty to take California," he instructed his men at Monterey, "but to preserve it afterwards as a part of the United States. . . ."[16]

When news of American triumphs in California reached Washington, the President wrote to his brother, William Polk, "You may calculate I think that *California & New Mexico*— being now possessed by forces—will not be given up, but will be retained—to indemnify our claimants upon Mexico & to defray the expenses of the war. Indeed you need not be surprised if other Provinces also are secured in like manner. The longer the war shall be protracted by the stubbornness of Mexico, the greater will be . . . the indemnity required." In December a disturbed Andrew J. Donelson, writing from Europe, urged the administration to annex San Francisco and Monterey as the minimum objects of the war, but to terminate the conflict before it became a political liability. Buchanan assured him that annexation would not go beyond New Mexico and California, and that even for these territories the United States would pay liberally.[17] During the early months of the Mexican War the executive purpose varied little from that described in the instructions prepared for Slidell in November, 1845. Now, however, the principle of indemnity made the acquisition of these territories a necessary adjunct to any satisfactory treaty of peace.

§ 3

The conquest of California quickly crystallized the expansionist mood of the nation. Members of the metropolitan press met the reports with cheers of approval and a deep resolve that the province never be returned to Mexico. The New York *Herald* in May, 1846, swept aside the threats of the European press with one gesture: "Let the tyrants of Europe rave—they may tremble, before this crisis on the Rio Grande may be closed."

California still appeared eminently satisfactory as a territorial addition. To egocentric Americans one essential factor was the smallness of the Mexican population. Donelson affirmed the popular belief that Mexicans were unfit for incorporation into the United States. This problem caused him no anxiety, however, since he anticipated within five years a dominant Anglo-American population in California. Lewis Cass early in 1847 believed any amalgamation between the Mexican and American people deplorable. He warned the

Senate not to annex Mexicans either as citizens or subjects, but only such territory "which they nominally hold, generally uninhabited, or, where inhabited at all, sparsely so, and with a population, which would soon recede, or identify itself with ours." Buchanan, opposing the extension of the United States to the Sierra Madre Mountains, asked: "How should we govern the mongrel race which inhabit it?" Like Donelson and Cass, he had no fear of annexing California, for, he added, "The Californias are comparatively uninhabited & will therefore be almost exclusively colonised by our own people."[18]

There was little sentimentality in the *Democratic Review's* prediction that American pioneers in California would dispossess the inhabitants as they had the American Indians. It declared that evidently "the process which has been gone through at the North of driving back the Indians, or annihilating them as a race, has yet to be gone through at the south." Similarly the *American Review* saw Mexicans giving way to "a superior population, insensibly oozing into her territories, changing her customs, and out-living, out-trading, exterminating her weaker blood. . . ."[19]

American expansionists were concerned with the regeneration of California's soil. John Quincy Adams had quoted the command of Genesis to "subdue the earth and replenish it" as justification for the appropriation of Oregon lands. Similar rationalizations during the Mexican War condoned the confiscation of California. Queried the *Illinois State Register:* "Shall this garden of beauty be suffered to lie dormant in its wild and useless luxuriance . . . ?" As United States territory, predicted the editor, "it would almost immediately be made to blossom like a rose; myriads of enterprising Americans would flock to its rich and inviting prairies; the hum of Anglo-American industry would be heard in its vales; cities would rise upon its plains and sea-coast, and the resources and wealth of the nation be increased in an incalculable degree." The Baltimore *American* pointed to the blessings already scattered over the Sacramento Valley by American pioneers.[20]

Visions of American commercial greatness in the Pacific were yet the prime realities behind the quest for territory. Within fifty years, predicted one South Carolinian in July, 1846, the United States would dominate the "commerce of the Pacific and the wealth of China and India," and the Republic would one day control as much wealth and power in the Pacific Ocean as in the Atlantic. One editor proclaimed that there was "something grand enough in the dream of a world of empire, embracing all Oceanica, and the Asiatic and American shores of the South Seas."[21] What was required to fulfill this dream, shouted the expansionists, was merely the retention of the California ports.

§ 4

Although Polk's territorial ambitions enjoyed wide approval and California enthusiasts over the nation anticipated and lauded his every move, the President hesitated to declare his war aims publicly. The principle of indemnity, clearly recognized under the law of nations, was acceptable only to those Americans who placed responsibility for the war on Mexico. On the academic debate over Taylor's instructions rested the decision whether California would constitute indemnity or conquest. Obviously politicians who attacked the war could not logically favor the annexation of California as a fruit of that struggle. Polk observed the attacks on the war and did not wish to add the connotation of conquest to the conflict by revealing his territorial aims. To the American public, therefore, he remained silent on the subject of California as it related to the war.

One day in December, 1845, several months before the outbreak of the Mexican War, while Slidell in Mexico was armed with specific instructions, a correspondent of the New York *Herald* approached the President to learn his intentions regarding California. "This I did not choose to communicate to him," Polk recorded. "My answers were general and indefinite. . . ." He could not have written a more cogent description of his tactics. Even when diplomacy receded before the force of arms, the President maintained the same guarded attitude outside his official family. In his war message he declared it his simple desire "not only to terminate hostilities speedily, but to bring all matters in dispute between this Government and Mexico to an early and amicable adjustment." The official policy, noted the Washington *Union*, was that of seeking peace through war. A few days later a public circular to American ministers and consuls reiterated the military objectives as the conquest of an "honorable and permanent peace." Only Polk's vehement objections prevented Buchanan from inserting a statement that the United States had no designs upon either New Mexico or California.[22] Polk preferred the risk of European intervention to a public announcement that would broach the subject of United States territorial aims.

By July, however, the Whigs in Congress began to question the military goals of the administration. Senator Reverdy Johnson, of Maryland, called at the White House to see the instructions issued to the governors relating to volunteers. "I read them to Mr. Johnson," the President confessed, "and, as they showed on their face, they disclosed the plans of the Government of a projected campaign by land and sea into Upper California, and I submitted to Mr. Johnson that if made public it would probably defeat our object & . . . excite the jealousy of England and France, who might interfere to prevent the accomplishment of our objects." Fortunately for the administration, Polk was able to convince the Senator that the publication of these instructions would be injurious to the public interest. A few days later the President assured Senator John A. Dix, a member of the disaffected Van Buren clique of New York, that he had no intention of holding Mexican territory beyond the guarantee of peace.[23] Polk's public declarations at least bore the merit of consistency. The object of the war was peace and not territorial indemnity.

Such noncommittal declarations of policy did not satisfy the opposition. Declared Daniel Webster, "The people . . . appear to me to demand, and with great reason, a full, distinct, and comprehensive account of the objects and purposes of this war of invasion." Whigs were quick to guess the aims of the administration. "The conquest of Mexico and California is the prize for which the game has been played," thought Giddings. The action of Congress authorizing a call for volunteers led the New York *Morning News* to remark, "Are we going to swallow Mexico at one gulp?"[24] During May and June the questions of the press became increasingly embarrassing. Quite pointedly the St. Louis *New Era* noted that the prosecution of war when no territory was desired merely confirmed the charge of conquest. Similarly the editor of the Augusta *Chronicle* announced that he would willingly withdraw every expression for peace if anyone could show good cause for prolonging the war. There was danger, moreover, that continued advance of American arms would nullify all prospects of peace. "If the United States were to take the whole or the half of Mexico," warned the Richmond *Times,* "the Government would be compelled to keep the country under military law until the enterprise of Anglo-Saxon Americans should push off the Mexicans, as they have done the Indians."[25] Everywhere Whigs demanded either a declaration of war aims or an immediate cessation of hostilities.

Increasingly the Mexican War placed Polk in a dilemma. While Whig pressure against expansion prevented any public statement of objectives, he would not terminate the war until his objectives were won. In his diplomacy with Mexico he had hoped to secure California by treaty. His eagerness to expedite such a settlement had provoked a clash of arms. Now his administration was forced to conduct a bitterly assailed war which it did not want, while it insisted upon using that war to achieve its undeclared purposes. Benton knew the administration well and saw its predicament clearly when he wrote:

It is impossible to conceive of an administration less warlike, or more intriguing, than that of Mr. Polk. They were men of peace, with objects to be accomplished by means of war; so that war was a necessity and an indispensability to their purposes. They wanted a small war, just large enough to require a treaty of peace, and not large enough to make military reputations, dangerous for the presidency. Never were men at the head of government less imbued with military spirit, or more adicted to intrigue. How to manage the war was a puzzle. Defeat would be ruin: to conquer vicariously, would be dangerous.[26]

So anxious was the President to be rid of the war, provided his goals could be attained, that he initiated an intrigue for peace before the war had fully commenced. He knew well that at the bottom of his earlier inability to negotiate with Mexico was the want of a Mexican government that dared to recognize an American emissary or possessed sufficient stability to guarantee any contract which might be consummated.

Polk recalled opportunely that a Colonel Atocha had informed him in February that Santa Anna intended to return to Mexico from Havana during the early summer of 1846 to resume power. This naturalized Mexican, moreover, informed him that Santa Anna favored a boundary adjustment which included granting the United States possession of both the Rio Grande and San Francisco bay. The President acted quickly. On May 13 Bancroft addressed an order to Commodore David Connor, anchored off Vera Cruz: "If Santa Anna endeavors to enter the Mexican ports, you will allow him to pass freely." The President, moreover, promised Santa Anna liberal compensation for any satisfactory settlement. The Mexican chieftain's subsequent perfidy thwarted Polk's expectations for an immediate peace. Meanwhile, as part of the President's peace offensive, he instructed Taylor in northern Mexico "to conciliate the inhabitants, and to let them see that peace is within reach the moment their rulers will consent to do us justice."[27]

Less than three months after the outbreak of war, Polk embarked upon a second peace venture. His war message, in which he had professed a willingness to accept any Mexican peace proposal, prompted Webster late in June to recommend a formal embassy to Mexico. Such an overture, the Senator believed, would convince the world that the United States had no ulterior motive. Since this was the stronger nation, the United States might well initiate a movement toward peace. Webster could see no practical alternative. "The people of the United States cannot wish to crush the republic of Mexico," he declared with conviction; "it cannot be their desire to break down a neighboring republic. . . ."[28]

Polk was attentive to such concrete proposals. On July 27 Buchanan's brief dispatch informed the Mexican minister of foreign relations that the President desired to terminate the war and assured the Mexican government that a minister would be assigned to Mexico City upon the receipt of the offer's acceptance.[29] The official explanation to Congress a week later followed Webster's reasoning. The obvious superiority of American arms removed all question of honor. But Polk saw clearly that his problem of making peace would be far more difficult than the Whig pacificists would concede. He understood privately that the real crisis would occur when the Mexicans received the American boundary proposals.

During the summer of 1846 the President found his efforts at peace complicated by the actions of Great Britain. Upon the settlement of the Oregon controversy in June, Pakenham, British Minister at Washington, followed the logical step of proposing British arbitration in the Mexican War. Then for several months his policy evinced hesitation. The British Foreign Office had determined to render Mexico no assistance in holding California, but Pakenham was distressed at the thought that Polk would demand San Francisco Bay. This would not only make negotiations difficult, but would also be "painful to the mediating Power to be a Party to the bargain." A British offer of arbitration was equally disturbing to the American press. British policy, warned the *Missouri Reporter*, would hew to the "Balance of Power" and must therefore be cast aside. The New York *Sun* agreed that British mediation would be a limiting factor. England never tolerated such interference in her affairs, never compromised her rights, observed the New York *Journal of Commerce*. The argument struck home. When Pakenham presented formal arbitration proposals in September, the President's answer was definite. It concluded that until a reply from Mexico was received, "the formal acceptance by the United States of the mediation of a Foreign Power might rather tend to protract the War than to facilitate an adjustment."[30] British sentiments toward American expansion were well known to Polk. He preferred to seek his objectives unhindered by European restrictions.

Polk knew that no administration in Mexico City could long remain in power if it ceded territory, unless it could receive, at the moment of the treaty, sufficient funds to support an army. Again his appraisal of the Mexican problem led him to consider the feasibility of securing a grant from Congress to aid in the establishment of a settlement. Convinced of the wisdom of that course, he followed his proposal to the Mexican government in July with a request to Congress for $2,000,000 to assist in overcoming the chief obstacle to peace, "the adjustment of a boundary between the two republics." Congress did not fully recognize the significance of the solicited appropriation. The bill was talked to death in the closing minutes of the session.

This request for funds served to increase the confusion in Congress over war aims. Its purpose, Polk admitted, was to adjust the boundary, but he refused to describe or even to hint at the boundary he desired. Richard Rush shortly inquired of Buchanan, "What may be the executive plans precisely in regard to Mexico?"[31] On the House floor, David Wilmot regretted that the President had not disclosed his views, for he disliked to work in the dark. Better to have the truth and if necessary go into secret session. Wilmot revealed his perplexity: "We claim the Rio Grande as our boundary—that was the main cause of the war. Are we now to purchase what we claim as a matter of right?" He assumed quite logically that the President desired territory on the Pacific. Even to this he had no objection, provided the region could come into the possession of the United States "by fair and honorable means, by purchase or negotiation—not by conquest." John Davis of Kentucky, like Wilmot, revealed a certain acquisitiveness toward California, but opposed its annexation by any mode other than negotiation. Yet he understood the administration sufficiently well to prophesy that if it failed to acquire the region by treaty, Polk would prosecute the war until Mexico was *"whipped into its cession."*[32]

§ 5

Davis was right. When Mexico responded unsatisfactorily to the peace overture in September, the President reversed completely the conduct of the war. The Mexican executive had refused to assume responsibility, but agreed to present the American note to the Mexican congress when it convened in December. Polk interpreted this delay as a complete refusal to negotiate. He warned Mexico that until she evinced a disposition to treat, the United States would "prosecute the war with vigor." He informed the Secretaries of War and Navy of his intention to change the entire character of the war. Instead of conciliating the Mexican people and paying liberally for all supplies, he was now determined, he recorded, "to quarter upon the enemy by laying contributions upon them, or seizing the necessary supplies for the army without paying for them, making proper discriminations in favour of such Mexicans as were ascertained to be friendly to the United States."[33]

Marcy informed Taylor of the Mexican habit of procrastination in refusing negotiations and instructed him to push the enemy until it begged for peace. By Marcy's own admission, Taylor could have known nothing of these instructions before his lenient treatment of the Mexicans following the battle of Monterey. Yet so severe and complete was the reversal of military policy that, according to General Scott, Taylor was very nearly recalled for his generosity. His high reputation alone saved him.[34]

Polk's immediate desire to seize Tampico led eventually to the campaign against Vera Cruz and the "rapid crushing movement" on Mexico City. This new offensive the President was prepared to announce publicly when Congress reconvened in December, 1846. In his message he called for action: "The war will continue to be prosecuted with vigor, as the best means of securing peace." In a second dispatch to Mexico the President informed the Mexican government that he would await the final decision of the Mexican congress. His intimation that a long war would entail heavy expenditures was a hint to the wise. Yet in his communication Polk again hesitated to mention the matter of boundary adjustments. Although the acquisition of territory was essential to an acceptable peace, he believed that "to announce the fact now that Mexico was to pay the expenses of the war, would excite that stubborn and impracticable people and prevent them from entering into negotiations."[35]

By the autumn of 1846 national leaders outside the administration agreed with Polk that the greatest barrier to a successful termination of the war was the Mexican government, not the Mexican army. Webster, as early as August, 1846, expected no more hard fighting, but he saw no prospect of peace. "Mexico is an ugly enemy," he wrote to his son. "She will not fight—& will not treat." He admitted that even the President desired peace but did not know how to achieve it. So anarchical was the Mexican nation that American victories had little effect on peace sentiment. Since only those in the line of combat felt the pressure of war, the slightest intimation that Mexico might lose territory was enough to invoke cries from the Mexican press that the war should rather continue. The London *Times* observed in November that the

Mexican War presented "the strange picture of a victorious army in a foreign country which is more nearly reduced to the necessity of effecting a peace than the State that it has conquered and subdued."[36]

The prospect of never finding a government in Mexico with which to conclude peace presaged the eventual reasoning of the *Democratic Review* that there could be no peace short of annihilation of the Mexican nation. Polk voiced his private apprehensions to Donelson: "Such is the distracted state of things in that unfortunate country, that I fear no party in power, will feel secure in making such a Treaty as ought to be satisfactory to the U. States."[37]

Obviously it was Polk's desire to force extensive territorial concessions from Mexico that prompted his vigorous military policy. To Congress, however, he again declared his purpose to obtain "an honorable peace and thereby secure *ample indemnity* for the expenses of the war, as well as to our much injured citizens. . . ." Yet he cleverly avoided any precise definition of such indemnification. In fact, his entire December message revealed extremely careful preparation in its discussion of Mexican policy without disclosing objectives other than an honorable peace. Polk admitted the need of establishing civil government in New Mexico and California without declaring any intention of retaining them. In requesting again an appropriation from Congress, he referred to the reasons given in his August message.[38] The famous Three Million Bill of January, 1847, which was the product of this request, merely stated as its purpose the defrayment of "any extraordinary expenses which may be incurred in order to bring the existing war with Mexico to a speedy and honorable conclusion."

During the first half year of the Mexican War, Polk committed himself to a clear-cut expansionist policy. His objects, however, were of such a nature that they could be achieved only through private negotiation so that he might present a *fait accompli* to a bitterly partisan nation. As late as December, 1846, the only hope lay in a continued vigorous prosecution of the war and the hopeful anticipation of the day when a Mexican regime would be permitted to make peace on the terms of the Polk administration.

Chapter 9

WARTIME POLITICS AND EXPANSION

§ 1

American expansionism toward California had developed free of domestic politics. Any acquisitiveness toward the Mexican province prior to May, 1846, had been favored equally by spokesmen of both the Democratic and Whig Parties. Webster's intentions toward the region never varied from those of Jackson, Calhoun, and Polk; for all were motivated primarily by a search for ports. Nor was the metropolitan press that focused attention on California in 1845 partisan. Not until Polk's Mexican policy degenerated into war did that expansionist goal leave its traditional nonpartisan sphere. Polk in absorbing the Whig attacks on the Mexican War sought conscientiously to preserve the issue of expansion from the political onslaught. It was for this end that he maintained a rigid secrecy regarding his war aims. But he could not isolate the question of the war's morality from that of its covert objectives. When finally the future of California became the subject of Congressional debate, it became increasingly doubtful whether Polk would acquire his territorial intentions. By December, 1846, politics had altered considerably the expansionist temper of the Whigs.

Polk's opposition returned to Congress strengthened by the November elections and conscious of the growing frustration of the American people toward the conduct of the Mexican

War. Driven to excesses by the administration's apparent defenselessness and the pleasant anticipation of building political fences through undermining the President's leadership, the Whigs continued, privately and publicly, to condemn the waging of the war. Joshua Giddings, with his customary passion, declared that the object of inquiry was everywhere the administration's responsibility for the crimes, misery, and suffering resulting from the war. "It is," he cried "the absorbing topic in our social circles, in stage-coaches, in railroad cars, and in steamboats; in our pulpits and religious meetings; in our political conventions, our State Legislatures; in Congress and in the Executive Cabinet. It is discussed in the United States, in Mexico, and in Europe."[1]

Tom Corwin attacked the war with venom in February, 1847: "It will be soon a 'bye word,' a curse, a hissing, and scorn with all honest men." Two months later the *American Review* termed the war "the great political and moral crime of the period." It was, charged the editor, "a war of foreign invasion and conquest, as little excusable in its origin and objectives as any that could be conceived of. . . ."[2]

Polk's continued veiled generalities on the purposes of the war added to the confusion and vituperation in the new session of Congress. Whigs challenged the administration to reveal its object in pursuing the armies of Mexico so relentlessly. When and under what conditions would the war end? If its purpose was the conquest of peace, at what stage in the progression of American victories would a peace be conquered? In complete disgust, Giddings attacked the President's message of December: "The people of the nation are demanding of the Executive a statement of the objects of the war. What are the ulterior designs of the government in its prosecution?" The Ohioan recounted the deeds of American arms in Mexico, professedly done in the name of defense, and continued: "What estimation must the author of this message have placed upon the intelligence of this body, and of the nation, when he penned these statements? Such absurdities defy argument."³

Robert Winthrop urged the President to abandon the senseless idea of obtaining peace by conquering it. "The only conquest which is now needed, in order to secure peace," he shouted, "is the noblest of all conquests, in which fortune has no share, a conquest over himself. . . ." Again it was the total absence of logic in pressing a defensive war on a defeated foe that brought forth Corwin's caustic diatribe: "I am not willing to scourge Mexico thus, and the only means left me is to say to the commander-in-chief, 'Call home your army, I will feed and clothe it no longer. . . .' "⁴

The American press was no less perplexed than the politicians in analyzing the significance of United States military conquests, especially those in California. Such expansionist organs as the New York *Journal of Commerce* assumed early that the coastal regions would never be given up. The Richmond *Enquirer,* on the other hand, predicted that the United States would hold California only until Mexico had paid all indemnity owed American citizens and had defrayed the cost of the war. The New Orleans *Picayune* pictured a similar future for California and other Whig presses agreed.⁵ Such mistaken notions were not corrected by Polk's public declarations.

Only the authorization of the New York Volunteer Regiment offered any tangible evidence of Polk's territorial objectives. Governor Silas Wright had looked askance at the arrangement, for it bespoke annexation. Marcy assured him, however, that the government had sought to avoid a return trip solely in the interest of economy. But in February, 1847, Alexander Stephens, of Georgia, on the floor of the House subjected to rigorous scrutiny the motivation behind the dispatching of this regiment to California. He questioned the President's sincerity in his continued insistence that the war was not being waged for conquest. He wondered whether the Democrats would do the President the injustice of believ-

ing him when the New York regiment was infallible proof
that Polk intended the dismemberment of Mexico.[6]

As the Twenty-ninth Congress wore on during the early
months of 1847, evidence of Democratic expansionism was
accumulating despite Polk's public denials. Administration
spokesmen in Congress increasingly argued the need of requiring territorial indemnity. Alexander Sims, of South Carolina, sought to counter the Whig opposition by insisting that
for the United States to take nothing would make of the war
an idle joust and would challenge national honor. Democrats
proceeded to delineate the areas of proper indemnification.
John Tibbatts, of Kentucky, informed the House early in
January that California, New Mexico, Chihuahua, and Ta-
maulipas would, in his estimation, suffice as territorial compensation.

Several days later Ambrose Sevier, of Arkansas, one of
Polk's chief spokesmen in the Senate, admitted that he could
not speak precisely for the President but supposed that no
Senator would agree to any treaty which conveyed to this
nation less than New Mexico and California. Lewis Cass
referred to "certain territorial acquisitions," important to the
United States and not held premanently by Mexico, which
would furnish satisfactory indemnity.[7] Such declarations of
leading Democrats, plus the call for additional arms, provided
some evidence of war aims. Whig leaders were learning by
inference in 1847 what many had suspected at the opening of
military action, that the Mexican War was a war of expansion
in which the minimum goals were California and New
Mexico. Polk's declared objective of peace with indemnity
carried rather specific overtones discernible to all astute
observers.

§ 2

Of Congress the President required men and supplies to
pursue the war. With a clear majority of Democrats in both
houses, Polk still anticipated the new session with some

serenity. He expected little of the Whigs but resented their rampant partisanship. Reluctantly he admitted that his initial hope of interparty cooperation in "bearing the American flag to honorable triumph" had been quickly dispelled. But not until he observed that Whig attacks were destroying the confidence of the nation in his administration did he rebuke them openly for spreading "erroneous views" and for giving "aid and comfort" to the enemy.[8] This inference of treason enraged the Whigs even further. By the end of December political rancor had driven them completely from the administration. The President recorded that members of the opposition party no longer attended White House receptions.

Partisanship also pervaded the military administration of the war. Polk quickly lost faith in the loyalty, and eventually in the efficiency, of the army's two ranking generals. The Whigs never forgot, nor allowed the nation to forget, that Winfield Scott and Zachary Taylor were members of their party. Scott, as commander of all American forces, could prevent the second-guessing of Congress on matters of strategy, but he never ceased to embarrass and antagonize the administration, for he also could not forget that he was a Whig.

Before the war was two months old, Scott began to complain openly that all general appointments were going to Democrats; he bluntly accused the Secretary of War of proscribing Whigs. He also advised Marcy that he did not intend to leave the capital until September to avoid placing himself in a peculiar position of having "a fire upon [his] rear, from Washington, and the fire, in front, from the Mexicans." Polk scrutinized the letter, amazed. "It proved to me," he noted "that Gen'l Scott was not only hostile, but recklessly vindictive in his feeling towards my administration."

Simultaneously Polk discovered that Scott and other Whig officers were using their influence in Congress to block the passage of a bill authorizing the appointment of several additional general officers. Polk believed such conduct highly censurable. He accused the officers of attempting to throw every obstacle in the path of his successful prosecution of the war.[9] In his next communication to the War Department Scott was more cordial and promised to abide by the decisions of the administration. Hardly had this feud with Scott receded before another of equal intensity developed with General Taylor.

Polk discovered early that old "Rough and Ready" in Mexico had an inordinate capacity to attract favorable attention to himself from all segments of the American public. As Taylor's political star began to rise, Polk's opinion of his generalship sank correspondingly lower. By September the President thought the general lacking in initiative. He complained that Taylor "simply obeys orders and gives no information to aid the administration in directing his movement."[10] Yet Polk dared not censure him openly. "After the late battles, which were well fought," admitted the beleaguered President, "the public opinion seems to point to him as entitled to the command."

Polk wanted victories, rapid and decisive, for the war's popularity was waning. His indignation toward Taylor reached a new high, therefore, when he learned of the armistice following the smashing American victory at Monterey. Taylor had permitted the Mexican commander to retire with his army intact. Polk lectured the General in his diary: "He had the enemy in his power & should have taken them prisoners, deprived them of their arms, discharged them on their parole of honour, and preserved the advantage which he had obtained. . . ." The President, influenced perhaps by a private letter from Gideon J. Pillow, became convinced that Taylor's generosity would allow the Mexican army to reorganize and prolong the north Mexican campaign. At that moment only its fear of public reaction prevented the administration from superseding Taylor in command. Scott quickly balanced the mutual antipathy between Taylor and Polk by informing the general of a plot in Washington to replace him and his staff with six new generals, all Democrats. Scott praised Taylor on his victory at Monterey and hoped that he would continue to defeat his enemies "in *front* and in *rear*."[11]

During the autumn months the administration decided on a second campaign at the heart of Mexico, commencing with an assault on Vera Cruz. Polk rejected Taylor completely for the new command, for he now suspected the General of political ambitions. "He is evidently a weak man and has been made giddy with the idea of the Presidency," guessed Polk, and proceeded to accuse Taylor of ingratitude. "He is most ungrateful, for I have promoted him, as I now think beyond his deserts, and without reference to his politics. I am now satisfied that he is a narrow minded, bigotted partisan, without resources and wholly unqualified for the command he holds." Polk was fully convinced that Whig politicians and editors, such as Bailey Peyton and George W. Kendall, editor of the New Orleans *Picayune,* were grooming him for a political future.[12] His apparent political connections, concluded the President, rendered the General untrustworthy to conduct administration military policy on the field of battle.

Polk wanted Scott out of Washington, for he observed that his presence there had become embarrassing to the Secretary of War. But only in desperation did he convey to him the command of the Vera Cruz expedition. Until his departure for Mexico in January, however, Scott reported that Polk and Marcy lavished both kindness and confidence upon him. The departure seemed propitious. Scott wrote to the Secretary, "On setting out, on my present mission, I laid down *whiggism* without taking up *democracy;* but without reference to party or politics, I have felt very like a Polk-man." Still the President failed to place complete reliance upon Scott. He knew that the General in entering the field of battle would be in an excellent position to establish a high military reputation. Polk's brother reminded him in November that there "is nothing which possesses so strong a charm to win public favour as the recitation of military services, or the exhibition of honorable scars received in the service of the country."[13]

During the early weeks of the new session of Congress Polk plotted cautiously to resolve the question of partisan military leadership. He suggested to Ambrose Sevier, recently elected chairman of the Senate Foreign Relations Committee, and to several other key Democrats that Congress authorize the appointment of a lieutenant general to serve as supreme commander in Mexico. These party leaders agreed both to the plan and to the President's choice of Benton for the new command. The unpredictable Missourian was at that moment a confidant of the President and closely aligned with the Van Buren group in Congress, whose recent support of administration policy required official acknowledgment. The Senator, to the astonishment of his closest friends, appeared delighted at the prospect of a military reputation.[14] "Poor Benton!" wrote Joel Poinsett. "He seems crazed indeed. What in heaven's name is he going to do? The army will be in opposition to such a leader and he can never manage those fiery spirits."

Congress defeated the administration's proposal. It conveyed only another commission of major general. This Benton declined, for he regarded both Scott and Taylor unfit and would accept no less than the supreme command in the field.[15] Without power to supersede them, the President followed the actions of the two Whig generals in Mexico with mounting fear and distrust. "I am held responsible for the conduct of the War," he confided to his diary, "and yet Congress refused to give me a commander in whom I have confidence, & I am compelled to employ the officers whom the law provided, however, unfit they may be." Scott was equally furious. He promptly bared his feelings toward Polk's attempt to replace him. "This is, from a high quarter," he charged, "opening a fire upon my rear, even before I have been able to draw the fire of the enemy in front."[16]

By February, 1847, the President was accusing both Taylor and Scott of converting their camps into political arenas and mistreating the Democratic officers. Nor was the President's opinion of Taylor elevated by the costly American triumph at Buena Vista. Polk could retain Taylor in northern Mexico, but he could not repress the soaring popularity of the Whig officer. Polk bitterly accused the Whig press of "moral treason" for attempting to make Taylor politically "available" by attributing the victories in Mexico to his generalship. "Our forces are the best troops in the world," he struck back privately, "& will [would] gain victories over superior forces of the enemy, if there was not an officer among them." But the President was forced to conclude that Taylor was "a Whig and the Federal party will make a hero of him if they can, and will make a candidate for the Presidency of him if they shall think him their most available candidate."[17]

§ 3

With a united Democratic Party behind him, Polk might have withstood unscathed the Whig onslaught against his wartime leadership. The momentous issues of 1846, however, seriously undermined his power. The subtreasury alone had ruined the Van Buren administration, but during the spring and summer of 1846 the Twenty-ninth Congress had wrestled with the tariff, river and harbor legislation, the subtreasury, the Oregon question, and the Mexican War. This was too much for any administration to carry. For Polk's, already crippled by schism that dated back to the Baltimore Convention of 1844, the issues were disastrous. With the Mexican War, moreover, the expansionist wing of the Democratic Party regained the ascendency in the party's directorship, and with it the wartime patronage. The Calhoun and Van Buren cliques looked on, their enthusiasm for administration causes waning as the war progressed.

Internal tensions threatened to cleave the Democratic Party to its roots. "All around is dissention and distrust," wrote one Virginia Democrat in December, 1846. "Gloom overspreads the party." Key organizations of New York, Virginia, Ohio, and Pennsylvania, he noted, were too divided and apathetic to render the national administration much support. One Calhounite added, "The administration is almost unanimously deserted." From Philadelphia came the observation, "I never saw an administration that was so little looked to or cared for."[18]

Van Burenites had never fully accepted Polk's leadership, and they tended to blame the President rather than his enemies for his failure to control Congress. One New Yorker phrased the faction's sentiments, "I have no faith either in Providential, or accidental Presidents." To his chief he wrote in March, 1847, "What an Eternal shame it is that this *Great Country* should be governed by such *little* men." James K. Paulding asserted that the President was simply devoid of character, influence, and personality, without "honesty of purpose, or frankness of heart." He concluded that any high-minded person in the President's weakened position would have found it unbearable. To the Van Buren clique the Mexican War was, in short, an unforgivable blunder that was undermining the strength of the party. "The truth is," wrote one Indianan, "the Mexican War is not popular with the thinking and reflecting Majority of our party." John Dix criticized the President for allowing "mercenary & needy men about him" to drive him into a position which the party could not sustain "in the face of the country or the civilized world."[19] The war, predicted one member of the faction, would furnish popular Whig presidential candidates for a decade.

These Van Burenites, however, abstained from an open attack on the war. "I know this is high-treason, and, therefore, desist," Dix assured Van Buren. Poinsett, at one time a member of Van Buren's cabinet, agreed that Polk's position on the war was untenable but guarded his public statements for fear of being suspected of "unamerican feelings." Benton never recognized the necessity of war, but he accepted the obligation of rendering full support to the administration in prosecuting it. The recently defeated governor of New York and staunch Van Burenite, Silas Wright, urged this policy of cooperation on his friends in Congress. To Dix he admitted that he would not "swap chances with Mr. Polk. What the poor man is to do, and how he is to get on with the Mexican War, are matters which trouble me more than my defeat." Wright urged an early peace to save the administration. He hoped Polk would demand no more of Mexico than what would have comprised a satisfactory arrangement before the outbreak of war. Francis P. Blair wrote in a similar vein, ". . . whatever we do in this quarrel with distracted & feeble Mexico would be safer & better done, if accompanied with a display of moderation and magnanimity."[20]

Unlike the Van Burenites, Calhoun deserted the administration completely and openly used his political prestige to undermine and embarrass it. During the spring of 1846 the Calhoun circle in Congress, about to capitalize on the Oregon, tariff, and river and harbor issues, commanded a dominant position in the party. Then the Mexican War forced Calhoun to the wall. If Texas annexation were its cause, and Benton among the Democrats never ceased to insist that it was, the burden would fall on Calhoun for his role in negotiating the treaty of annexation. In self-defense Calhoun denounced Polk for the Slidell mission and the "thoughtless and unwarranted movement of our troops to the Del Norte." Annexation had caused a diplomatic rupture, he admitted, but ordinary prudence could have prevented hostilities. "That Mexico was chafed, chagrined; that she threatened much, and blustered much; talked about war, and even the existence of hostilities—is all true," but, Calhoun insisted, skillful diplomacy could have avoided war.[21] He readily joined the Whigs in accusing the President of usurping power and involving the nation in an undeclared war.

But other motives were more subtle. Like the politically conscious Van Burenites he viewed the growing popularity of

Taylor as a major blunder. "In their folly and profligacy," he accused members of the administration, "they made the Mexican War, without seeing, that the successful general will ever be sure to turn the party, in this country, out of power, which makes the war." The South Carolinian feared above all that the war would defeat the proposed low Walker Tariff of 1846 and produce a revolution in United States tariff policy. What terrified the free traders was the Whig logic that tariff reduction was illogical in wartime. The tariff passed, but Calhoun's anxiety persisted. New military expenditures would leave nothing for his "inland seas" project of internal improvements by which he hoped to capture the West. The Mexican War, moreover, might afford a pretext to renew high protective duties in the future. He predicted a struggle long and expensive, and other Calhounites reflected his dismay. F. W. Byrdsall reported that one New York merchant openly proclaimed the hope that the war would involve the nation in a huge debt to compel the restoration of high tariffs. The war will "bankrupt the treasury, endanger the cause of free trade, and create discontent in every section of the Union," lamented one Alabama correspondent.[22] This was a war against the federal treasury. One Virginian warned Polk that only an early peace would guarantee the success of the "glorious free-trade experiment."

Increasingly Polk's resentment toward Congressional obstruction centered on Calhoun's small core of Democrats in the Senate. This "Balance of Power Party," the President observed, voted more frequently with the Whigs than the Democrats. Aided by the united Whig Party, this group had defeated Polk's proposal for the appointment of a lieutenant general. When he learned in February that Calhoun's clique had defeated his request for ten additional regiments, the President concluded painfully that Calhoun had formally broken with the administration. Added the President, "I now consider him the most mischievous man in the Senate to my administration."[23] Polk attributed Calhoun's enmity and his willingness to paralyze the national leadership to the Senator's dissatisfaction over patronage and cabinet appointments.

This open Democratic disaffection soon went beyond the Calhoun faction. John Wentworth and other Democrats defeated the wartime tax on tea and coffee in the House. The President noted dejectedly in his diary, "I have a nominal majority of Democrats in both Houses of Congress, but am in truth in a minority in each house." As the session entered its third month, disharmony among Democrats still prevented action on all administration war measures. Polk passed judgment on the Democratic revolt: "I am perfectly disgusted with the want of patriotism which seems to control the votes and course of a portion of the Democratic members."[24]

Thomas Ritchie's Washington *Union* took up the administration's fight against Calhoun and the Whigs. In February its correspondent accused Congress of maintaining the cause of Mexico "with zeal and ability." Upon the rejection of the ten regiment bill, the writer continued, "If Santa Anna, Ampudia, or any other Mexican general could snatch from our soldiers a corresponding victory, we should place them upon the same elevation where their compatriots, friends, and fellow-soldiers in the Senate now stand." Immediately Senator D. L. Yulee of Florida, a member of Calhoun's faction, led a successful maneuver to bar Ritchie from the chamber. "It is a second Duane case," lamented the President, "& strikes a blow at the liberty of the press."[25]

In one succinct paragraph in February, 1847, the President summarized all the political pressures beating against the vigorous execution of his expansionist policy toward Mexico:

It is now in the third month of the Session and none of my war measures have yet been acted upon. There is no harmony in the Democratic party. . . . In truth faction rules the hour, while principle & patriotism is forgotten. While the Democratic party are thus distracted and divided and are playing this foolish and suicidal game, the

Federal party are united and never fail to unite with the minority of
the Democratic party, or any faction of it who may break off from the
body of their party, and thus postpone and defeat all my measures. I
am in the unenviable position of being held responsible for the conduct of the Mexican War, when I have no support either from Congress or from the two officers highest in command in the field. How
long this state of things will continue I cannot foresee.[26]

Polk sought the means to drive the Democrats into line
before they sank him and the entire party. He urged the
cabinet to confer with leaders in Congress from their regions
and impress upon them the need for harmony and action in
war measures. Before the end of January the President considered taking his cause to the electorate. "I am resolved,"
he declared, "to do my duty to the country & if I am not sustained by Congress I will fearlessly appeal to the people." He
would send a special message to Congress to exert public
pressure on that body and throw upon it the responsibility for
the failure of the administration to prosecute the war successfully.

Polk still had some vigorous support in Congress. Leadership of the Polk Democrats fell to Lewis Cass, who regarded
himself as the administration's spokesman in the Senate. He
was an ardent expansionist and the essence of Midwestern
Anglophobia. He practiced on the drum and trumpet, noted
one observer, and his appearance was "redolent of gunpowder."
In this boisterous minority were also Allen of Ohio, Johnson
of Tennessee, Douglas of Illinois, and Sevier of Arkansas.
They turned on the Whigs, and their words bore weight, for
they possessed the appeal of patriotism. Orlando Ficklin, of
Illinois, cried, "The Whigs must get themselves into line,
and be either for the war or against the war, for the United
States or for Mexico." Nor did Calhoun escape the denunciation of the party. "I have no sympathy or confidence left
for or in him," wrote one Gideon Welles correspondent, while
from Athens, Georgia, came a note of disgust: "Mr. Calhoun,
I see, is getting farther and farther off. . . . I think I shall
have to read him out before long."[27]

§ 4

Slavery added a new, more serious dimension to the political confusion of Congress. If partisanship alone was insufficient to destroy the President's program in Congress, the reintroduction of the Wilmot Proviso by Preston King in January, 1847, to prevent the expansion of slavery into new territory, challenged all military progress. Polk was soon dismayed over the ceaseless debates over slavery, for that institution had no connection, he insisted, with either war or peace. "Its introduction in connection with the Mexican War," he recorded, "is not only mischievous but wicked." The distraught President reminded members of Congress that slavery could not exist in New Mexico or California. The issue when applied to war objectives was unrealistic. He was not alone in this impression, and Wilmot was among those who agreed. But the debate continued. "The state of things in Congress is lamentable," he wrote two weeks later. "Instead of coming up to the mark as patriots and sustaining the administration and the country in conducting a foreign War, they are engaged in discussing the abstract question of slavery. . . ."[28] The President concluded that he would be forced to discontinue the war for lack of legislative support.

Polk saw in the debate a drive of Democratic politicians of the North and South to gain political ascendency over the party. He condemned both factions equally. "Both desire to mount slavery as a hobby, and hope to secure the election of their favorite upon it," he observed. "They will both fail and ought to fail. . . . I am utterly disgusted at such intriguing of men in high places, & hope they will be rebuked by the people."

Slavery by 1847 challenged all national expansion. Philip Hone, the New York Whig and bitter partisan, anticipated the day when the Wilmot Proviso would "alter the whole organization of political parties in the country, and defeat the *great objects* of the annexation of Texas and its consequence, the unrighteous war with Mexico." He spoke for those ardent Whigs and abolitionists from New England to Ohio who viewed the Mexican War as the diabolical conspiracy of a coalition of slaveholders and pro-Southern influences in the Polk administration. This sensitive minority hated the war and wanted it stopped. The *Ohio State Journal* declared in May, 1846: "The administration, in attempting to consum· mate a scheme for the extension and strengthening of Slavery and the Slave Power, has involved the country in a War, which the people are now compelled to take off its hands and prosecute."[29] The slavocrats, believed these critics, had started their career of rapine and plunder with Texas and would not cease their exertions until they had extended slavery to the Pacific. It was slavery, therefore, that was responsible for the debasement of the country, for the murder of thousands of helpless Mexicans.

Fearing that the benefits of war would therefore accrue to another section, these "Conscience Whigs" became abusive in their attacks on expansionism. Giddings, like many abolitionists, believed that slavery would reach the Pacific to degrade the "freedom of Ohio . . . to the level of Mexican slaves." James Russell Lowell reduced his famed castigation of slaveholding expansionism to verse in his *Biglow Papers*:

> They jest want this Californy
> So's to lug new slave-states in
> To abuse ye, an' to score ye,
> An' to plunder ye like sin.

In New Hampshire a Whig convention solemnly announced that the Mexican War was being pursued "for the dismemberment of a sister republic upon pretexts that are false, and for a purpose that is abhorrent to all feelings of humanity and justice." In New York the Reverend Samuel D. Burchard cautioned his parishoners against accepting the war: "I fear—

I *do* fear that conquest is our object, that we may extend over that vast territory the dark realm of slavery.[30]

For many Southerners the Wilmot Proviso destroyed quite as completely all enthusiasm for expansion. John M. Berrien, Georgia Whig, warned his friends in the Senate that "the duty of the South, the interests of the South—the safety of the South, demands that we should oppose ourselves to any and to every acquisition of territory." Waddy Thompson, giving similar evidence of Southern fears, condemned all expansion which might find "southern men madly rushing upon destiny by the acquisition of another cordon of free states. . . ."[31]

Fear of disunion drove conservative Whigs into an equally vociferous antiexpansionist position. To them the desire for Mexican soil and the conflict over slavery were grave threats to the security of the nation. Stephens, of Georgia, anxiously reviewed the impact of the slavery debate on American politics: "The North is going to stick the Wilmot amendment to every appropriation and then all the South will vote against any measure thus clogged. Finally a tremendous struggle will take place and perhaps Polk in starting one war may find half a dozen on his hands. I tell you the prospect ahead is dark, cloudy, thick, and gloomy."[32] Corwin was haunted by visions of a nation on the crumbling brink of a "bottomless gulf of civil strife," with "bloody eddies whirling and boiling" before him.

Already the debate was severing the Democratic Party and threatening to divide the Whig Party and the Union itself. Astute politicians had long predicted that the nation would remain united only as long as the parties maintained their national character. Such men in 1847 could no longer detect the compromising spirit of the past that had held the parties together. Their only hope of saving the Union was to destroy the issue by which it was threatened—territorial expansion. They accepted as their program Berrien's proposed amendment of February, 1847, which declared that "the war with Mexico ought not to be prosecuted by this Government with any view to the dismemberment of the republic, or to the acquisition by conquest of any portion of her territory."[33]

§ 5

By February the Whig stand against expansion was official. That decision comprised the party's final effort to maintain party unity and reap political capital from the war. Corwin attacked the Democratic plea that America needed room. "Sir, look at this pretense of want of room," he stormed at Cass in the Senate. "With twenty millions of people, you have about one thousand millions of acres of land, inviting settlement by every conceivable argument—bringing them down to a quarter of a dollar an acre, and allowing every man to squat where he pleases . . . and yet you persist in the ridiculous assertion, 'I want room.' "

Whigs belabored the doctrine of territorial indemnity. Again Corwin shouted, "You want *'more room!'* This has been the plea of every robber from Nimrod to the present day." The Cincinnati *Atlas* pointed to the American policy of "wrenching territory from Mexico by force" and the "enormous outrage and crime of mutilating and dismembering that country." Waddy Thompson limited American claims to "the ruffian, the robber right of conquest." The *National Intelligencer* suggested that the American nation be warned by the history of previous conquerors.[34]

Politics and slavery together had driven the Whigs into the antiexpansionist position which Polk had fought to avoid. Both the fear of political disunion and the gradual realization that the Mexican War had territorial objectives forced the Whigs to condemn expansion. For some the condemnation came hard. Their conservatism was too deep, their interests too broad, to permit any resounding denunciation of the war. Polk's will-o'-the-wisp, California, had once beckoned Webster as it had enslaved the boot and shoe industry of his beloved Massachusetts. He would not even designate the struggle a war of aggression, and he approved the efforts of his son, Edward, to recruit a company of volunteers. Winthrop, mindful of New England's ambitions, acknowledged in January, 1847, that he still favored the acquisition of additional maritime facilities on the Pacific; but he repudiated, as an afterthought, a policy of wresting good harbors from Mexico through force of arms.[35] Webster and Winthrop had no more desire to see California slip beyond their grasp than did the President.

These Whigs efficiently bearded the administration, stalled and delayed Congressional action, and referred to "Polk, the Mendacious," but they eventually voted the men and supplies for the very hostilities which they condemned. With a sagacity unknown to the Federalists of 1812, they continued alternately to abuse and concede in the simple conviction that if they gave the administration enough rope it would hang itself. The absurdities of their position did not deter them. "They denounced the war enough to incriminate themselves when they supported it," Justin H. Smith has observed, "and they supported it enough to stultify themselves when they condemned it."[36]

One small minority accepted completely the logic of the Whig position and to the end stood firmly against the war and all expansion. It consisted of extremes—Northern pacifists and abolitionists and such unionists as Corwin. The specter of Webster, representing New England business and unconvincingly opposing the war, was deeply perturbing to Northern antislavery elements. Ralph Waldo Emerson lamented the Senator's Whiggism as a "feast of shells, idolatrous of the forms of legislature; like a cat loving the house, not the inhabitants." Again he recorded in his journal, "The Whig party are what people would call *first-rate* in opposition. . . . Perhaps they have not sufficient fortitude."[37]

Congress did not appease the President when at last in February and March it authorized the calling of additional troops. Had it acted earlier, Polk commented coldly, "The troops would probably by this time have been on the theater of War ready to render active and important service."[38] Congress was no longer to be trusted; for the first time Americans in large numbers had turned against the acquisition of California. Private diplomacy with Mexico remained the only solution to the administration's political predicament.

Chapter 10

THE TRIST MISSION

§ 1

A disturbed Polk confided to his diary in January, 1847: "I am the more solicitous to open negotiations & conclude a peace with Mexico because of the extraordinary delay of Congress to act upon War measures which I have recommended to them."[1] Increasingly the President found himself in the unenviable position of conducting a bitterly assailed and burdensome war while he insisted on employing American military triumphs to secure California by treaty. Incessant Whig invectives against any expansion by conquest prevented a public statement of war aims, but Polk was still determined privately to continue the war until he could attain his territorial objectives. His failure to negotiate with Mexico during the autumn of 1846 led to demands for more ruthless warfare. Thereafter American arms added victory to victory, but alone they did not assure the success of his policy. The occupation of California by United States forces exerted little pressure on the Mexican government; the refusal of Congress to adopt his military measures thwarted Polk's repeated efforts to win California through a thorough chastisement of Mexico.

During the early months of 1847 Polk's purpose of re-establishing diplomacy with Mexico through the friendly services of Atocha again ended in failure. For such obstinacy, the President had but one answer. The time had come, he harangued the cabinet, to lay aside the technical rules of warfare, discard the cumbersome baggage trains, and instead move forward with lightning strokes to destroy the enemy wherever he might be found. Soon, however, Congressional trifling, added to the gloomy implications of the slavery debate on American expansionism, forced the President again to seek an early peace. In desperation he searched for a new solution. Perhaps a secret diplomatic mission might avail itself of the expected triumphs of General Winfield Scott on the road to Mexico City or a sudden shift in Mexican politics. In mid-April the President quietly dispatched Nicholas P. Trist, weighted down with instructions, to join the army of Scott in Mexico.

California was not lost. Through private negotiation Polk and Trist together achieved a settlement with Mexico whereby the United States could acquire an empire in the Southwest. Their ephemeral relationship produced one of the strangest and most important episodes in American diplomatic history. So novel was it, in fact, that Philip Hone could characterize it accurately with his witty observation that the Mexican treaty was "negotiated by an unauthorized agent, with an unacknowledged government, [and] submitted by an accidental President to a dissatisfied Senate."[2] Despite its uniqueness, however, the Trist mission was completely logical, for it was the natural sequel to Polk's wartime California policy.

In Trist's negotiations Polk enjoyed one advantage not present in the Oregon crisis. On California his party had assumed no official position. Democrats, especially the expansionist wing, had never opposed the apparent territorial objectives of his administration. It was doubtful by December, 1847, that even the small abolitionist element in the North would object to the acquisition of Mexican lands.

Trist met all the political requirements of the wartime administration. His adherence to the Democratic Party dated back to Jackson's presidency, when for a time he served as Jackson's private secretary.[3] The selection of the chief clerk in the Department of State, a position of no political importance, afforded the President the opportunity of opening negotiations without offending any faction of the party. In commissioning Trist as an executive agent, Polk left the way open for a subsequent full-fledged diplomatic mission under Buchanan should it become necessary. Since Trist, furthermore, had no standing within the party, he could not deprive the administration of full credit for any successful negotiations. The fact that Trist was destroyed by his connection with the Treaty of Guadalupe Hidalgo, whereas Polk has won unending acclaim from it, indicates that these political considerations were of considerable importance.

This Virginian, Trist, was not as mediocre in ability as certain of his later critics would have us believe. Many who knew him attested to his scholarly attainments, his integrity and honor, and to his industry. Schuyler Hamilton, Scott's aide-de-camp, later wrote that he had "met with few men whose conduct entitled them to so much confidence, as did that of Mr. Trist under trying circumstances."[4] He spoke French and Spanish fluently, and this accomplishment, added to a long residence in Havana as United States Consul, well equipped him for his mission to Mexico. There was nothing in Trist's previous experience or his coming negotiations to merit the historian Jesse Reeves's assertion that Trist lacked the diplomatic abilities necessary for this undertaking. The treaty he secured with Mexico was not the product of incompetence.

Trist did lack two important qualities, good judgment and humility. He possessed a rare measure of the intellectual quality of "abstruse investigation and searching analysis." He could not, therefore, resist the inclination to fathom every secret about him, to approach each problem from every conceivable direction. Thus his letters were lengthy, verbose, and heavy in abstractions. He wrote easily and, when angered, could pour forth invectives with remarkable facility. Francis P. Blair, who knew Trist well, wrote to Martin Van

Buren in August, 1847, that the Virginian would wear out even the Spanish patience, which he understood was durable enough to last a thousand years. He recalled that "Trist's letters to Jackson (almost exclusively about his own health & the physic he took & how it operated) arrived . . . to at least a thousand pages."[5]

These failings have exposed Trist to criticism that has obscured the chief reason he has become an important figure in American diplomatic history. Scott recognized his real significance—that his negotiations in Mexico rather than his quarrel with the administration altered considerably the destiny of the United States. To Andrew J. Donelson, the choice of Trist seemed propitious, and he assured Polk that through his agent he would eventually announce an acceptable treaty to the American people.[6]

Trist's official baggage contained detailed instructions from Buchanan plus the *projet* for a treaty hurriedly prepared by the State Department. These documents revealed clearly the purposes of the Polk administration—a peace with territorial indemnity. Trist was instructed to secure the Rio Grande boundary as well as New Mexico and both Californias, to be separated from Mexico by the southern boundary of New Mexico, the Gila River, and the Colorado. Should lower California be excluded, the boundary was to extend down the Colorado "to a point directly opposite the division line between Upper and Lower California; thence due west, along said line, which runs north of the parallel of 32° and south of San Miguel, to the Pacific Ocean. . . ."[7] San Diego Bay had become, with San Francisco, the official goal of the administration. Territorial acquisitions had now assumed the form of war indemnity, but Polk agreed to compensate Mexico as much as twenty-five million dollars for New Mexico and Upper California alone. With the ratification of an acceptable treaty, moreover, Trist could draw upon the United States Treasury for any sum not to exceed three million to bolster the Mexican regime that signed it.

§ 2

Since the Polk administration at the time of Trist's departure had still avowed publicly no objective beyond peace, the indemnity clauses in Trist's instructions dictated absolute secrecy. Trist slipped quietly out of Washington, impressed by the admonitions of the President. At Charleston, South Carolina, two days later, he sought an inconspicuous lodging, but reported that the fates were against him. All the omnibuses of the city belonged to some hotel; his took him to the renowned Charleston House. He left Charleston with considerable relief and continued by rail and post coach to Montgomery, Alabama, where he boarded a vessel bound for the coast and New Orleans. One week after leaving Charleston he reported to his wife that he was "perfectly well escondido" in an obscure French *auberge* (Hotel d'Orleans), under the name of "Docteur Tarro." His knowledge of French was being employed to good purpose. Almost immediately he traveled back down the Mississippi to Southwest Pass to await the cutter *Ewing*. Only when he attempted to board his ship did he face difficulty. It required a lengthy argument with the collector of customs to keep his name off the customhouse form. After a fast trip of eight days his vessel anchored at Vera Cruz.[8] That the news of his mission shortly flooded the press was not the fault of Trist.

Polk sought above all to protect his efforts to renew negotiations from political attacks at home. His indignation was boundless, therefore, when two letters published soon after Trist's departure, showing remarkable accuracy of detail, appeared in the New York *Herald* and the Boston *Post*. When the *National Intelligencer* reprinted the news, the mission became widely known at the capital. Polk interrogated the cabinet. He threatened removals. Buchanan even accused Mrs. Trist of revealing the information.[9] Although little mention was made of Trist's departure from New Orleans, a correspondent at Vera Cruz not only noted Trist's arrival for the American public, but also predicted accurately his subsequent movements. Before the middle of June the New York *Herald's* Washington correspondent had secured for his paper Polk's boundary proposals.

Thomas Ritchie's Washington *Union* attempted to counter such intelligence. Polk had informed the editor confidentially of Trist's mission so that he could "shape the course of his paper in reference to it." So consistent were Ritchie's denials of Trist's activities that J. C. Rives once declared that if an "opposition paper were to charge that Mr. Polk read the Bible every Sabbath, Mr. Ritchie would deny it, for fear it would make the Jury inimical to the President." The administration never ceased to show its displeasure at the "scribblings" of the press. Secretary of War Marcy termed the correspondents "gifted wiseacres who know more than every thing some days before events transpire or exist."[10] While Polk and his cabinet fumed, the metropolitan press continued to condemn, praise, question, and outguess Trist at every turn. Any further effort of the administration to deny its war aims now became futile.

By July the administration had further cause for apprehension. News had reached Washington of the verbal feud between Trist and General Scott. When the General, motivated by an abiding distrust of the Polk administration, failed to comply with the President's instructions to him, Trist chose to absorb Scott's abuse of the administration. He read a lengthy lecture to the General, confiding to his wife, "If I have not *demolished* him, then I give up." The letter almost drove Scott to derangement. His first impulse, he answered Trist, was to return the "farrago of insolence, conceit, and arrogance to the author," but he decided instead to preserve it "as a choice specimen of diplomatic literature and manners." He declared that Trist, armed with "an ambulatory guillotine," would be "the personification of Danton, Marat, and St. Just, all in one." A few days later Scott tendered his resignation to the War Department and censured the President for sending the commissioner: "To have such a flank battery planted against me, amidst critical military operations, is a great annoyance."[11]

Washington braced itself against the expected epistolary flood, for it knew the adeptness of both men with the pen. Blair observed wittily that Scott and Trist would produce "a most voluminous, if not a luminous correspondence." Marcy predicted that their writing would be "the most *piquant* & interesting in the war series."[12] To the administration the feud was especially reprehensible since, as Polk had feared, many ardent Whigs interpreted Trist's presence in Mexico as an effort of the President to confine Scott's popularity. "It would appear," observed the London *Globe*, ". . . that President Polk, having made a war for 'political capital,' is not less anxious to make a peace, now he finds the capital accruing to Gen. Scott. . . . He has been sending a certain Mr. Trist to Mexico, it is said, to attempt negotiation, and—it is farther said by 'the well-informed friends of Gen. Scott—as a spy upon the public conduct of the General, and if possible to ruin him.' "

One outraged Whig editor added: "It is not a matter of every day occurrence for a government to supersede its own generals, by appointing over them civilians of neither rank or character. Jealousy has frequently arisen at home, of successful warriors carrying the arms of their country, into distant lands; but a decent respect . . . for the dictates of justice, has prevented it from seeking its gratification by so ignoble and baseminded a resort as this."[13]

To the President, in turn, Scott's actions stemmed purely from political motivation. "The truth is," he recorded, "that I have been compelled from the beginning to conduct the war against Mexico through the agency of two Gen'ls highest in rank who have not only no sympathies with the Government, but are hostile to my administration." Polk decided against the removal of Scott, but he instructed his fellow Democrat and close supporter, General William O. Butler, to prepare himself for the command in Mexico. Privately Buchanan informed Trist that Scott was being held responsible and extended to him an added assurance: "Your friends here will take care of you."[14]

During his continuing quarrel with Scott, Trist never forgot his purpose in Mexico. When he arrived at Puebla early in June, Trist addressed a letter to Charles Bankhead, British Minister at the capital, requesting him to notify the Mexican government of his presence in Mexico. Bankhead immediately dispatched Edward Thornton of the British legation to Puebla to inform Trist of the status of Mexican affairs. Late in June Thornton returned with news that Santa Anna was peacefully disposed. He suggested, however, that negotiations might be facilitated by an artful application of gold. Trist quickly rationalized away his initial indignation. It was inconceivable, he thought, that Polk would desire him to neglect any opportunity to approach the Mexican General when the President himself had been instrumental in reinstating Santa Anna to the Mexican presidency.[15]

Although only a reconciliation between Scott and Trist could terminate the endless review in the Whig press of the motivation behind the Trist mission, the administration was hardly prepared for the next significant intelligence from Mexico. Trist's early efforts at negotiation convinced him that he needed Scott's cooperation in making a treaty, for the General alone could delay the army at Puebla and make funds available for a first installment to the wily Santa Anna. Scott's response to Trist's overture was cordial, and soon the two men became fast friends. Scott reported to Marcy that he regarded Trist as "able, discreet, courteous, and amiable." He added: "So far as I am concerned, I am perfectly willing that all I have heretofore written to the Department about Mr. Trist, should be suppressed." Similarly Trist praised the General to the State Department. To his wife he wrote that

Scott was "the soul of honour and probity, and full of the most sterling qualities of heart and head: affectionate, generous, forgiving, and a *lover of justice*."[16] When Trist suddenly became ill, Scott placed him under the care of their mutual friend, General Persifer F. Smith, sent him some guava marmalade from his personal stores, and finally made the commissioner his guest at headquarters.

Quite naturally the administration viewed this arrangement as politically ominous, for it appeared to place Scott in a position of influence during any future negotiations with Mexico. For the moment Marcy thought the new friendship deserving of ridicule. "This is a changeable world in which we live," he wrote to his intimate, P. M. Wetmore. "I believe I will hereafter adopt the maxim of dealing with your friends as if you might become enemies & with your enemies as if you might become friends. Hereafter you must not expect in my letters much confidential matters unless I make you an exception."[17]

During the late summer months affairs in Mexico produced another crisis with the administration in Washington. As the American army in August took breath before the gates of Mexico City after the two notable victories of Contreras and Churubusco, Santa Anna, through the British legation, asked for an armistice to save the capital "from the horrors of war." Both Scott and Trist believed an armistice justified in the interests of peace. Before Trist could forward the Mexican offer of the Nueces and San Francisco alone to Washington, the armistice broke down. Immediately Scott ordered the reconnaissance that led to the storming of Molino del Rey and Chapultepec. By mid-September the United States army had entered the seat of the Montezumas. The weeks since Puebla had alienated Scott from his staff, but had brought Trist and Scott closer together. One American officer noted shortly after the occupation of Mexico City, "Mr. Trist is the only fellow-liver with the general."[18]

§ 3

Before the end of September news of the August armistice
had filtered across the nation through the New Orleans press,
prompting the impatient Polk to regard the Trist mission as
a political liability. George W. Kendall's letter to the *Picayune* indicated that the entire negotiation looked like one of
Santa Anna's old tricks to gain time and "plan some new
scheme of trickery and dissimulation." He predicted that
Mexico would demand too much: " 'Give them an inch, and
they'll take an ell,' is applied to many people in the world—
give a Mexican an inch and he'll take at least seven miles and
a half." Some members of the press declared that Trist had
conceded even the harbor of San Francisco. The cabinet
feared the implications of the unusual delay in the official reports from Mexico. Marcy expressed alarm: "The negotiations should only have lasted for a brief period—I fear the
negotiators have got to writing—if so all is over—the Mexicans
are the most famous people in the whole world for protracting
business and both Trist & Scott are interminable writers.
When they begin they never know where to stop."[19]

By October the Mexican terms, printed widely throughout
the United States, quickly crystallized the belief that the
armistice had been a hoax. The New York *Herald* warned its
readers to take care when they read the proposals, or they
would be thrown into convulsions.[20] Polk had no quarrel
with the peaceful sentiments of his officials in Mexico, but
Trist, by agreeing to submit to the administration the Mexican
proposal, appeared to be ignoring his instructions. The President determined to recall him. A brief diary notation explained his action: "Mr. Trist is recalled because his remaining any longer with the army could not, probably, accomplish
the objects of his mission, and because his remaining longer
might, & probably would, impress the Mexican Government
with the belief that the United States were so anxious for

peace that they would ultimate[ly] conclude one upon the Mexican terms. Mexico must now first sue for peace, & when she does we will hear her proposition."

When Trist's report reached Washington the President commented again: "He had no right to depart from his instructions, and I disapprove his conduct in doing so. . . . Mr. Trist has managed the negotiation very bunglingly and with no ability. . . . I thought he had more sagacity and more common sense than to make the propositions he has made." Under Polk's direction Buchanan repeated the order of recall, but he revealed privately his own embarrassment at doing so. "I am extremely sorry to be obliged to write to you this Despatch," admitted Buchanan. "It was unavoidable. You have placed us in an awkward position & the President feels it deeply." He informed Trist, however, that Polk bore no great animosity, and added a further assurance: "You may always confidently rely upon my friendship; & I hope that portion of your conduct which the President disapproved may not subject you to any public criticism."[21] Trist's recall was the product of the President's frustration, not of his antipathy.

The failure of the August armistice again forced the administration to formulate measures that would bring the Mexican government to acceptable terms. Not even the seizure of the Mexican capital seemed to bring peace any nearer. The London *Chronicle* predicted in November that a long time might still elapse before the United States could end the war. W. J. Hammersley, an astute political observer of Hartford, Connecticut, wrote his misgivings: "The strange people with whom we are at war, governed as they are by no ordinary rules of action, furnish us with little safe ground for prophecy."

It was inconceivable to many Americans that any Mexican regime would be permitted to conclude a peace satisfactory to the United States. "Nothing is easier than to make a revolution in Mexico," observed the *American Review* in October, "and nothing is plainer to our minds than that no chief or party in that country, who shall enter into a provisional treaty to cede away to us New Mexico and California, can hold the reins of government long enough to consummate so wicked a purpose." John Parrott wrote from Vera Cruz in December that Mexico was not ready for peace, for too many areas had not been subjected to American arms.[22] Recently returned from Mexico, John P. Gaines, Whig Congressman from Kentucky, informed official Washington that he had met no one who believed that Trist could make a treaty.

In his message to the Thirtieth Congress in December, 1847, Polk officially denied all possibility of peace and based his future Mexican policy on that assumption. The capture of the Mexican capital left him two alternatives in military policy for securing his wartime goals. One plan, widely accepted by politicians as well as army officers in Mexico, favored the establishment of an indemnity line which could be patrolled by a small force for an indefinite period and eventually secured by treaty. A New York *Herald* correspondent summarized this solution to the Mexican problem: "Draw your line, proclaim it, hold it, hold the Mexican ports to pay the costs, and when she acknowledges the line, break up and open the blockade."[23] To the President, however, the answer lay in the continued destruction of Mexican resistance. He urged Congress to increase the tempo of war as the only means of securing a peace.

For the first time since the inception of the war Polk gave his call for arms real meaning by pressing the need of acquiring New Mexico and California. During the autumn months the Mexican disinclination to treat deepened the conviction in the United States that Mexico be punished by the seizure of territory. Congress had, asserted the New York *Sun,* "contemplated territorial acquisitions when it nationalized the war, or else it contemplated a farce, as ridiculous as shameful, for its members knew that Mexico had no other means of indemnity." Assuming this argument, Polk reminded Congress that "the doctrine of no territory is the doctrine of no indemnity; and, if sanctioned, would be a public acknowledgment that our country was wrong, and that the war declared by Congress with extraordinary unanimity was unjust, and should be abandoned."[24]

Even while Polk was declaring at last his territorial objectives, new developments on the American political scene were complicating the expansionist goals of the nation. The prolongation of the war and the ephemeral qualities of the Mexican government aggravated among Democratic expansionists a determination that the United States meet her destiny and annex the entire Mexican Republic. Such sentiment was everywhere in evidence in banquet toasts to returning officers, at Democratic conventions, and even in the halls of Congress. Early in January, Senator R. M. T. Hunter, of Virginia, regretfully acknowledged the annexationism whirling about him. "Schemes of ambition, vast enough to have tasked even a Roman imagination to conceive," he cried, "present themselves suddenly as practical questions."[25] Both Buchanan and Walker of the cabinet, as well as Vice President George Dallas, openly concurred in these views.

Polk, however, was not alienated from his limited, although realistic, objectives by the growing all-of-Mexico movement. He assured Congress in December that he had not entered the ranks of the annexationists when he declared: "It has never been contemplated by me, as an object of war, to make a permanent conquest of the Republic of Mexico, or to annihilate her separate existence as an independent nation." During January Polk refused, despite expansionist pressure, to alter his official stand. As late as February 4, Sevier, chairman of the Senate Foreign Relations Committee, informed his colleagues that the President desired only a fair indemnity, that California and New Mexico would be sufficient.[26] Polk's private belief that increased military expenditures might eventually require additional indemnity was never made public. To the end of the Mexican War, the two Mexican provinces remained the official objectives of the administration.

Unfortunately Polk's tardy affirmation of his war aims

brought them no nearer fulfillment. Much had occurred since the adjournment of Congress in March, 1847, to make the Thirtieth Congress even more vituperative than its predecessor. Calhoun predicted some stormy deliberations. "I foresee a session of great distraction and confusion . . . ," he wrote to Duff Green in November. The autumn elections had weakened further Polk's Democratic coalition. American victories which annihilated the Mexican government but secured no peace brought public sentiment in the United States to a new stage of insistence and criticism. The New York *Herald* observed rightly, "The theater of war is no longer the plains of Mexico, but the halls of Congress. . . ."[27]

In January, 1848, *Niles' Register* observed that "never before were there half as many contradictory issues to divide and distract the people." The Mexican War, with its mounting costs and casualties, presented enough conflicting and far-reaching topics for debate to tax the oratorical energies of any Congress. Week after week the Ten Regiment Bill supplied the vehicle for Whig invectives against the administration and the war. The Wilmot Proviso still held its terrors. Webster spoke for all conservatives when he charged various groups in the United States with trying to induce the Senate "to take any bit of parchment, or any bit of paper, which could be called or concluded to be a treaty, to clench it, and confirm it, with our eyes blindfolded; no, Sir, with our eyes dead sightless as the eyes of a marble statue, to all the future."[28]

Southerners viewed the all-of-Mexico movement with dread and also lost their appetite for new acquisitions, for they understood clearly that the vast reaches in the Southwest could not become slave territory.[29] While Polk's conquest of peace called for further military action, Congress threatened to scuttle the war effort completely. As late as February, 1848, the President could foresee no final triumph for his expansionist program. Congress had effectively destroyed his power to pursue further a vigorous war for specific ends against an ephemeral enemy.

§ 4

Through the diplomacy of its commissioner in Mexico the Polk administration was yet able to extricate itself successfully from its Mexican dilemma. Trist's decision to disregard the President's instructions and to remain in Mexico was highly irregular, but his subsequent negotiations indicate that it was the proper one. It was not so viewed by the administration, partially because of its lack of knowledge of what was taking place. Communications were inadequate to keep Washington abreast of the rapidly changing political scene in Mexico that suddenly in late November made peace more than a possibility. The entreaties of Mexican officials, the British legation, and even Scott himself convinced Trist that on his willingness to negotiate rested all hope of peace. "I am sure you will, and I leave it to your kindness, I may almost say charity for this unhappy nation," wrote Thornton, "to lend a helping hand towards the preservation of her nationality. I look upon this as the last chance, for either party, of making peace."[30]

Early in December Trist suggested to the Mexican commissioners that he would be willing to resume negotiations on the basis of a boundary line "running up the middle of the Rio Bravo from its mouth to the thirty-second degree of latitude, and thence along that parallel to the Pacific Ocean." The Mexican authorities agreed. On December 4, Trist announced to Thornton his decision to remain in Mexico: "What is my line of duty to my government and my country in this most extraordinary position in which I find myself? Knowing as I do, that peace is the earnest wish of both, is it, *can* it be my duty to allow this last chance for peace to be lost . . . ? Upon full reflection, I have come to the conclusion that my duty is, to pursue the opposite course; and upon this conclusion I have taken my stand."[31] Two days later he explained his decision to Buchanan. He assured the Secre-

tary that his action still left the administration "perfect liberty
to disavow his proceeding, should it be deemed disadvan-
tageous to our country."

Trist's diplomacy secured a treaty of peace from Mexico at
a time when American generals, politicians, the press, members of the cabinet, and the President himself believed it impossible. Perhaps few other Americans could have succeeded
at the task. Trist knew the character of Mexico well, adapted
himself to it, and consequently impressed its authorities favor-
ably. Trist's painstaking efforts in the preparation of recom-
mendations for the Mexican commissioners throughout the
month of January, 1848, required enormous energy and long
hours. For two days only he maintained a journal. "Every
day and night after that I worked until exhaustion compelled
me to bed," he recorded.[82] No longer did he have time for
the parties and dinners of November and December with
American generals and members of the British legation, or
visits to the Aztec Club, organized by American officers in
Mexico City.

Although Trist assumed the sole responsibility for the
cause of the United States, he did not labor alone. Percy W.
Doyle, newly arrived head of the British legation, rendered
him impartial advice; Thornton served as translator and copy-
ist. Trist's American friends added their encouragement. "I
hope for our country as well as your own sake that your un-
tiring exertions may be crowned with success," wrote one;
and he added, "Congress and the President and the Nation
are deeply solicitous for peace."

Trist's diplomatic role was equally appreciated by the Mexican officials. One wrote to Trist, "You have understood Mexico and the Mexicans better than any statesman of your father
land, from Poinsett down to Polk, and this has enabled you
to obtain that which was as desirable for your country as for
Mexico—an honourable peace. I doubt if others could have
accomplished what you did." The Mexican commissioners

avowed such sentiments later before the Mexican congress. "Happy has it been for both countries," ran their evaluation, "that the choice of the American Government should have been fixed upon a person of such worth, upon a friend of peace so loyal and sincere: of him there remains in Mexico none but gratified and honouring recollections."[33]

Trist's second major diplomatic accomplishment was the creation of a boundary which secured San Diego Bay for the United States. The administration assumed that this harbor was north of 32° and instructed Trist to follow that parallel from the Rio Grande to the Pacific. At Mexican insistence he quickly conceded the Gila River line between New Mexico and the Colorado. The short segment of boundary from the Colorado to the Pacific presented greater difficulty, however, for the Mexicans were determined to hold San Diego. Trist understood well that Polk's disappointment at the anticipated loss of this site in his negotiations of August, 1847, had led to his recall. Late in October Buchanan had reminded Trist that this port was "for every commercial purpose of nearly equal importance to the United States with that of San Francisco. It was *to secure to us the port & harbor of San Diego beyond all question* . . . that, in my original instructions, I directed, that if you could not obtain *Lower* California, the 4th Article of the Projet should, in terms, fix this line as running 'North of the parallel of 32°, & south of San Miguel, to the Pacific Ocean.' "[34]

Buchanan based his instructions on the earliest of the 1847 editions of Disturnell's new map of Mexico, which placed the line dividing Lower and Upper California far south of San Diego. Mexico's commissioners, using especially Mofras's atlas, sought to prove that San Diego had always been located in Lower California. Trist was willing to concede to Mexico the historic boundary separating the two Californias. His task lay in securing evidence that would challenge the Mexican reading of history.

Trist shortly resolved his dilemma by showing that San
Diego traditionally belonged to Upper California. Four notes
in the Trist papers established his proof. The first was a
memorandum from Thornton; the second, a brief note from
Lieutenant Robert E. Lee, who had examined several maps for
Trist. The third was a communication from General Smith
which said, "Mr. Trist You will see that I was mistaken—it
is in Northern California." A fourth note from one of the
Mexican commissioners, who had examined Mofras's two-vol-
ume work, agreed in essence with the first three.[35] Trist now
reconstructed the boundary line to join the mouth of the Gila
on the Colorado with a point on the Pacific one league south
of San Diego Bay. This line completed the American quest
for frontage on the Pacific.

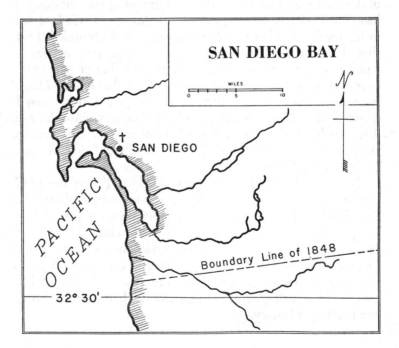

§ 5

It was, finally, Trist's superior evaluation of Mexican politics that achieved both peace with Mexico and the administration's war aims. The President might have been expected, therefore, to acknowledge his error, laud Trist's sagacity, and forgive his commissioner's insubordination. Trist, however, was completely rejected. Although forewarned, he had become involved in the political turmoil of the American high command in Mexico and was regarded thereafter by the Polk administration as a traitor to the Democratic cause. He had become enmeshed in the well-known controversy between Scott and three high-ranking officers, chose the wrong side, and was discarded by the administration even before it had knowledge of his decision to remain in Mexico.

Heading this trio in American headquarters who opposed Scott was Gideon J. Pillow, Polk's former law partner and now volunteer major general, second in command to Scott and placed there at the suggestion of the President. Pillow was a party man above all, had headed the Tennessee delegation to the Baltimore Convention of 1844, and boasted to his fellow Tennessean in the White House that he had secured his nomination. Some called Pillow the President's alter ego; they noted that he claimed unlimited influence in the distribution of executive favors. Although he lacked any great military ability, he enjoyed the full confidence of the administration. When he was severely criticized for ineptness at Cerro Gordo, the Washington *Union* rushed to his defense. In agreement with Pillow in matters of strategy, and equally at variance with Scott, were the regular army officer, General William Jenkins Worth, whose distinguished military career dated back to the War of 1812, and Colonel James Duncan, a close friend of both Pillow and Worth.[36] Scott was convinced that the machinations of the two generals had secured a brevet for Duncan, and finally the more substantial reward of colonel and inspector-general.

Scott had complained repeatedly of misstatements in the battle reports of both Pillow and Worth when a letter attributed to Pillow, but published over the signature of "Leonidas," appeared in the New Orleans *Delta*. It assigned all the credit for the victories of Contreras and Chapultepec to Pillow and predicted that they would "stand unparalleled in the history of the world." This letter, moreover, ridiculed the armistice of August and indicated that both of these generals had bitterly opposed it. The repeated references to the "brave and gallant" Pillow were too much for Scott. He issued a general order directed at these officers to prevent the repetition of such offenses.

Trist was quickly caught in the whirl of this dissension. He was on good terms with Scott and at the same time was still in high standing with the administration. "Between these two facts," he recorded, "stood Gideon J. Pillow." Both Pillow and Worth had shown considerable interest in Trist as well as in his mission. When Pillow suddenly found himself in a serious quarrel with Scott, he sought to avoid the consequences by securing the "friendly services" of Trist. He wrote to Trist in October: "Will Mr. Trist do me the favour of calling to see me. I wish to see him *specially*. Please say when you can call in." The General even intimated to Trist that any aid from him would bring an appointment from the President. The Commissioner, however, believed Pillow to be a "barefaced impostor" and refused to intercede. Both Scott and General James Shields, Trist wrote later, warned him of an impending attack from the administration: "You don't know what party-spirit is capable of. They will torture you. They will put you on the rack."[37]

Pillow repudiated the "Leonidas" letter and was again amply upheld by the administration. Wrote the Washington *Union*: "General Pillow has been twice falsely charged with writing his own praises. As if, indeed, the pen of impartial history would not render full justice to his splendid services to his country." When Scott finally placed the three officers under arrest and requested a court-martial for their trial, Pillow injected a breath of scandal into the dispute and brought it before the administration. In a letter to the President he so recounted the conversation at a July conference of officers at Puebla as to imply that Trist and Scott had attempted to bribe Santa Anna.

Polk was infuriated. He wrote: "The whole cabinet and myself condemned the proceedings unqualifiedly, and resolved to have the matter investigated." The President was convinced that Pillow was being abused because of his friendship for the administration. His chief concern was to prevent Pillow's name from becoming associated with the Santa Anna intrigue of July. Shortly thereafter Shields arrived in Washington and offered some comfort to Polk by defending Pillow's bravery and gallantry. But he informed the President that Trist had not been present at the ill-fated conference and that no bribe had been intended.[38] The President was not convinced; he awaited further details from Pillow.

Before the end of December the Secretary of War brought more shocking news—the charges of Scott against Pillow, Worth, and Duncan. Quite naturally, the administration turned on Scott. The charges, concluded Polk, stemmed from Scott's "vanity and tyrannical temper" and his "want of prudence and common sense." He believed Scott to be jealous of the Democratic generals because he had not been made the exclusive hero of the war in the American press. Within two weeks the President issued orders relieving Scott of his command and substituting a court of inquiry for the court-martial. Buchanan warned him that this creation of a less severe court would be interpreted by the Whigs as a show of favoritism toward his political friends. Even the British minister observed that it would be difficult thereafter for the administration to satisfy its opposition that party considerations did not govern its relation with Scott.[39] In February, 1848,

Scott received his new instructions and immediately gave the command of his army to General Butler.

Trist was rejected as completely as Scott. His reconciliation with the General had made him a very dangerous member of the administration's household, and it aroused increasing disapproval in Washington. The President, therefore, interpreted Trist's refusal to pour oil on troubled waters as a personal affront. Wrote the irate Polk on December 30: "Mr. Trist, from all I can learn, has lent himself to Gen'l Scott and is his mere tool, and seems to be employed in ministering to his malignant passions, in persecuting Gen'l Pillow and others who are supposed to be friendly to me."

Trist's decision to remain in Mexico threw what was left of party rancor against him, for he appeared to be acting on the advice of Scott. When Polk learned of it early in January, he recognized only one explanation: "He seems to have entered into all Scott's hatred of the administration, and to be lending himself to all Scott's evil purposes. He may, I fear, greatly embarrass the Government." He termed Trist's lengthy explanation of December 6 "arrogant, impudent, and very insulting to his Government, and even personally offensive to the President." His reasoning was repetitious. "It is manifest to me," he recorded, "that he has become the tool of Gen'l Scott and his menial instrument, and that the paper was written at Scott's instance and dictation."[40]

Strangely enough, Polk took no immediate action against Trist, although he knew throughout the month of January that Trist was engaged in negotiations. Jefferson Davis informed Polk before the end of December that intelligence from Mexico indicated that an American commissioner could then conclude a peace with Mexico. On the following day the Washington *Union* published a report from "Mustang" of the New Orleans *Delta*, dated December 13, that Trist would probably return to the United States with a treaty. Mexican commissioners, he noted, had already arrived at the capital to confer with Trist. "Whether they have succeeded, no person as yet is apprized," he observed, "but I hope, for the interests of our country that he will, if he is so enabled, go home with the treaty in his pocket." Rumors of Trist's negotiations mounted in volume throughout the month of January. Editors found themselves puzzled, however, by Polk's reticence to speak out on this subject. They knew that Trist was already in disrepute, yet the administration refused to condemn his negotiations publicly. "This discrepancy ought to be cleared up," chided the New York *Herald*. "It belongs to the personal character of the President and his cabinet to have it done."[41] Continued silence might prove embarrassing to the administration if the treaty were based on Trist's original instructions.

In his perplexity Polk concluded simply that Trist and Scott had conspired to embarrass him. Not until late in January, however, did he finally address an order to Butler to terminate any negotiation in which Trist might be engaged. Even then Buchanan warned the President that such a letter might commit the administration to the rejection of a very desirable settlement.[42]

§ 6

Following a close scrutiny of the treaty, Polk accepted it with both hands. "Mr. Trist has acted very badly," he recorded upon receipt of the document from Buchanan. But as he paged through the neatly-written manuscript, he reflected that "if on further examination the Treaty is one that can be accepted, it should not be rejected on account of his bad conduct." But Polk's hatred of Trist continued. Three weeks later he wrote, "Trist has proved himself to be an impudent and unqualified scoundrel." The President never again recognized Trist publicly or privately, but he showed no inclination to disqualify the product of Trist's endeavors, for the treaty contained the indemnity clauses he required. The New York *Herald* predicted with truth that Polk would be content with the "dazzling object of his ambition," California and New Mexico. The administration might feel chagrin at Trist's insubordination, observed the New Orleans *Picayune,* but it would "ultimately swallow its disappointment, and California and New Mexico at the same time."[43]

On February 20 Polk took the preliminary step of submitting the treaty to his cabinet for its careful analysis. Buchanan and Walker urged the President to withhold it from the Senate, but Polk, with the concurrence of the other four members, favored its submission. The initial attack in the Senate was not aimed at the document, but at the method and conditions of its negotiation. Every member of the Foreign Relations Committee except Sevier favored its rejection. Polk reminded the Arkansan that it was the treaty, not Trist, that was under consideration. To renegotiate a treaty, he continued, "would be worse than an idle ceremony." The President's political enemies took pleasure in his discomfiture. Blair remarked that the manner of negotiation was the treaty's chief *asset.* Trist and Scott began by declaring war on each other, recalled the Van Burenite; then after being soundly rebuked by the "exalted dignitaries at home," they patched up a peace between themselves and declared war on the administration.[44] Now the clerk had given the administration no choice but to send his insult to be ratified by the Senate.

Finally the Senate's decision to debate the treaty on its own merits assured its eventual acceptance. Such administration Democrats as Sevier and Cass, supported by Calhoun, pushed the treaty toward ratification. Only the vociferous Democratic minority, who now favored the whole of Mexico, and the Whig minority, who feared the divisive effect of new territorial acquisitions, opposed it. Extremes, observed Polk with considerable truth, "sometimes meet and act effectively for negative purposes." The treaty became the law of the land, but the President refused to compensate its author for his expenses in Mexico. Recalled Benton regretfully: "Certainly those who served the government well in the war with Mexico, fared badly with the administration. . . . Trist, who made the treaty which secured the objects of the war, and released the administration from its dangers, was recalled and dismissed."[45]

Polk gladly accepted the fruits of Trist's diplomacy to rid himself of a politically dangerous war. By 1848 the administration had extended the war so long that peace had become a prime requisite. It had learned to its dismay that it could acquire no territory from Mexico through a little war. "It was not brief, cheap, and bloodless," observed Benton; "It had become long, costly, and sanguinary." Yet Polk illogically condemned the very deliberations which extricated him from this embarrassing conflict. In fact, he did nothing to stop Trist's efforts until the end of January, 1848, less than a week before the treaty was signed and a full month after rumors of Trist's negotiations began to flood the American press. The administration was either insincere in its indignation or it had determined in advance to avail itself of every opportunity for peace, even the efforts of its rejected commissioner. Certain critics of the Polk administration even believed that it purposely showed hostility toward Trist so that it could avail itself of the treaty without assuming any responsibility for the negotiations.[46]

It was within the power of the President to accept both Trist and his treaty with a minimum of embarrassment. During the lengthy deliberations in Mexico the President might have recognized the actions of his agent and thus rendered them admissible to Congress and the American people. But Polk preferred to risk Congressional rejection of the settlement rather than to condone the negotiations publicly. Trist's decision to remain in Mexico considered alone should not have dictated this course of action, for his success in a difficult diplomatic situation proved the validity of his contentions. He assumed the risk of repudiation, but his diplomacy had not failed. Trist's mistake lay elsewhere. He made the fatal error of siding with the administration's most dangerous political enemy, Winfield Scott. Thereafter, his decision to remain in Mexico was viewed by the President as a revolt against the Democratic administration rather than an honest effort to establish peace with Mexico.

Chapter 11

EMPIRE ON THE PACIFIC

§ 1

Manifest destiny persists as a popular term in American historical literature to explain the expansion of the United States to continent-wide dimensions in the 1840's. Like most broad generalizations, it does not bear close scrutiny. Undoubtedly, the vigor of the American people in that decade, their restless and sometimes uncontrollable energy, their idealism and faith in their democratic institutions convinced them of a peculiar American mission. Perhaps for many expansionists the American purpose remained that of spreading democracy over the land from ocean to ocean.

Public sentiment in 1844 seemed to favor the extension of the United States into Oregon. But lands along the Pacific were not for the taking, and public opinion is never simply defined or casually conveyed into specific proposals by a national administration. This was especially true in the forties when political leaders at no time were in agreement on precise objectives on the Pacific. There was, in fact, sufficient disagreement over expansionist purpose that the territorial gains of the Polk administration were achieved amid vigorous political opposition. Nor did these acquisitions prevent the American people from voting from power the party that gave them their immense foothold on the distant sea. Diverse are the elements which shape the course of history.

The concept of manifest destiny, as a democratic expression, represented an expanding, not a confining or limiting, force. As an ideal, it was not easily defined in terms of precise territorial limits. In 1844, when the claims of the ideal had fully taken hold, American expansionism looked far beyond Texas and Oregon. Indeed, it had no visible limit. The New York *Herald* prophesied that the American Republic would in due course embrace all the land from the Isthmus of Panama to the polar regions and from the Atlantic to the Pacific. One Texas correspondent wrote that "the fact must be no longer disguised, that we, the people of the United States must hold, and govern, under free and harmonious institutions, the continent we inhabit."

Some suggested that American laws be extended to include the downtrodden peons of South America. "And who does not wish to have them finally reach Cape Horn if their democratic character can be preserved?" demanded one expansionist. "Certainly no friend of the largest liberty of oppressed humanity."[1] In their enthusiasm to extend the "area of freedom," many even looked beyond the continental limits to Cuba, the Sandwich Islands, the far-flung regions of the Pacific, and even to the Old World itself. This was a magnificent vision for a democratic purpose, but it hardly explains the sweep of the United States across the continent.

For American expansion to the Pacific was always a precise and calculated movement. It was ever limited in its objectives. American diplomatic and military policy that secured the acquisition of both Oregon and California was in the possession of men who never defined their expansionist purposes in terms of a democratic ideal. The vistas of all from Jackson to Polk were maritime and they were always anchored to specific waterways along the Pacific Coast. Land was necessary to them merely as a right of way to ocean ports—a barrier to be spanned by improved avenues of commerce. Any interpretation of westward extension beyond Texas is meaningless unless defined in terms of commerce and harbors.

§ 2

Travelers during the decade before 1845 had created a precise vision of the western coasts of North America. It was a vision born of the sea. With the exception of Fremont, every noted voyager who recorded his impressions of Oregon and California had approached these regions via the Pacific. Some traders had sailed these coasts directly from Boston; others had first traversed the broad Pacific world as captains of merchant vessels or as explorers. But whatever their mission on the great ocean, they were without exception struck by the excellent quality of the Strait of Juan de Fuca, San Francisco Bay, and the harbor of San Diego, as well as the possible role of these ports in the development of Pacific commerce.

Charles Wilkes, as the commander of the United States exploring expedition to the Pacific, studied minutely not only the islands and sea lanes of the entire area, but also the important harbors and bays along the North American coast from Fuca Strait to San Francisco. Wilkes was not certain that these coastal regions, separated as they were in the early forties by almost two thousand miles of wilderness from the settled portions of the Midwest, would become other than a prosperous and independent maritime republic. Eminently qualified, however, to speculate on these Western harbors as stations in a Pacific commerce, he predicted a sizable stream of traffic emanating from them:

This future state is admirably situated to become a powerful maritime nation, with two of the finest ports in the world,—that within the straits of Juan de Fuca, and San Francisco. These two regions have, in fact, within themselves every thing to make them increase, and keep up an intercourse with the whole of Polynesia, as well as the countries of South America on the one side, and China, the Philippines, New Holland, and New Zealand, on the other. Among the latter, before many years, may be included Japan. Such various climates will furnish the materials for a beneficial exchange of products, and an intercourse that must, in time, become immense; while this western coast, enjoying a climate in many respects superior to any other in the Pacific, possessed as it must be by the Anglo-Norman race, and having none to enter into rivalry with it but the indolent inhabitants of warm climates, is evidently destined to fill a large space in the world's future history.[2]

American officials and expansionists refused to accept his prediction of a separate commercial nation across the mountains. The threat of European encroachment convinced them that the grandeur of the Pacific Coast must accrue to the wealth, prosperity, and commercial eminence of the United States. By 1845 the American press accepted the dreams of Webster and Calhoun who had anticipated an American Boston or New York situated on some distant harbor. For those who perpetuated the expansionist program after Polk's inaugural, ports of call in Oregon and California were as vital as had been land empires in Texas during the preceding year. Except for what remained of the whole-of-Oregon fever, American expansionism had lost its broad nationalism and had become anchored to the mercantile interests of the United States.

After California entered the American consciousness, the expansionist purpose increasingly embraced both Oregon and California as two halves of a single ambition. Thereafter the complete vision of empire on the Pacific included the harbors from Puget Sound to San Diego. It called for a peaceful settlement of the Oregon controversy at 49° and the acquisition of Upper California. Writing to President Polk in July, 1845, Charles Fletcher pictured an American Union stretching from the Atlantic to the Pacific and from the thirtieth to the forty-ninth degree of north latitude. The St. Louis *Missourian* demanded both the Strait of Fuca and San Francisco harbor to fulfill the maritime destiny of the United States. Quite typically William Field, a Texan, advised the President to accept the parallel of 49° and then purchase California for as much as fifty million if necessary. He wrote, "I will only remark that if you can settle the Oregon difficulty without war and obtain California of Mexico, to the Gulf of California and the river Gila for a boundary, you will have achieved enough to enroll your name *highest* among those of the benefactors of the American people."[3]

By 1846 this unitary but limited view of the Pacific Coast had penetrated the halls of Congress, where Meredith P. Gentry, of Tennessee, observed: "Oregon up to the 49th parallel of latitude, and the province of Upper California, when it can be fairly acquired, is the utmost limit to which this nation ought to go in the acquisition of territory."[4]

With the Oregon treaty of 1846 the United States had reached the Pacific. Its frontage along the sea from 42° to Fuca Strait and Puget Sound fulfilled half the expansionist dream. On those shores the onward progress of the American pioneer would stop, but commercial expansionists looked beyond to the impetus that the possession of Oregon would give to American trade in the Pacific. "Commercially," predicted Benton, "the advantages of Oregon will be great—far greater than any equal portion of the Atlantic States."[5] This Missourian believed that Oriental markets and export items would better complement the mercantile requirements of the United States than would those of Europe.

Through Fuca Strait, moreover, lay the new passage to the East which would bring to America the wealth and splendor which had always gone to those who commanded the trade of the Orient. The editor of the Baltimore *American* declared that

The commerce of the world is to be ours, and both oceans are to be subject to us. The splendors of Eastern cities which grew into greatness by the trade between the Valley of the Nile and the Valley of the Ganges, will shine but dimly, even in the enhanced illumination of fancy and tradition, when compared with the stately magnificence and colossal structure of the cities which are to concentrate the rich elements of the Valley of the Mississippi. The ruins of Thebes and Memphis, of Palmyra and Balbee remain still to attest a wonderful degree of former greatness; but they grew up by means of a caravan trade on camels, or by a commerce of galleys on the Red Sea and the

Persian Gulf. From such a traffic let the eye turn to the rivers, canals, and railroads of this continent of ours, to the mighty agency of steam, propelling innumerable vessels and cars, and the immense expanse of alluvial soil, fertile in products under the culture of a people who for enterprise, energy and invention have no superiors—we may say no equals.[6]

For decades after 1846 British travelers in the Far Northwest recognized the magnitude of this American diplomatic achievement. With a Columbia River boundary, complained one British observer in 1872, Canadian shipping in the north Pacific might have competed with that of the United States. Upon viewing the waters of Puget Sound, another English traveler acknowledged dejectedly the significance of the American triumph in Oregon: "It is not easy to conceive what reasons for claiming the country north of the Columbia could be urged by the United States Government. But they knew the prospective value of the magnificent inland waters of Puget Sound, and acted upon that knowledge. With the possession of that grand inlet, British Columbia could easily compete with California and Oregon; without it, it becomes a difficult matter to do so."[7] British observers in western Canada agreed that the American negotiators knew the value of the waterways they sought, whereas the British did not.

Following the outbreak of the Mexican War in May, 1846, metropolitan editorialists soon regarded that conflict as the agency whereby the United States might consummate her westward movement and annex the harbors of California. To them the Oregon settlement had been made particularly acceptable by the anticipation of adding certain Mexican ports to the American Union. In May the New York *Herald* urged the Polk administration to seize San Francisco Bay so that men would forget the whole of Oregon. One California correspondent predicted the result of the speedy occupation of the Pacific ports by the American naval squadron: "We shall have then a country, bounded at the North latitude by 49 degrees, to the Pacific—and the South on the same ocean by 32 degrees—and the western and eastern boundaries, being what Nature intended them, the Pacific, with China in the outline, and the Atlantic with Europe in the background."[8]

Such prospects pleased the editor of the New York *Herald*. He noted that the proposed boundaries gave the United States 1,300 miles of coast on the Pacific, several magnificent harbors, and "squared off our South-Western possessions." One writer for the New York *Journal of Commerce* in December, 1846, rejoiced that with the acquisition of New Mexico and California the territory of the United States would "spread out in one broad square belt from one ocean to the other, giving us nearly as much coast on the Pacific as we possess on the Atlantic."[9] The imaginary line of 42° meant little to these commercial expansionists of a century ago.

This vision was not lost on the Midwest. The Mississippi Valley responded eagerly to the call to arms, stimulated perhaps by the prospect of conquering Mexican soil. Such enthusiasm was not misplaced, for future trade routes through the great valley lay in the direction of California as well as Oregon. During the Oregon debates Andrew Kennedy and John McClernand had revealed the significance of the Strait of Fuca to the grain regions of the Midwest. Now this agrarian concept of commercial empire in the Pacific encompassed also the harbors of California. It was the editor of the Baltimore *American* who analyzed cogently in September, 1847, the possible mercantile relationships between this Mexican province and the broad prairies of the Mississippi Valley:

The Mississippi River . . . stretches out its arms east and west to lay hold of both oceans. That vast alluvial region, the garden of the civilized world . . . is to be, and that before many generations shall have passed, the centre of the world's commerce and its most prolific source. It must have access to the sea coast on both shores, and along the whole extent, communicating freely with the Atlantic sea board, which we already possess, entire, and with the Pacific which we must possess, entire. . . . Besides, it is clear that California must have its connections with the Mississippi Valley. . . . Without these connections California would be insulated. Confined to her own resources

. . . her fine harbors without the materials of commerce would not avail her much. But once drawn into the embrace of the great valley and suffused with the rich currents of its ample products, California, from her position alone, becomes important, and her commercial greatness stands revealed.[10]

American expansion over contiguous territory was complete with the Treaty of Guadalupe Hidalgo. Thereafter United States frontage on the Pacific remained unchanged. In 1848, it is true, some did not believe that American continental expansion had run its course. Tom Corwin anticipated demands for even greater annexations in the future. He wrote to William Greene in March, 1848, that the treaty gave to the United States a third of Mexico immediately "with the implied understanding that the ballance is to be swallowed when our anglo-saxon gastric juices shall clamor for another Cannibal breakfast." The New York *Herald* recognized the same feeling but with considerably more pleasure: "We will take a large portion now, and the balance at a more convenient season."[11] Both were wrong, for American expansion was a deliberate movement, and the United States had achieved what two decades of observers had thought essential for this nation's future development.

§ 3

Polk alone could fulfill the expansionist goals of the forties. Although he was an advocate of agrarian democracy, his expansionist outlook as President was as narrowly mercantile as that of Webster or Winthrop. He accepted the wisdom of compromise in Oregon for the precise reasons that the Whigs and the metropolitan press called for a settlement along the forty-ninth parallel. His wartime expansionist policy was aimed primarily at San Francisco and San Diego, and as the war neared completion Polk acknowledged no other objectives to Congress. In his message of December, 1847, he declared that the bay of San Francisco and other harbors on the

California coast "would afford shelter for our navy, for our numerous whale ships, and other merchant vessels employed in the Pacific ocean, [and] would in a short period become the marts of an extensive and profitable commerce with China, and other countries of the East."[12]

With the ratification of the Treaty of Guadalupe Hidalgo, the weary President could at last contemplate the success of his arduous foreign policy. In July he delivered to Congress a personal appraisal of his success in expanding the boundaries of the United States. Again his eyes were focused solely on the ports of San Diego, Monterey, and San Francisco. These, he declared, "will enable the United States to command the already valuable and rapidly increasing commerce of the Pacific." Under the American flag they would "afford security and repose to our commercial marine; and American mechanics will soon furnish ready means of ship-building and repair, which are now so much wanted in that distant sea." The President prophesied the growth of great commercial cities on these capacious harbors which would secure "the rich commerce of the East, and shall thus obtain for our products new and increased markets, and greatly enlarge our coasting and foreign trade, as well as augment our tonnage and revenue."[13]

Democratic spokesmen in 1848 likewise measured the diplomatic settlements of the Polk administration in terms of harbors and trade. Lucien Chase of Tennessee limited the important acquisitions of the United States to Puget Sound, Monterey, San Diego, and San Francisco. His particularism focused his attention even more narrowly. "In the Bay of San Francisco," he wrote, "will converge the commerce of Asia and the model Republic. It possesses advantages over every other harbor upon the western coast of North or South America. . . . The vast and increasing commerce of Asia, and the islands of the East, is now open to our adventurous seamen. . . ."[14]

Similarly a Democratic electioneering pamphlet singled out the California ports as the key acquisition of recent United

States expansionist policy which had placed the American nation firmly on the distant coast. "From our cities on the Pacific," it predicted, "a speedy communication will be opened with China, and a profitable trade enjoyed, which must soon pour the wealth of that nation into our laps."[15] For Whigs who had flayed Polk's Mexican policy, San Francisco Bay possibly made somewhat more palatable the huge swallow of territory acquired by the war.

During the succeeding years observers at San Francisco continued to appraise the acquisition of California in commercial terms. The French consul at this port viewed the region as the controlling element in the development of Pacific trade. He concluded in 1852 that "all the archipelagoes of the Pacific Ocean, the entire American continent from Sitka to the Straits of Magellan, China, Japan, are destined to submit to the influence of this state [and] to be attracted into the sphere of its commercial activity."[16] One Californian in the fifties revealed the importance of that region's waterways to the total commercial growth of the United States in the following words:

The commerce of the Pacific is in the hands of New York, Boston, New Bedford, Bangor, Cape Cod, and all-along-shore to New Orleans, and whatever benefits commerce derives hereby, is felt throughout the whole country. Neither are other portions of the sunny south, or the rich valleys of the west unrepresented there. Though the ships may be of Eastern construction, and commanded by the indomitable and enterprising Yankee skipper, yet he and his hardy crew are but the carriers for the products of the East and South.[17]

§ 4

Historians have tended to exaggerate the natural urge of the American people to expand in the forties. For that reason they have attributed an unrealistic importance to the impact of pioneers, public sentiment, and war on American continental expansion. None of these had any direct bearing on the determination of United States boundaries along the Pacific. American frontiersmen never repeated the role they played in the annexation of Texas. In time they might have secured possession of California, but in 1845 hardly a thousand had reached that province. More numerous in Oregon, American pioneers were still limited to regions south of the Columbia. If they prompted the British to retreat from that line, they hardly explain why the United States insisted on that British retreat.

What mattered far more in the definition of American purpose were the travelers who toured the Pacific coasts and recorded the location and significance of waterways. These men, not pioneers, formulated the objectives of American officials from Adams to Polk. For two decades the official analysis of United States needs on the Pacific changed imperceptibly. Pioneers undoubtedly strengthened the American urge to expand westward, but they had little effect on the extent to which the nation would expand.

Public opinion as reflected in the spirit of manifest destiny played no greater role in the determination of United States ocean frontage than did the pressure of pioneers. Politicians had aroused sufficient interest in Oregon by 1844 to turn it into a popular issue. But to the extent that the Oregon settlement was a mandate, the American people voted for 54° 40′, a boundary which they never acquired.

California was never a campaign issue at all. Its annexation was never the result of popular demand. After the metropolitan press turned its attention to that region in 1845, the Mexican province undoubtedly became a coveted objective for thousands of Americans. Yet for the mass of citizens it remained a remote, unknown region. California persisted probably as an area of vital concern for those relatively few merchants, politicians, travelers, and officials who appreciated its commercial significance. Whig success in attacking Democratic expansionist policy during 1848 reveals an extensive lack of interest in Polk's diplomatic achievement. The Washington *National Intelligencer* interpreted the Whig victory as proof that the American people had rejected the seductive visions of manifest destiny.

American triumphs in Mexico were essential to the success of the expansionist program, but they had no bearing on administration goals. These had been defined by Polk and his cabinet before the war was hardly under way. Manifest destiny revealed itself in the Mexican War only when it clamored for the whole of Mexico, but even that final burst of agrarian nationalism was effectively killed by the Treaty of Guadalupe Hidalgo. Polk's objectives, clear and precise, were ever limited to two ocean ports. Victories along the road to Mexico City were important only in that they eventually brought to the President the opportunity to secure what he had once hoped to achieve by diplomacy alone.

Nor can Nicholas P. Trist be overlooked in the fulfillment of United States territorial growth, for in the final analysis it was he, lonely and unobserved, who secured the southern boundary of California. If the nation achieved all this through the dictates of manifest destiny, that destiny revealed itself through some exceedingly devious patterns.

Particularism had its way in both the Oregon and Mexican treaties. Administration goals, therefore, had to be achieved through private diplomacy, England assuming the leadership in the former negotiations. This was essential, for only thus could the President defy that public opinion and avoid those pressures of American politics that sought to prevent both the peaceful settlement of the Oregon question and the acquisition of California.

Indeed, manifest destiny is an inadequate description of American expansionism in the forties. The mere urge to expand or even the acceptance of a destiny to occupy new areas on the continent does not create specific geographical objectives. Nor do these factors take into account the role of chance or the careful formulation and execution of policy. It was not by accident that the United States spread as a broad belt across the continent in the forties. It was rather through clearly conceived policies relentlessly pursued that the United States achieved its empire on the Pacific.

NOTES

Chapter 1

1. Nicholas P. Trist to Mrs. Trist, February 2, 1848, Trist to James Buchanan, February 2, 1848, Mrs. Trist to Trist, February 23, 1848, Trist Papers (Division of Manuscripts, Library of Congress); Mobile *Herald*, February 13, 1848; New Orleans *Picayune*, February 13, 1848; Washington *National Intelligencer*, February 21, 1848.

2. See, for example, Dan Elbert Clark, "Manifest Destiny and the Pacific," *Pacific Historical Review*, I (1932), 2–7.

3. See Samuel Eliot Morison, *Maritime History of Massachusetts 1783–1860* (Boston, 1923), 225–26.

4. Foster Rhea Dulles, *The Old China Trade* (Boston, 1930), 201; *Hunt's Merchants' Magazine*, X (1844), 425, 481, XII (1845), 44.

5. *DeBow's Commercial Review*, III (1847), 5, 490; *Hunt's Merchants' Magazine*, VIII (1843), 226, XII (1845), 49. Both publications predicted a commerce in the Pacific equal to that in the Atlantic.

6. Morison, *op. cit.*, 264.

7. See *ibid.*, 260–61; Dulles, *op. cit.*, 63–64; William Sturgis, "The Northwest Fur Trade, and the Indians of the Oregon Country, 1788–1830," *Old South Leaflet*, No. 219, 2–7.

8. Morison, *op. cit.*, 266–68; Adele Ogden, "Boston Hide Droghers Along California Shores," *California Historical Society Quarterly*, VIII (December, 1929), 290–96.

9. *Hunt's Merchants' Magazine*, XIV (1846), 105, XVI (1847), 319, XX (1849), 184; Larkin to John C. Calhoun, December 9, 1844, George P. Hammond (ed.), *The Larkin Papers* (Berkeley, 1952), II, 309.

10. Allen Nevins (ed.), *The Diary of Philip Hone 1828–1851* (New York, 1936), 809; *Hunt's Merchants' Magazine*, XV (1846), 162–63.

11. George W. Featherstonhaugh, *Excursion Through the Slave States* (New York, 1844), 64.

12. *Ibid.*, 68–69; Nevins, *op. cit.*, 809; Jesse Benton Fremont, *The Origin of the Fremont Explorations,* pamphlet, Fremont Collection (Bancroft Library, University of California).

13. For a more detailed survey of these explorations, see Ray Allen Billington, *Westward Expansion* (New York, 1950), 554–64.

14. John C. Fremont, *Narrative of the Exploring Expedition to the Rocky Mountains in the Year 1842, and to Oregon and North California in the Years 1843–44* (Washington, 1845), 246–47; Journal of Titian Ramsey Peale, Assistant Naturalist of the Wilkes Expedition, MSS (Division of Manuscripts, Library of Congress), VII, 32–33.

15. Quoted in James Christy Bell, Jr., *Opening a Highway to the Pacific 1838–1846* (New York, 1921), 183.

16. Oliver Dyer, *Great Senators of the United States Forty Years Ago* (New York, 1889), 185–86; John Wentworth, *Congressional Reminiscences* (Chicago, 1882), 21.

17. Gadsden to Calhoun, May 3, 1844, Dixon H. Lewis to Calhoun, March 6, 1844, J. Franklin Jameson (ed.), *The Correspondence of John C. Calhoun, Annual Report of the American Historical Association* (1899), II, 936, 952–53; Calhoun to Hammond, May 17, 1844, *Ibid.,* p. 589; Thomas Hart Benton, *Thirty Years' View* (New York, 1856), II, 617–18.

18. Maxcy to Calhoun, December 10, 1843, Jameson, *op. cit.*, 903.

19. Quoted in Henry Clyde Hubbart, *The Older Middle West, 1840–1880* (New York, 1936), 16.

20. Benjamin Poorley Poore, "Reminiscences of Washington," *The Atlantic Monthly,* XLVI (1880), 666; Dyer, *op. cit.*, 129–30.

21. Poore, *op. cit.*, 799.

22. Ephraim D. Adams, *The Power of Ideals in American History* (New Haven, 1913), 93.

23. Quoted in Albert K. Weinberg, *Manifest Destiny: A Study of Nationalist Expansionism in American History* (Baltimore, 1935), 107.

24. "The Great Nation of Futurity," *Democratic Review,* VI (1839), 427, 429–30.

25. "The Texas Question," *Democratic Review,* XIV (1844), 429; *Congressional Globe,* 28 Cong., 2 Sess., Appendix, 68.

26. Jackson to Brown, February 12, 1843, *Niles' Register,* March 30, 1844.

27. Gadsden to Jackson, May 3, 1844, Miscellaneous Papers (Division of Manuscripts, Chicago Historical Society).

28. *Nashville Whig* quoted in the *Whig Banner,* June 22, 1844; Washington *National Intelligencer,* November 11, 1844; Nevins, *op. cit.,* 690–91, 702.

29. Giddings to Oran Follett, November 18, 1844, L. Belle Hamlin (ed.), "Selections from the Follett Papers, III," *Quarterly Publication of the Historical and Philosophical Society of Ohio,* X (1915), 20.

30. *Cong. Globe,* 28 Cong., 1 Sess., Appendix, 705.

31. S. D. Ingham to Duff Green, February 12, 1844, Green Papers (Division of Manuscripts, Library of Congress).

32. Stephens to James Thomas, May 17, 1844, U. B. Phillips (ed.), *The Correspondence of Robert Toombs, Alexander H. Stephens, and Howell Cobb, Annual Report of the American Historical Association* (1911), II, 57–58.

33. Story to William W. Story, January 25, 1845, William Wetmore Story, *Life and Letters of Joseph Story* (Boston, 1851), II, 510–11.

34. Corwin to Crittenden, November 15, 1844, Mrs. Chapman Coleman, *The Life of John J. Crittenden* (Philadelphia, 1871), I, 225.

35. Corwin to Follett, February 22, 1845, March 7, 13, 1845, L. Belle Hamlin (ed.), "Selections from the Follett Papers, II," *op. cit.,* IX (1914), 80–81, 84.

36. Lewis to Richard Cralle, March 19, 1844, Cralle Papers (Division of Manuscripts, Library of Congress); Davezac to Polk, July 11, 1844, Polk Papers (Division of Manuscripts, Library of Congress); Andrew Johnson to William M. Lowery, March 30, 1844, Johnson Papers (Division of Manuscripts, Library of Congress).

CHAPTER 2

1. "A Trip Down the Oregon Coast," *Life,* August 10, 1953, 59; Charles Wilkes, *Narrative of the United States Exploring Expedition During the Years 1838, 1839, 1840, 1841, 1842* (Philadelphia, 1845), V, 157, 240.

2. See Frederick Merk, *Albert Gallatin and the Oregon Problem: A Study in Anglo-American Diplomacy* (Cambridge, 1950), 67–69.

3. Eugène Duflot de Mofras, *Travels on the Pacific Coast,* ed. and trans. Marguerite Eyer Wilbur (Santa Ana, California, 1937), II, 132; Thomas J. Farnham, *Travels in the Great Western Prairies, October 21–December 4, 1839,* in Reuben Gold Thwaites (ed.), *Early Western Travels 1748–1846,* XXIX (Cleveland, 1906), 95.

4. See Robert G. Cleland, "Asiatic Trade and the American Occupation of the Pacific Coast," *Annual Report of the American Historical Association* (1914), I, 283–84; Joseph Schafer, "The Western Ocean as a Determinant in Oregon History," in H. Morse Stephens and Herbert E. Bolton (eds.), *The Pacific Ocean in History* (New York, 1917), 288, 291.

5. John C. Fremont, *Narrative of the Exploring Expedition to the Rocky Mountains in the Year 1842, and to Oregon and North California in the Years 1843–44* (Washington, 1845), 405.

6. Quoted in Clarence B. Bagley, "The Waterways of the Pacific Northwest," in Stephens and Bolton, *op. cit.*, 306–07.

7. Wilkes, *op. cit.*, IV, 293; Mofras, *op. cit.*, 56; Robert Greenhow, *The History of Oregon and California* (Boston, 1844), 23; Farnham, *op. cit.*, 80.

8. Mofras, *op. cit.*, 58–59; Farnham, *op. cit.*, 61–62; Greenhow, *op. cit.*, 24–25; Wilkes, *op. cit.*, IV, 305.

9. Canning quoted in Merk, *op. cit.*, 46.

10. Canning to the Earl of Liverpool, June 24, July 7, 1826, in Edward J. Stapleton (ed.), *Some Official Correspondence of George Canning* (London, 1887), II, 62, 74.

11. Pageot to Guizot, November 27, 1843, quoted in George Vern Blue, "France and the Oregon Question," *Oregon Historical Quarterly*, XXXIV (March, 1933), 46–47.

12. Sir George Simpson to the Governor, Deputy Governor, and Committee of the Hudson's Bay Company, March 1, 1842, Joseph Schafer (ed.), "Letters of Sir George Simpson, 1841–1843," *American Historical Review*, XIV (October, 1908), 83.

13. Simpson to Sir John H. Pelly, March 10, 1842, *ibid.*, 86–87.

14. Gallatin quoted in Merk, *op. cit.*, 93.

15. See James Christy Bell, Jr., *Opening a Highway to the Pacific 1838–1846* (New York, 1921), 92–95; Oscar Osburn Winther, *The Great Northwest: A History* (New York, 1947), 120–21.

16. Joseph Schafer, *A History of the Pacific Northwest* (New York, 1943), 143–45; Bell, *op. cit.*, 117; Farnham, *op. cit.*, 48–50; Wilkes, *op. cit.*, V, 236–37, 239; Lansford W. Hastings, *The Emigrant's Guide to Oregon and California* (Cincinnati, 1845), 63.

17. Albert Gallatin, *The Oregon Question*, in Henry Adams (ed.), *The Writings of Albert Gallatin* (Philadelphia, 1879), III, 515–16.

18. Joel Palmer, *Journal of Travels over the Rocky Mountains to the Mouth of the Columbia River, made during the Years 1845 and 1846*, in Reuben Gold Thwaites (ed.), *Early Western Travels 1748–1846*, XXX (Cleveland, 1906), 158–60.

19. Daniel W. Howe, "The Mississippi Valley in the Movement

for Fifty-Four Forty or Fight," *Proceedings* of the Mississippi Valley Historical Association (1911–1912), 100–01; Bell, *op. cit.*, 108-11.

20. Quoted in Winther, *op. cit.*, 145.

21. Robert L. Schuyler, "Polk and the Oregon Compromise of 1846," *Political Science Quarterly*, XXVI (1911), 445-46; Melvin Jacobs, *Winning Oregon* (Caldwell, Idaho, 1938), 176–77; A. F. Pollard, *Factors in American History* (New York, 1925), 181.

22. *Cong. Globe*, 28 Cong., 2 Sess., Appendix, 136, 202; *Cong. Globe*, 28 Cong., 1 Sess., Appendix, 244, 264; Hubert Howe Bancroft, *History of Oregon* (San Francisco, 1886), I, 447.

23. *Cong. Globe*, 28 Cong., 1 Sess., Appendix, 239; *Cong. Globe*, 28 Cong., 1 Sess., 678.

24. For declarations favoring this policy see *Cong. Globe*, 28 Cong., 1 Sess., Appendix, 238-39, 308; *Cong. Globe*, 28 Cong., 2 Sess., 226. For speech of Atchison see *Cong. Globe*, 28 Cong., 1 Sess., Appendix, 240.

25. For speech of Winthrop see *ibid.*, 318.

26. *Cong. Globe*, 28 Cong., 2 Sess., Appendix, 163, 179; *Cong. Globe*, 28 Cong., 2 Sess., 226. For Ingersoll's remarks see *Cong. Globe*, 28 Cong., 2 Sess., Appendix, 241.

27. Choate's speech in Senate, March 21, 1844, *Cong. Globe*, 28 Cong., 1 Sess., Appendix, 585-87.

28. *Ibid.*, 238.

29. *Ibid.*, 98, 239, 245.

30. Speech of Dayton in Senate, February 23, 26, 1844, *ibid.*, 275, 279.

31. *Cong. Globe*, 28 Cong., 2 Sess., Appendix, 47, 292.

32. *Cong. Globe*, 28 Cong., 1 Sess., Appendix, 584.

CHAPTER 3

1. See F. W. Beechey, *Narrative of a Voyage to the Pacific and Beering's Strait in the Years 1825, 26, 27, 28* (London, 1831), II, 15, 17–19, 37–38; Susanna Bryant Dakin, *The Lives of William Hartnell* (Stanford, 1949), 37–38; Adele Ogden (ed.), "New England Merchant in Mexican California," *California Historical Society Quarterly*, XXIII (September, 1944), 194–96; Eugène Duflot de Mofras, *Travels on the Pacific Coast*, translated by Marguerite Eyer Wilbur (Santa Ana, 1937), I, 165.

2. Captain Benjamin Morrell, *A Narrative of Four Voyages to the South Sea* (New York, 1832), 208; Charles Franklin Carter (ed.), "Duhault-Cilly's Account of California in the Years 1827–28," *Cali-*

fornia Historical Society Quarterly, VIII (June, 1929), 151; W. S. W. Ruschenberger, *A Voyage Round the World in 1835, 1836, and 1837* (Philadelphia, 1838), 507–08; Sir George Simpson, *Narrative of a Journey Round the World, During the Years 1841 and 1842* (London, 1847), I, 370–71.

3. Mofras, *op. cit.,* 216–17; Simpson, *op. cit.,* 365; Carter, *op. cit.,* 150; Ogden, *op. cit.,* 206–07; Herman Leader (ed.), "A Voyage from the Columbia to California in 1840, From the Journal of Sir James Douglas," *California Historical Society Quarterly,* VIII (June, 1929), 113–15; Richard Henry Dana, *Two Years Before the Mast* (Boston, 1911), 133–34, 143–44; Sir Edward Belcher, *Narrative of a Voyage Round the World Performed in Her Majesty's Ship Sulphur during the Years 1836–1842* (London, 1843), I, 326–27.

4. Simpson, *op. cit.,* 330–31; Charles Wilkes, *Narrative of the United States Exploring Expedition During the Years 1838, 1839, 1840, 1841, 1842* (Philadelphia, 1845), V, 216–17.

5. Journal of Titian Ramsey Peale, Assistant Naturalist of the Wilkes expedition, MSS (Division of Manuscripts, Library of Congress), VII, 38; Wilkes, *op. cit.,* 223.

6. Dana, *op. cit.,* 93–94, 107–08, 170–72.

7. *Ibid.,* 100, 475–76; Samuel Eliot Morison, *Maritime History of Massachusetts, 1783–1860* (Boston, 1923), 266–68.

8. Francis A. Thompson to Mrs. Lydia Thompson, October 27, 1832, D. Mackenzie Brown (ed.), *China Trade Days in California: Select Letters from the Thompson Papers, 1832–1863* (Berkeley, 1947), 8; John C. Jones to Alpheus B. Thompson, November 7, 1833, *ibid.,* 10–11; Simpson, quoted in H. H. Bancroft, *History of California* (San Francisco, 1886), IV, 477.

9. *Ibid.,* 475.

10. Ogden, *op. cit.,* 199–200; William Sturgis Hinckley to Thomas O. Larkin, July 21, 1841, George P. Hammond (ed.), *The Larkin Papers* (Berkeley, 1951), I, 97.

11. Wilkes, *op. cit.,* 168; Ogden, *op. cit.,* 201; also Adele Ogden, "Boston Hide Droghers Along California Shores," *California Historical Society Quarterly,* VIII (December, 1929), 299–300.

12. Bancroft, *op. cit.,* 224–25, 280.

13. Larkin to James G. Bennett, February 10, 1843, Hammond, *op. cit.,* II, 6–7; also Robert G. Cleland, *Early Sentiment for the Annexation of California 1835–1846* (Austin, 1915), 59.

14. Alfred Robinson to Larkin, March 3, 1844, Hammond, *op. cit.,* II, 79.

15. The Washington *Union,* May 22, 1846, advertised the books

of Greenhow, Gregg, Hastings, Robinson, Fremont, as well as Mitchell's map.

16. New York *Herald*, June 12, 1845; Sir George Simpson, *An Overland Journey Round the World, During the Years 1841 and 1842* (Philadelphia, 1847), 162.

17. Wilkes, *op. cit.*, 175.

18. Bidwell quoted in Bancroft, *op. cit.*, 347n. For the quality of the California horses see Rufus B. Sage, *Rocky Mountain Life; or Startling Scenes and Perilous Adventures in the Far West, During an Expedition of Three Years* (Boston, 1859), 245; *National Intelligencer*, November 22, 1847.

19. Wilkes, *op. cit.*, 211.

20. Simpson, *An Overland Journey*, 211; John Bidwell, "Life in California Before the Gold Discovery," *Century Magazine*, XIX (December, 1890), 170–173; Wilkes, *op. cit.*, 176, 182.

21. John C. Fremont, *Narrative of the Exploring Expedition to the Rocky Mountains in the Year 1842, and to Oregon and North California in the Years 1843–1844* (Washington, 1845), 357–60.

22. Quoted in J. D. B. Stillman, *Seeking the Golden Fleece* (San Francisco, 1877), 15–17.

23. See Larkin to John C. Calhoun, September 16, 1844, December 12, 1844, Hammond, *op. cit.*, II, 229, 332; Jones to Thompson, November 7, 1833, Brown, *op. cit.*, 11.

24. Dana, *op. cit.*, 86, 98; Mofras, *op. cit.*, 211–13.

25. Alice Eastwood (ed.), "Archibald Menzies' Journal of the Vancouver Expedition," *California Historical Society Quarterly*, II (January, 1924), 313.

26. Erwin Gustav Gudde (ed.), "Edward Vischer's First Visit to California," *California Historical Society Quarterly*, XIX (September, 1940), 196; Carter, *op. cit.*, 156; Dana, *op. cit.*, 67, 85–87, 114.

27. Jones to Larkin, July 16, 1841, Hammond, *op. cit.*, I, 16.

28. Carter, *op. cit.*, 164–65, 246, 248; Dana, *op. cit.*, 115–16, 130; Simpson, *Narrative*, I, 402–04.

29. *DeBow's Commercial Review*, VII (1847), 24; Eastwood, *op. cit.*, 330–31; Dana, *op. cit.*, 117–18.

30. Mofras, *op. cit.*, 170, 255–56; Dana, *op. cit.*, 187–88; Morrell *op. cit.*, 200; Belcher, *op. cit.*, 325; Carter, *op. cit.*, 217.

31. Morrell, *op. cit.*, 210–11; Wilkes, *op. cit.*, 163; Simpson, *Narrative*, I, 282, 285-86; Fremont, *op. cit.*, 369.

32. Carter, *op. cit.*, 143–44, 239–40; Dana, *op. cit.*, 463; Wilkes, *op. cit.*, 162; Simpson, *Narrative*, I, 283–84, 306.

33. Hinckley to Larkin, December 30, 1841, Thomas Cummins to Larkin, October, 1842, Hammond, *op. cit.*, I, 146, 304.

34. Thomas J. Farnham, *Life ond Adventures in California* (New York, 1846), 352, 355; *Niles' Register*, October 31, 1846; Morrell, *op. cit.*, 210–11; Lansford W. Hastings, *The Emigrant's Guide to Oregon and California* (Cincinnati, 1845), 79; Dana, *op. cit.*, 290.

35. *DeBow's Commercial Review*, VI (1847), 222.

36. St. Louis *Missouri Reporter*, June 24, 1845; Hastings, *op. cit.*, 131; *Hunt's Merchants' Magazine*, XVI (1847), 36–37.

CHAPTER 4

1. Eugène Duflot de Mofras, *Travels on the Pacific Coast*, translated by Marguerite Eyer Wilbur (Santa Ana, 1937), I, xxviii–xxix, 227n; Sir George Simpson, *Narrative of a Journey Round the World, During the Years 1841 and 1842* (London, 1847), I, 253; Rufus Kay Wyllys, "French Imperialists in California," *California Historical Society Quarterly*, VIII (June, 1929), 125.

2. See Abraham P. Nasatir (ed.), *French Activities in California: An Archival Calendar-Guide* (Stanford, 1945), 4; Charles Franklin Carter (ed.), "Duhault-Cilly's Account of California in the Years 1827–28," *California Historical Society Quarterly*, VIII (June, 1929), 132.

3. Mofras, *op. cit.*, xxiii; Abraham P. Nasatir (ed.), "The French Consulate in California, 1843-1856, Part I," *California Historical Society Quarterly*, XI (September, 1932), 202–03.

4. Mofras, *op. cit.*, II, 27–28; Gasquet to Minister of Foreign Affairs, 1843, Nasatir, "French Consulate," *op. cit.*, 216.

5. F. W. Beechey, *Narrative of a Voyage to the Pacific and Beering's Strait in the Years 1825, 26, 27, 28* (London, 1831), II, 63–64.

6. Simpson quoted in Nasatir, *French Activities in California*, 20; also Herman Leader (ed.), "A Voyage from the Columbia to California in 1840, From the Journal of Sir James Douglas," *California Historical Society Quarterly*, VIII (June, 1929), 107; Simpson, *op. cit.*, 407.

7. Alexander Forbes, *California: A History of Upper and Lower California* (London, 1839), 287; Pakenham, quoted in Ephraim Douglas Adams, "English Interest in the Annexation of California," *American Historical Review*, XIV (July, 1909), 746.

8. Charles Francis Adams (ed.), *Memoirs of John Quincy Adams* (Philadelphia, 1876), XI, 347–48; John Forsyth to Anthony Butler, August 6, 1835, Instructions to Mexico MSS, Department of State, National Archives, Vol. XV.

9. Powhatan Ellis to Forsyth, September 24, 1836, Dispatches

from Mexico MSS, Department of State, National Archives, Vol. VII; Mofras, *op. cit.*, II, 127; *Hunt's Merchants' Magazine*, XII (1845), 444–45.

10. Webster to Thompson, June 27, 1842, C. H. Van Tyne (ed.), *The Letters of Daniel Webster* (New York, 1902), 269–70; George Bancroft to Martin Van Buren, March 28, 1844, Van Buren Papers (Division of Manuscripts, Library of Congress); Thompson to Webster, April 29, 1842, Dispatches from Mexico, Vol. XI.

11. See Foster Rhea Dulles, *America in the Pacific* (Boston, 1938), 43; Richard W. Van Alstyne, "International Rivalries in the Pacific Northwest," *Oregon Historical Quarterly*, XLVI (September, 1945), 206; Adams, *Memoirs*, XI, 355.

12. Thomas O. Larkin to John C. Calhoun, August 18, 1844, George P. Hammond (ed.), *The Larkin Papers* (Berkeley, 1952), II, 205–06; William McKendree Gwin, "Memoirs on History of United States, Mexico, and California," MS (Bancroft Library, University of California), 4; Duff Green, *Facts and Suggestions* (New York, 1866), 85.

13. Richard Henry Dana, *Two Years Before the Mast, a Personal Narrative of Life at Sea* (New York, 1840), 210–12.

14. Wilkes, *op. cit.*, 152; Carter, *op. cit.*, 150–51; Mofras, *op. cit.*, I, 167; Sir George Simpson, *An Overland Journey Round the World, During the Years 1841 and 1842* (Philadelphia, 1847), 179, 197.

15. Thomas J. Farnham, *Life and Adventures in California* (New York, 1846), 352–53; Beechey, *op. cit.*, 9–10; Dana, *op. cit.*, 144; Mofras, *op. cit.*, I, 228–29; Carter, *op. cit.*, 218.

16. Mofras, *op. cit.*, II, 31; London *Times*, April 21, 1845; Simpson, *An Overland Journey*, 222–23; Gasquet to Minister of Foreign Affairs, 1843, Nasatir, "French Consulate," *op. cit.*, 216–17.

17. Baron Alleye de Cyprey to Thiers, August 21, 1840, Nasatir, *French Activities in California*, 153; Pageot to Guizot, January 27, 1843, *ibid.*, 70.

18. Cyprey to Guizot, February 23, 1843, *ibid.*, 171; Gasquet to Minister of Foreign Affairs, 1843, Nasatir, "French Consulate," *op. cit.*, 217.

19. Quoted in Adams, "English Interest," *op. cit.*, 749.

20. Pakenham to Aberdeen, February 24, 1843, Barron to Aberdeen, April 15, 1843, Nasatir, *French Activities*, 486–87; Simpson, quoted in Joseph Schafer (ed.), "Letters of Sir George Simpson, 1841–1843," *American Historical Review*, XIV (October, 1908), 92; Pakenham, quoted in Adams, "English Interest," *op. cit.*, 746.

21. See Pakenham to Palmerston, August 30, 1841, *ibid.*, 745–46.

22. Thompson to Webster, April 29, July 30, 1842, Dispatches from Mexico, Vol. XI.

23. Thompson to Webster, January 30, 1843, Webster Papers (Division of Manuscripts, Library of Congress); Green to Calhoun, October 28, 1844, J. Franklin Jameson (ed.), *Correspondence of John C. Calhoun, Annual Report of the American Historical Association* (1899), II, 978–79.

24. Beechey, *op. cit.*, 67; Mofras, *op. cit.*, II, 28, 32; Simpson, *Narrative*, I, 326–27; Barron to George Seymour, January 28, 1845, Foreign Office, Mexico, Vol. 189 (Justin Smith Transcripts, New York Public Library, Vol. II); Pageot to Guizot, December 28, 1845, Gueroult to Minister, August 13, December 10, 1845, Nasatir, *French Activities*, 76, 182–83, 185; Sam Houston to Charles Elliot, May 13, 1843, Public Record Office MSS, Foreign Office, Texas (Justin Smith Transcripts, New York Public Library, Vol. I).

25. Simpson, *Narrative*, I, 327–28; London *Times,* April 21, 1845; New Orleans *Picayune,* December 19, 1845.

26. London *Times,* April 21, October 1, 1845, February 11, 1846; *European Times* and Liverpool *Mercury,* quoted in New York *Herald,* September 21, 1845; other British papers quoted in New York *Herald,* August 19, September 21, 1845.

27. Quoted in *American Review,* III (January, 1846), 91–92.

28. Aberdeen to Bankhead, October 1, 1845, Public Record Office, Foreign Office, Vol. LXXXIX, Part II (Photostat, Manuscripts Division, Library of Congress).

29. Gasquet to Cyprey, October 14, 1845, Nasatir, "French Consulate," *op. cit.,* 344.

30. Cyprey to Minister, May 2, 1843, Cyprey to Guizot, May 21, 1844, Pageot to Guizot, June 12, July 15, 1845, Nasatir, *French Activities,* 73–75, 176–77; Guizot, quoted in *Niles' Register,* July 5, 1845.

31. Wyllys, *op. cit.,* 128–29; Adams, "English Interest," *op. cit.,* 747, 756–60, 763; George Lockhart Rives, *The United States and Mexico, 1821–1848* (New York, 1913), II, 98.

32. London *Times,* quoted in New York *Journal of Commerce,* November 12, 1845. See also *Foreign Quarterly Review* in *American Review,* III (January, 1846), 90.

CHAPTER 5

1. Baltimore *American,* quoted in *Niles' Register,* March 15, 1845.

2. James Schouler, *History of the United States of America Under the Constitution* (New York, 1894), IV, 498; conclusions on

public sentiment are based on a wide examination of the important newspapers and manuscripts for the period.

3. *Cong. Globe,* 28 Cong., 2 Sess., 88; New York *Herald,* July 2, 1845; St. Louis *Missouri Reporter,* May 31, 1845; New York *Journal of Commerce,* March 5, 1845; also William E. Dodd, "The West and the War with Mexico," *Journal of the Illinois State Historical Society,* V (1912), 163.

4. Robert Glass Cleland, *A History of California: The American Period* (New York, 1922), 156–57.

5. New York *Herald,* June 12, 1845; *Niles' Register,* June 7, 1845; New York *Sun,* May 28, 1845; Thomas O. Larkin to John C. Calhoun, March 22, June 6, 1845, Larkin to Moses Y. Beach, May 28, 1845, George P. Hammond (ed.), *The Larkin Papers* (Berkeley, 1952), III, 80–81, 202, 227.

6. St. Louis *Missouri Reporter,* June 9, 1845; New York *Herald,* May 31, 1845; *Niles' Register,* May 31, June 14, 1845; Justin H. Smith, *The War with Mexico* (New York, 1919), I, 322; Larkin to Calhoun, March 24, 1845, Jones to Larkin, August 10, 1845, Hammond, *op. cit.,* 95–96, 304.

7. New York *Herald,* July 2, 1845; Andrew Jackson to Robert J. Walker, March 11, 1844, Miscellaneous Papers (Division of Manuscripts, Chicago Historical Society); Duff Green, *Facts and Suggestions* (New York, 1866), 84.

8. New York *Journal of Commerce,* February 20, 1845; New York *Herald,* February 2, 1845; New York *Morning News,* quoted in the St. Louis *Missouri Reporter,* May 5, 1845.

9. James Gordon Bennett to James K. Polk, March 10, 1845, Robert H. Morris to Polk, August 9, 1845, Polk Papers (Division of Manuscripts, Library of Congress); Bennett to E. L. Childs, December 5, 1846, Moses Y. Beach to Larkin, December 24, 1845, Larkin Papers (Bancroft Library, University of California). For Ritchie's attitude, see Thomas Ritchie to W. Heiss, April 13, 1845, Polk Papers.

10. Washington *Union,* January 24, 1846.

11. Washington *Semi-Weekly Union,* June 16, 1845.

12. Cushing's letter appeared in *Niles' Register,* November 8, 1845, Washington *Union,* November 5, 1845, and February 17, 1846, St. Louis *Missouri Reporter,* February 28, 1846, and *American Review,* III (January, 1846), 88, 94; Thompson, quoted in *Niles' Register,* June 20, 1846; *DeBow's Commercial Review,* I (1846), 64.

13. "Reflections on the 'Balance of Power,'" *Democratic Review,* XVIII (April, 1846), 280–81; New York *Sun,* April 29, June 20, 1845; St. Louis *Missouri Reporter,* August 19, 1845; George S. Neuill

to William Allen, January 18, 1846, William Allen Papers (Division of Manuscripts, Library of Congress).

14. New York Herald, October 1, 1845; "Progress in America," Democratic Review, XVIII (1846), 92.

15. Niles' Register, May 31, 1845; H. H. Bancroft, History of Oregon (San Francisco, 1886), 508; Jacob P. Leese to Larkin, May 23, 1845, Hammond, op. cit., 192; Larkin to James Buchanan, November 4, 1845, Consular Letters MSS, Department of State, National Archives, Vol. I.

16. Hunt's Merchants' Magazine, XIV (1846), 353, 436; New York Herald, August 1, 1845; Cincinnati Enquirer, May 19, 1845; New Orleans Tropic, quoted in Niles' Register, May 17, 1845; Alfred Robinson to Larkin, May 29, 1845, Hammond, op. cit., 205.

17. Albert K. Weinberg, Manifest Destiny: A Study of Nationalist Expansionism in American History (Baltimore, 1935), 160–64; Cong. Globe, 28 Cong., 2 Sess., Appendix, 178.

18. "Annexation," Democratic Review, XVII (1845), 9; New York Herald, May 20, July 30, August 1, 1845; Robert Greenhow quoted in Washington Union, May 20, 1845.

19. John Law to Polk, June 26, 1845, Polk Papers.

20. Democratic Review, XVII (1845), 9; St. Louis Missourian quoted in the St. Louis Missouri Reporter, September 1, 1845.

21. Washington Semi-Weekly Union, May 22, 1845; New York Herald, October 24, 1845.

22. New York Sun, October 10, 1845; New York Journal of Commerce, October 11, 1845; New York Herald, January 30, 1846; Larkin to New York Journal of Commerce, July, 1845, Larkin Papers.

23. Lansford W. Hastings, The Emigrant's Guide to Oregon and California (Cincinnati, 1845), 40–41, 81–82, 91, 133, 152.

24. Cong. Globe, 28 Cong., 2 Sess., 219; Columbus Ohio State Journal, December 1, 1845; Larkin to New York Journal of Commerce, July, 1845, Larkin Papers.

25. Democratic Review, XVII (1845), 9; Charles Fletcher to Polk, July 24, 1845, Polk Papers; Whitney to Buchanan, June 4, 1845, Buchanan Papers (Manuscripts Division, Pennsylvania Historical Society).

26. Asa Whitney, "Intercommunication Between the Atlantic and Pacific Oceans," DeBow's Commercial Review, IV (1847), 166–67; New York Herald, July 11, 1845; Washington National Intelligencer, April 6, 1845; New York Sun, November 11, 1845; American Review, I (1845), 432; Robert R. Russel, Improvement of Communication with the Pacific Coast as an Issue in American Politics, 1783–1864 (Cedar Rapids, 1948), 11–13.

27. *DeBow's Commercial Review,* III (1847), 447, 477–78, 483; *Niles' Register,* November 29, 1845; Washington *Union,* January 9, 1846, May 5, 1847; Albert Gilliam, *Travels in Mexico, During the Years 1843 and 1844* (Aberdeen, 1847), 269; Josiah Gregg to A. Yell, December 16, 1845, Polk Papers.

28. Russel, *op. cit.,* 12–13; New York *Herald,* September 28, December 12, 1846; Fletcher to Polk, July 8, 1845, Polk Papers.

29. *DeBow's Commercial Review,* I (1846), 23–24; *Hunt's Merchants' Magazine,* XVII (1847), 385; C. Darragh in *Cong. Globe,* 29 Cong., 1 Sess., 171.

30. *DeBow's Commercial Review,* III (1847), 211; Russel, *op. cit.,* 15; Sam Cartwright to Robert J. Walker, November 30, 1845, Walker Papers (Division of Manuscripts, Library of Congress); Fletcher to Polk, July 8, 1845, Polk Papers; Columbus *Ohio State Journal,* December 1, 1845; C. Goodyear in *Cong. Globe,* 29 Cong., 1 Sess., 109.

31. Quoted in New York *Herald,* December 20, 1846. See also H. S. Clark in *Cong. Globe,* 29 Cong., 1 Sess., 247.

32. Gilliam, *op. cit.,* 269, 281.

33. Larkin quoted in Richard W. Van Alstyne, *American Diplomacy in Action* (Stanford, 1944), 510; Gilliam, *op. cit.,* 287; Webster to Fletcher Webster, March 11, 1845, Fletcher Webster (ed.), *The Private Correspondence of Daniel Webster* (Boston, 1857), II, 204. Farnham concluded that San Francisco would become "the seat of the ruling maritime power of that half of the world."

34. St. Louis *Missouri Reporter,* September 1, 1845.

35. "California," *American Review,* III (1846), 85–86.

36. Gilliam, *op. cit.,* 287–88.

CHAPTER 6

1. Quoted in Oscar Osburn Winther, *The Great Northwest* (New York, 1947), 147–48.

2. See Thomas Hart Benton, *Thirty Years' View* (New York, 1856), II, 661; Robert L. Schuyler, "Polk and the Oregon Compromise," *Political Science Quarterly,* XXVI (September, 1911), 446–47; James Buchanan to Louis McLane, July 12, 1845, John Bassett Moore (ed.), *The Works of James Buchanan* (Philadelphia, 1909), VI, 193–94.

3. *Ibid.,* 190–91; Buchanan to Richard Pakenham, July 12, 1845, *ibid.,* 203–04.

4. New York *Sun,* July 8, 1845; Milo Milton Quaife (ed.), *The*

Diary of James K. Polk (Chicago, 1910), I, 63, 75; John Mason to McLane, August 12, 1845, Polk Papers (Division of Manuscripts, Library of Congress). McLane was warned to make no further overtures for a compromise.

5. Quaife, *Diary of Polk*, I, 4–5, 106–07.

6. *Cong. Globe*, 29 Cong., 1 Sess., Appendix, 3.

7. Calhoun to Green, April 19, 1844, Instructions to Mexico MSS, Department of State, National Archives, Vol. XV.

8. Robert Armstrong to Polk, August 4, October 19, 1845, Polk Papers.

9. William Parrott to Buchanan, May 13, 1845, Dispatches from Mexico MSS, Department of State, National Archives, Vol. XII.

10. Larkin to Buchanan, July 10, 1845, Larkin to New York *Journal of Commerce*, July, 1845, George P. Hammond (ed.), *The Larkin Papers* (Berkeley, 1952), III, 266–67, 292–93; Buchanan to Larkin, October 17, 1845, Abraham P. Nasatir (ed.), "The French Consulate in California, 1843–1856, Part I," *California Historical Society Quarterly*, XI (September, 1932), 201; Buchanan to Louis McLane, October 14, 1845, Polk Papers.

11. New York *Herald*, September 15, 1845.

12. *Cong. Globe*, 29 Cong., 1 Sess., 7; Quaife, *Diary of Polk*, I, 71; Buchanan to Larkin, October 17, 1845, John Bassett Moore (ed.), *The Works of James Buchanan* (Philadelphia, 1909), VI, 275-77.

13. Norfolk *Herald*, November 11, 1845, quoted in *Niles' Register*, November 15, 1845.

14. Ingersoll to Polk, March 23, 1845, Polk Papers; Larkin to New York *Journal of Commerce*, July, 1845, Hammond, *op. cit.*, 294–95.

15. Waddy Thompson to Webster, January 30, 1843, Webster Papers (Division of Manuscripts, Library of Congress); Talmadge to Polk, March 30, 1845, Polk Papers; Coxe to Buchanan, August 4, September 5, 1845, Buchanan Papers (Division of Manuscripts, Pennsylvania Historical Society).

16. Thompson to Webster, November 30, 1842, Dispatches from Mexico, Vol. XI.

17. Washington *Semi-Weekly Union*, July 3, 1845.

18. Ben Green to Upshur, April 8, 1844, Dispatches from Mexico, Vol. XII; New Orleans *Picayune*, September 27, 1845.

19. A. Yell to Polk, September 10, 1845, Polk Papers; New York *Herald*, September 17, 1845.

20. St. Louis *Missouri Reporter*, August 19, 1845; Aaron Leggett to William Marcy, October 16, 1845, *California Historical Society Quarterly*, XI (March, 1932), 33–34.

21. Polk to Buchanan, August 7, 1845, Buchanan Papers; Polk to A. O. J. Nicholson, July 28, 1845, Polk to Armstrong, July 28, 1845, Charles J. Ingersoll to Polk, August 20, 1845, Polk to William H. Haywood, August 9, 1845, Polk Papers; St. Louis *Missouri Reporter,* July 29, 1845.

22. Buchanan to Polk, August 11, 1845, J. Catron to Polk, August 16, 1845, Polk Papers; *Niles' Register,* November 15, 1845.

23. Washington *Semi-Weekly Union,* October 20, 1845.

24. Levi D. Stamm to Polk, October 2, 1845, David Lambert to Polk, December 16, 1845, Polk Papers; Buchanan to Larkin, October 17, 1845, Nasatir, *op. cit.,* 201.

25. Bancroft to John D. Sloat, June 24, 1845, Major Edwin A. Sherman, *The Life of the Late Rear-Admiral John Drake Sloat* (Oakland, 1902), 51.

26. Parrott to Buchanan, August 26, 1845, Dispatches from Mexico, Vol. XII; Quaife, *Diary of Polk,* I, 33, 35, 91–92; Bankhead to Pakenham, October 16, 1845, Foreign Office, Mexico, Vol. 187 (Justin Smith Transcripts, New York Public Library, Vol. II).

27. Buchanan to Slidell, November 10, 1845, Instructions to Mexico MSS, Department of State, National Archives, Vol. XVI.

28. Polk to A. J. Donelson, June 15, 1845, Donelson Papers (Division of Manuscripts, Library of Congress); New York *Journal of Commerce,* November 26, 1845.

29. Buchanan to Slidell, November 10, 1845, Instructions to Mexico, Vol. XVI.

30. Buchanan to Larkin, October 17, 1845, Moore, *op. cit.,* 275; Quaife, *Diary of Polk,* I, 34–35, 71; William Sturgis to Bancroft, August 22, 1845, Bancroft Papers (Division of Manuscripts, Massachusetts Historical Society); Bancroft to Sloat, June 24, 1845, Sherman, *op. cit.,* 51.

31. Washington *Union,* June 13, 1846; Bankhead to Aberdeen, December 30, 1845, Foreign Office, Mexico, Vol. 187 (Justin Smith Transcripts, New York Public Library, Vol. II); London *Times* correspondent, quoted in New York *Journal of Commerce,* March 24, 1846.

32. Slidell to Buchanan, January 14, 1846, Dispatches from Mexico, Vol. XII; Alexander Slidell Mackenzie to Trist, January 2, 1846, Trist Papers (Division of Manuscripts, Library of Congress).

33. Quaife, *Diary of Polk,* I, 306–11.

34. *Ibid.,* 312, 317.

CHAPTER 7

1. Albert K. Weinberg, *Manifest Destiny: A Study of Nationalist Expansionism in American History* (Baltimore, 1935), 145.

2. *Cong. Globe*, 29 Cong., 1 Sess., 134, 200; *Democratic Review*, XVIII (1846), 93.

3. See Nathan Sargent, *Public Men and Events from the Commencement of Mr. Monroe's Administration, in 1817, to the close of Mr. Fillmore's Administration, in 1853* (Philadelphia, 1875), II, 278–79; *Cong. Globe*, 29 Cong., 1 Sess., 342, 136.

4. Daniel W. Howe, "The Mississippi Valley in the Movement for Fifty-Four Forty or Fight," *Proceedings* of the Mississippi Valley Historical Association (1911–1912), 104; *Cong. Globe,* 29 Cong., 1 Sess., Appendix, 289; Chas. B. Stickney to Allen, January 2, 1846, John N. Barger to Allen, December 12, 1845, G. James *et al* to Allen, December 22, 1845, J. M. Clark to Allen, January 19, 1846, Saml. G. Mickles to Allen, January 9, 1846, Allen Papers (Manuscripts Division, Library of Congress). Letters in the James Buchanan papers for the period reveal the same spirit.

5. Thos. H. H. Cocke to Allen, April 10, 1846, Allen Papers; George Plitt to Nicholas P. Trist, March 19, 1846, Nicholas P. Trist Papers (Manuscripts Division, Library of Congress); George D. Phillips to Cobb, December 30, 1845, Ulrich B. Phillips (ed.), *The Correspondence of Robert Toombs, Alexander H. Stephens, and Howell Cobb, Annual Report of the American Historical Association* (1911), II, 70.

6. *Cong. Globe,* 29 Cong., 1 Sess., 249; John C. Calhoun to Thomas G. Clemson, June 11, 1846, J. Franklin Jameson (ed.), *The Correspondence of John C. Calhoun, Annual Report of the American Historical Association* (1899), II, 697.

7. *Cong. Globe*, 29 Cong., 1 Sess., Appendix, 117, 239.

8. *Ibid.*, 99.

9. William Sturgis to —————, June 6, 1845, Bancroft Papers (Division of Manuscripts, Massachusetts Historical Society); William Sturgis, *The Oregon Question: Substance of a Lecture Before the Mercantile Library Association, Delivered January 22, 1845* (Boston, 1845), 27–28.

10. *Cong. Globe*, 29 Cong., 1 Sess., Appendix, 212.

11. Sturgis, *op. cit.*, 25; Albert Gallatin, *The Oregon Question*, in Henry Adams (ed.), *The Writings of Albert Gallatin* (Philadelphia, 1879), III, 493–94.

12. Wilkes, quoted in Thomas J. Farnham, *Travels in the Great*

Western Prairies, October 21–December 4, 1839, in Reuben Gold Thwaites (ed.), *Early Western Travels 1748–1846,* XXIX (Cleveland, 1906), 76; R. R. Waldron to Bancroft, April 22, 1845, Bancroft Papers; *Cong. Globe,* 29 Cong., 1 Sess., Appendix, 218.

13. *Ibid.,* 277, 309–10.

14. *Cong. Globe,* 29 Cong., 1 Sess., Appendix, 216. For Calhoun's views on the importance of preserving Oregon's ports for the United States, see Robert G. Cleland, "Asiatic Trade and the American Occupation of the Pacific Coast," *Annual Report of the American Historical Association* (1914), I, 285–86.

15. Albert M. Gilliam, *Travels in Mexico, During the Years 1843 and 1844* (Aberdeen, 1847), 268–270; Thompson, quoted in *Niles' Register,* June 20, 1846.

16. Larkin to New York *Journal of Commerce,* July, 1845, Thomas O. Larkin Papers (Bancroft Library, University of California); New York *Journal of Commerce,* October 18, 30, 1845. See also Lyon Gardiner Tyler, *Letters and Times of the Tylers* (Richmond, 1885), II, 448.

17. London *Times,* May 15, 1846. This article was widely quoted in the United States.

18. Richmond *Enquirer,* June 25, 1846; New York *Herald,* February 3, 1846.

19. "The Oregon Question," *North American Review,* LXII (January, 1846), 214–16, 218–226.

20. Nashville *Union,* quoted in New York *Herald,* May 16, 1845. See also New York *Herald,* June 12, 1846; *American Review,* I (April, 1845), 427; New York *Journal of Commerce,* October 30, 1845; *Niles' Register,* March 22, 1845, May 2, 30, 1846; New Orleans *Picayune,* April 22, 1846; *Boston Daily Advertiser,* May 2, 1846. For the British view, see John McLaughlin to Sir George Simpson, March 3, 1845, Foreign Office, Vol. 89 (Photostat, Manuscripts Division, Library of Congress); *London Illustrated News,* October 11, 1845.

21. Columbus *Ohio State Journal,* June 20, 1846; New York *Journal of Commerce,* March 21, 1846; New York *Sun,* January 7, 1846.

22. J. Hamilton to Polk, March 2, 1846, Polk Papers (Division of Manuscripts, Library of Congress); Columbus *Ohio State Journal,* January 19, 1846; Allan Nevins (ed.), *The Diary of Philip Hone 1828–1851* (New York, 1936), 751.

23. "A Democrat" to Allen, January 10, 1846, Allen Papers. The *Louisville Journal* (January 14, 1846) expressed the same view. It insisted that the Northwest was not behind its ardent leaders in Congress.

24. Milo Milton Quaife (ed.), *The Diary of James K. Polk* (Chicago, 1910), I, 246; New York *Journal of Commerce,* quoted in St. Louis *Missouri Reporter,* January 9, 1846.

25. James Buchanan to Louis McLane, February 26, 1846, Hunter Miller (ed.), *Treaties and Other International Acts of the United States of America* (Washington, 1937), V, 60; New York *Herald,* January 4, April 6, 1846; Daniel Webster to Sears, January 17, 1846, Fletcher Webster (ed.), *The Private Correspondence of Daniel Webster* (Boston, 1857), II, 215.

26. Melvin Jacobs, *Winning Oregon* (Caldwell, Idaho, 1938), 242. For similar views, see Frederick Merk, "British Government Propaganda and the Oregon Treaty," *American Historical Review,* XL (1934), 38; Joseph Schafer, "The British Attitude toward the Oregon Question, 1815–1846," *American Historical Review,* XVI (1911), 275; Ray Allen Billington, *Westward Expansion* (New York, 1949), 507.

27. See St. George L. Sioussat, "James Buchanan," in Samuel Flagg Bemis (ed.), *The American Secretaries of State and Their Diplomacy* (New York, 1928), V, 260; Thomas P. Martin, "Free Trade and the Oregon Question, 1842–1846," *Facts and Factors in Economic History: Articles by Former Students of Edwin Francis Gay* (Cambridge, 1932), 485; Frederick Merk, "The British Corn Crisis of 1845–46 and the Oregon Treaty," *Agricultural History,* VIII (1934), 98–103.

28. Sioussat, *op. cit.,* 261; Miller, *op. cit.,* 48. This widely accepted thesis has been fully developed by Thomas P. Martin. See Martin, *op. cit.,* 490 ff. See also Thomas P. Martin, "Cotton and Wheat in Anglo-American Trade and Politics, 1846–52," *Journal of Southern History,* I (1935), 315.

29. Martin, *op. cit.,* 477–78, 488; Quaife, *Diary of Polk,* I, 191–92; New York *Herald,* January 17, 1846.

30. Merk has discounted the free-trade argument. See Merk, "The British Corn Crisis of 1845–46 and the Oregon Treaty," *op. cit.,* 106–19; *Cong. Globe,* 29 Cong., 1 Sess., 460; *Cong. Globe,* 29 Cong., 1 Sess., Appendix, 174.

31. Frederick Merk, "The Oregon Pioneers and the Boundary," *American Historical Review,* XXIX (1924), 696. For similar conclusions, see Jacobs, *op. cit.,* 219–20; Richard W. Van Alstyne, "International Rivalries in the Pacific Northwest," *Oregon Historical Quarterly,* XLVI (1945), 209; and Leslie M. Scott, "Influence of American Settlement upon the Oregon Boundary Treaty of 1846," *Oregon Historical Quarterly,* XXIX (1928), 1–19.

32. Aberdeen to Peel, September 25, 1844, October 17, 1845, in Miller, *op. cit.*, V, 25, 48.

33. Frederick Merk, "British Government Propaganda and the Oregon Treaty," *American Historical Review*, XL (1934), 40–41, 51, 55–58, 61; *The Edinburgh Review*, LXXXII, No. CLXV (July, 1845), 263–64; *London Illustrated News*, VII (December 27, 1845), 407; *Quarterly Review*, LXXVII, No. CLIV (March, 1846), 564–65, 603.

34. Julius W. Pratt, "James K. Polk and John Bull," *The Canadian Historical Review*, XXIV (1943), 341–349; Weinberg, *op. cit.*, 153.

35. Albert Gallup to Walker, March 14, 1846, Walker Papers (Division of Manuscripts, Library of Congress).

36. *Cong. Globe*, 29 Cong., 1 Sess., Appendix, 4; Quaife, *Diary of Polk*, I, 135; Miller, *op. cit.*, 60.

37. Buchanan to McLane, January 29, February 4, 26, 1846, in John Bassett Moore (ed.), *The Works of James Buchanan* (Philadelphia, 1909), VI, 367, 372, 377.

38. Crittenden to Letcher, March 9, 1846, in Mr. Chapman Coleman, *The Life of John J. Crittenden* (Philadelphia, 1871), I, 235; Quaife, *Diary of Polk*, I, 268, 275, 453.

39. *Cong. Globe*, 29 Cong., 1 Sess., 549; Hannegan, quoted in New York *Tribune*, June 8, 1847; Quaife, *Diary of Polk*, I, 273.

40. *Ibid.*, 268, 279.

41. Richard Rush to Nicholas P. Trist, September 21, 1846, Trist Papers, as quoted in Eugene Irving McCormac, *James K. Polk: A Political Biography* (Berkeley, 1922), 610n.

42. Webster, quoted in Miller, *op. cit.*, V, 89; Pakenham, quoted in *ibid.*, 90. See also Calhoun to Clemson, April 25, 1846, Jameson, *op. cit.*, 689. Wrote Calhoun, "This great change has been effected by the Senate against the entire influence of the Executive. . . ."

43. See Miller, *op. cit.*, V, 33, 59, 61, 63–66, 71, 77, 79–80.

44. *Cong. Globe*, 29 Cong., 1 Sess., Appendix, 867; New York *Herald*, June 12, 1846.

CHAPTER 8

1. *Cong. Globe*, 29 Cong., 1 Sess., Appendix, 643; *Cong. Globe*, 29 Cong., 2 Sess., Appendix, 223.

2. *Cong. Globe*, 29 Cong., 1 Sess., Appendix, 946; Joshua Giddings, *Speeches in Congress* (Boston, 1853), 188, 282–83; Corwin to Greene, June 16, 1846, L. Belle Hamlin (ed.), "Letters of Thomas Corwin to William Greene, 1841–1851," *Quarterly Publication of*

the *Historical and Philosophical Society of Ohio,* XIII (1918), 16; Giddings to Howells, June 8, 1846, Miscellaneous Papers (Division of Manuscripts, Chicago Historical Society); Robert C. Winthrop, *Addresses and Speeches on Various Occasions* (Boston, 1852), I, 560. Whig attacks on the Mexican War created such an enormous volume of evidence against the Polk administration that historians to this day have had trouble in extricating themselves from it.

3. Thomas H. Bradley to J. Knox Walker, August 17, 1845, Polk Papers (Division of Manuscripts, Library of Congress).

4. "Will There Be War with Mexico?" *American Review,* II (1845), 229; John C. Calhoun to Thomas G. Clemson, May 28, 1846, J. Franklin Jameson (ed.), *The Correspondence of John C. Calhoun, Annual Report of the American Historical Association* (1899), II, 692.

5. New York *Herald,* January 27, 1846; Abiel Abbot Livermore, *The War with Mexico Reviewed* (Boston, 1850), 50; Marcy to P. M. Wetmore, February 1, 1846, Marcy Papers (Division of Manuscripts, Library of Congress); James Buchanan to Polk, February 17, 1846, Slidell to Polk, December 29, 1845, Polk Papers.

6. New York *Herald,* March 1, 1846; St. Louis *Missouri Reporter,* April 18, 1846; Washington *Union,* April 27, 1846; Philadelphia *North American* in Richmond *Enquirer,* May 2, 1846; London *Times,* May 7, 1846.

7. *Democratic Review,* XXII (1848), 8–9, 115–17; Washington *Union,* August 28, 1847.

8. Winfield S. Scott, *Memoirs of Lieut.-General Scott* (New York, 1864), II, 381; R. W. Ripley, *The War with Mexico* (New York, 1849), I, 25–26.

9. Milo Milton Quaife (ed.), *The Diary of James K. Polk* (Chicago, 1910), I, 397.

10. *Ibid.,* 395–96, 400–401, 407, 437–38, II, 15.

11. *Ibid.,* I, 16, 473; George C. Strong to Marcy, March 2, 1845, Marcy to Wetmore, May 28, 1846, Marcy Papers; John Hogan to Polk, September 2, 1846, Polk Papers; New York *Sun,* August 6, 1846; *Niles' Register,* September 12, 1846; New York *Courier and Enquirer,* quoted in *Niles' Register,* August 29, 1846.

12. New York *Journal of Commerce,* September 24, 28, 1846; *Niles' Register,* September 19, 1846; Washington *National Intelligencer,* September 30, 1846; Marcy to Wetmore, September 27, November 14, 1846, Marcy Papers.

13. Bancroft to Samuel Hooper, June 16, 1846, Bancroft Papers (Division of Manuscripts, Massachusetts Historical Society).

14. Hooper to Bancroft, June 19, 25, 1846, *ibid.*

15. Quaife, *Diary of Polk*, II, 16; Bancroft to Hooper, June 22, 1846, Bancroft Papers.

16. For Bancroft's instructions of June 8, July 12, and August 13, 1846, see *House Ex. Doc. 60*, 30 Cong., 1 Sess., 237–41; Sloat, quoted in Major Edwin A. Sherman, *The Life of the Late Rear-Admiral John Drake Sloat* (Oakland, 1902), 85.

17. Polk to William H. Polk, October 2, 1846, Polk Letter Books (Manuscripts Division, Library of Congress); Donelson to Buchanan, December 22, 1846, Buchanan Papers (Division of Manuscripts, Pennsylvania Historical Society); Buchanan to Donelson, January 29, 1847, Donelson Papers (Division of Manuscripts, Library of Congress).

18. Donelson to Polk, May 23, 1846, Polk Papers; *Cong. Globe*, 29 Cong., 2 Sess., Appendix, 191; Buchanan to Genl. James Shields, April 23, 1847, Buchanan Papers.

19. "The War," *Democratic Review*, XX (1847), 100; *American Review*, V (1847), 239.

20. Springfield *Illinois State Register*, July 10, 1846; Baltimore *American* in New York *Herald*, July 29, 1847.

21. F. W. Pickens to Buchanan, July 5, 1846, Buchanan Papers; New York *Herald*, July 27, November 19, December 6, 13, 1846; Washington *Union*, September 1, 16, 1847, February 28, March 2, 1848; New York *Sun*, July 24, 1846; *Niles' Register*, September 11, 1847; New York *Tribune*, March 10, 1847; New York *Journal of Commerce*, December 17, 1846.

22. Quaife, *Diary of Polk*, I, 126–27, 397; *Cong. Globe*, 29 Cong., 1 Sess., 783; Washington *Union*, May 13, 21, 1846.

23. Quaife, *Diary of Polk*, II, 13–14; Dix to Silas Wright, July 10, 1846, Morgan Dix (ed.), *Memoirs of John Adams Dix* (New York, 1883), I, 202.

24. Daniel Webster, *The Works of Daniel Webster* (Boston, 1864), V, 160; Giddings, *op. cit.*, 190–91; New York *Morning News* quoted in Washington *National Intelligencer*, May 15, 1846.

25. Newspapers quoted in *National Intelligencer*, June 20, 1846.

26. Thomas Hart Benton, *Thirty Years' View* (New York, 1856), II, 680.

27. Quaife, *Diary of Polk*, I, 224–25, 228–30; Bancroft to Connor, May 13, 1846, *House Ex. Doc. 60*, 30 Cong., 1 Sess., 774; Marcy to Taylor, July 9, 1846, Marcy Papers.

28. *Cong. Globe*, 29 Cong., 1 Sess., 1015–16; *Niles' Register*, June 27, 1846.

29. Buchanan to Mexican Minister of Foreign Relations, July 27,

1846, Communications to Foreign Sovereigns and States MSS, Department of State, National Archives, Vol. II.

30. Pakenham to Aberdeen, June 28, 1846, Foreign Office, America, Vol. 497 (Justin Smith Transcripts, New York Public Library, Vol. II); Quaife, *Diary of Polk*, II, 129–30, 132; St. Louis *Missouri Reporter*, June 9, 1846; New York *Journal of Commerce*, July 10, 1846; New York *Sun*, August 10, 1846.

31. Quaife, *Diary of Polk*, II, 76–77; *Cong. Globe*, 29 Cong., 1 Sess., 1211; Rush to Buchanan, August 18, 1846, Buchanan Papers.

32. *Cong. Globe*, 29 Cong., 1 Sess., 1214–15.

33. Manuel Rejon to Buchanan, August 31, 1846, Notes from the Mexican Legation MSS, Department of State, National Archives, Vol. IV; Buchanan to Mexican Minister of Foreign Relations, September 26, 1846, Communications to Foreign Sovereigns and States, Vol. II; Quaife, *Diary of Polk*, II, 145.

34. Marcy to Taylor, September 22, October 13, 1846, Marcy to Wetmore, October 16, 1846, Marcy Papers; Scott to Crittenden, October 19, 1846, Crittenden Papers (Division of Manuscripts, Library of Congress).

35. Quaife, *Diary of Polk*, II, 157–58, 222–23; *Cong. Globe*, 29 Cong., 2 Sess., 9.

36. Webster to D. Fletcher Webster, August 6, 1846, C. H. Van Tyne (ed.), *The Letters of Daniel Webster* (New York, 1902), 343; Mexico City *El Republicano*, February 24, 1847, Polk Papers; London *Times*, November 9, 1846.

37. *Democratic Review*, XX (1847), 101; Polk to Donelson, December 29, 1846, Donelson Papers.

38. *Cong. Globe*, 29 Cong., 2 Sess., 9, 305. (Italics mine.)

CHAPTER 9

1. *Cong. Globe*, 29 Cong., 2 Sess., Appendix, 48.

2. Corwin to Oran Follett, February 4, 1847, L. Belle Hamlin (ed.), "Selections from the Follett Papers," *Quarterly Publication of the Historical and Philosophical Society of Ohio*, IX (1914), 90; *American Review*, V (1847), 325, VI (1847), 11.

3. Joshua R. Giddings, *Speeches in Congress* (Boston, 1853), 266–67.

4. Robert C. Winthrop, *Addresses and Speeches on Various Occasions* (Boston, 1852), I, 601–02; Josiah Morrow (ed.), *Life and Speeches of Thomas Corwin* (Cincinnati, 1896), 300.

5. Richmond *Enquirer*, May 28, 1846; New Orleans *Picayune*,

June 12, 1846; New York *Journal of Commerce,* May 25, July 16, November 30, 1846.

6. New York *Herald,* February 26, 1847; *Cong. Globe,* 29 Cong., 2 Sess., 401; *ibid.,* Appendix, 353.

7. *Cong. Globe,* 29 Cong., 2 Sess., 148, 290–91, 306.

8. *Ibid.,* 1; Milo Milton Quaife (ed.), *The Diary of James K. Polk* (Chicago, 1910), II, 288.

9. Scott to Marcy, May 21, 1846, *Senate Doc. 378,* 29 Cong., 1 Sess., 5; Quaife, *Dairy of Polk,* I, 414–15, 417–18.

10. *Ibid.,* II, 119, 139–40.

11. *Ibid.,* 181, 211, 229; Scott to Taylor, September 26, 1846, Scott to John J. Crittenden, October 19, 1846, Mrs. Chapman Coleman, *The Life of John J. Crittenden* (Philadelphia, 1871), I, 257–58, 260.

12. Quaife, *Diary of Polk,* II, 236, 249–50.

13. *Ibid.,* 242; Scott to Marcy, January 16, 1847, Marcy Papers (Division of Manuscripts, Library of Congress); Winfield S. Scott, *Memoirs of Lieut.-General Scott* (New York, 1864), II, 399; William H. Polk to Polk, November 6, 1846, Polk Papers (Division of Manuscripts, Library of Congress).

14. Quaife, *Diary of Polk,* II, 275-77, 281, 304; Poinsett to Kemble, March 10, 1847, Gilpin Papers (Division of Manuscripts, Pennsylvania Historical Society).

15. Benton to Martin Van Buren, January 26, 1847, Benton to Polk, March 10, 1847, Van Buren Papers (Division of Manuscripts, Library of Congress).

16. Quaife, *Diary of Polk,* II, 352, 355–56; Scott, *op. cit.,* 399–401; Scott to Marcy, January 27, 1847, Marcy Papers.

17. Quaife, *Diary of Polk,* II, 385–86, 452–53, 480, 482, 492–93.

18. George W. Thompson to Van Buren, December 23, 1846, Van Buren Papers; Calhoun to Coryell, November 7, 1846, J. Franklin Jameson (ed.), *The Correspondence of John C. Calhoun, Annual Report of the American Historical Association* (1899), II, 709.

19. H. D. Gilpin to Van Buren, April 6, 1847, G. A. Worth to Van Buren, March 30, 1847, J. K. Paulding to Van Buren, February 5, 1847, John Law to Van Buren, August 2, 1847, John Dix to Van Buren, May 16, 1846, Van Buren Papers.

20. Dix to Van Buren, May 16, 1846, Poinsett to Van Buren, May 26, 1846, Blair to Van Buren, November 27, 1846, Van Buren to Worth, May 23, 1847, *ibid;* Wright to Dix, November 5, 1846, R. H. Gillet, *The Life and Times of Silas Wright* (Albany, 1874), II, 1723–24.

21. Gideon Welles to Van Buren, July 28, 1846, Van Buren

Papers; Richard K. Cralle (ed.), *Speeches of John C. Calhoun* (New York, 1854), IV, 370, 380; Calhoun to James Edward Calhoun, July 2, 1846, Jameson, *op. cit.*, 698.

22. Calhoun to James Edward Calhoun, December 12, 1846, Calhoun to Thomas G. Clemson, July 11, 1846, James Hamilton to Calhoun, August 12, 1846, *ibid.*, 701, 714, 1089; Byrdsall to Calhoun, August 4, 1846, Fisher to Calhoun, September 24, 1846, James Chestney to Calhoun, November 23, 1846, Chauncey S. Boucher and Robert P. Brooks (eds.), *Correspondence Addressed to John C. Calhoun 1837–1849, Annual Report of the American Historical Association* (1929), 357, 360–61; Isaac S. Pennybacker to Polk, August 13, 1846, Polk Papers.

23. Quaife, *Diary of Polk*, II, 371.

24. *Ibid.*, 347–48.

25. *Ibid.*, 375–78; Nathan Sargent, *Public Men and Events* (Philadelphia, 1875), II, 311.

26. Quaife, *Diary of Polk*, II, 368.

27. *Ibid.*, 341, 348, 369, 371–72; Welles to Van Buren, July 28, 1846, Van Buren Papers; W. V. Pettit to Welles, January 5, 1847, incomplete letter, June 8, 1846, February, 1847, Welles Papers (Division of Manuscripts, Library of Congress); *Cong. Globe*, 29 Cong., 2 Sess., Appendix, 99; Matthias Martin to William Allen, February 16, 1847, Allen Papers (Division of Manuscripts, Library of Congress).

28. Quaife, *Diary of Polk*, II, 289, 307–08, 334, 340.

29. Allen Nevins (ed.), *The Diary of Philip Hone 1828–1851* (New York, 1936), 790; Columbus *Ohio State Journal*, May 19, 1846.

30. Giddings to Oran Follett, July 26, 1847, L. Belle Hamlin (ed.), "Selections from the Follett Papers, III," *Quarterly Publication of the Historical and Philosophical Society of Ohio*, X (1915), 31; James Russell Lowell, *The Biglow Papers* (Boston, 1876), 6; Samuel D. Burchard, *A Sermon Preached in the Thirteenth Street Presbyterian Church, New York, on Thanksgiving Day, November 25, 1847* (New York, 1848), 20.

31. *Cong. Globe*, 29 Cong., 2 Sess., 330; *Greenville* (S. C.) *Mountaineer*, October 15, 1847, in *Niles' Register*, October 30, 1847; Washington *Union*, October 25, 1847.

32. *Cong. Globe*, 29 Cong., 2 Sess., Appendix, 211, 218.

33. *Cong. Globe*, 29 Cong., 2 Sess., 326.

34. *Ibid.*, Appendix, 217; Sargent, *op. cit.*, 314; Cincinnati *Atlas*, quoted in Washington *National Intelligencer*, February 24, 1847; Thompson, quoted in *Niles' Register*, October 30, 1847.

35. Winthrop, *op. cit.*, 581.

36. Justin H. Smith, *The War with Mexico* (New York, 1919), II, 283.

37. Ralph Waldo Emerson, *Journals*, ed. by Edward Waldo Emerson and Waldo Emerson Forbes (Boston, 1912), VII, 547.

38. Quaife, *Diary of Polk*, II, 436.

CHAPTER 10

1. Milo Milton Quaife (ed.), *The Diary of James K. Polk* (Chicago, 1910), II, 340.

2. Bayard Tuckerman (ed.), *The Diary of Philip Hone, 1828–1851* (New York, 1910), II, 347.

3. For an excellent and sympathetic evaluation of Trist's life and character, see Louis Martin Sears, "Nicholas P. Trist, A Diplomat with Ideals," in *Mississippi Valley Historical Review*, XI (June, 1924), 85–98.

4. See Edward Livingston to Martin Van Buren, March 17, 1829, W. C. Rives to Van Buren, March 19, 1829, Schuyler Hamilton to Hamilton Fish, April 20, 1869, Trist Papers (Division of Manuscripts, Library of Congress); Aaron Vail to Buchanan, October 24, 1845, Buchanan Papers (Manuscripts Division, Pennsylvania Historical Society).

5. Letter of recommendation written for Trist by J. A. G. Davis, April 17, 1831, Trist Papers; Francis P. Blair to Van Buren, August 25, 1847, Van Buren Papers (Manuscripts Division, Library of Congress).

6. Andrew J. Donelson to James K. Polk, July 15, 1847, Polk Papers (Manuscripts Division, Library of Congress).

7. James Buchanan to Trist, April 15, 1847, Instructions to Mexico MSS, Department of State, National Archives, Vol. XVI; Quaife, *Diary of Polk*, II, 471–75; Robert Walker to Trist, April 15, 1847, Trist Papers.

8. Trist to Mrs. Trist, April 18, 25, 28, May 6, 1847, Trist to Denis Prieur, April 28, 1847, Trist Papers.

9. New York *Herald*, April 20, 21, 1847; Boston *Post*, quoted in *Niles' Register*, April 24, May 22, 1847; M. J. R. [Trist's sister] to Trist, May 22, 1847, Trist Papers.

10. Quaife, *Diary of Polk*, II, 480; J. C. Rives to Van Buren, May 12, 1847, Van Buren Papers; William L. Marcy to P. M. Wetmore, July 26, 1847, Marcy Papers (Manuscripts Division, Library of Congress).

11. Trist to Mrs. Trist, May 15, 21, 1847; Winfield Scott to

Trist, May 29, 1847, Trist Papers; Scott to Marcy, June 4, 1847, in Letter Group 94, Adjutant General, Letters Received, No. 882–S–1847, War Department (National Archives).

12. Blair to Van Buren, July 7, 1847, Van Buren Papers; Marcy to Wetmore, July 16, 1847, Marcy Papers.

13. London *Globe,* quoted in New York *Herald,* August 9, 1847; New York *Courier and Enquirer,* quoted in Washington *Union,* July 13, 1847.

14. Quaife, *Diary of Polk,* III, 57–59; Marcy to Scott, May 31, July 12, 1847, Marcy Papers; Polk to General William O. Butler, August 7, 1847, Polk Letter Books (Manuscripts Division, Library of Congress); for Buchanan's opinions of Trist, see Buchanan to Trist, June 14, July 13, 19, 1847, Trist Papers.

15. Trist to Charles Bankhead, June 6, 7, 1847, Trist to Buchanan, June 13, 1847, Trist Papers; Edward Thornton to Bankhead, June 14, 1847, Foreign Office, Mexico, Vol. 210 (Justin Smith Transcripts, New York Public Library, Vol. III). Trist's documentary proof of Polk's alleged purposes can be found in the Trist Papers, Vol. XXXI.

16. Trist to Scott, June 25, 1847, Trist Papers; Scott to Marcy, July 25, 1847, in Letter Group 94, Adjutant General, Letters Received, No. 883–S–1847, War Department. For Trist's opinions of Scott, see Trist to Buchanan, July 7, 23, August 24, 1847, Trist to Mrs. Trist, October 18, 1847, Trist Papers.

17. Marcy to Wetmore, September 26, 1847, Marcy Papers.

18. Pacheco to Buchanan, August 20, 1847, Bankhead to Trist, August 20, 21, 1847, Trist Papers; Scott to Marcy, August 28, 1847, Winfield Scott, *Memoirs of Lieut.-General Scott* (New York, 1864), II, 498–99; Robert Anderson, *An Artillery Officer in the Mexican War, 1846–1847* (New York, 1911), 317.

19. Kendall's letter was widely quoted in the American press. See New Orleans *Picayune,* September 9, 1847; New Orleans *Delta,* September 10, 1847; New York *Herald,* September 18, 19, 1847; *Niles' Register,* September 18, 1847; Marcy to Wetmore, September 26, 1847, Marcy Papers.

20. See New York *Herald,* October 4, 5, 6, 7, 1847.

21. Buchanan to Trist [Private], October 25, 27, 1847, Trist Papers.

22. London *Chronicle,* November 12, 1847; W. J. Hammersley to Gideon Welles, August 1, 1847, Welles Papers (Manuscripts Division, Library of Congress). For a similar view of Mexican affairs, see New York *Herald,* May 31, July 9, September 1, December 20, 1847.

23. New York *Herald,* October 22, 1847; Persifer Smith to Marcy, September 28, 1847, Marcy Papers; W. C. Rives to John Crittenden,

February 8, 1847, Crittenden Papers (Manuscripts Division, Library of Congress); Smith to Franklin Pierce, December 13, 1847, Pierce Papers (Manuscripts Division, Library of Congress); Harvey Curtis to Polk, May 20, 1847, Polk Papers.

24. New York *Sun,* November 30, December 9, 1847; *Cong. Globe,* 30 Cong., 1 Sess., Appendix, 2.

25. *Niles' Register,* January 22, 1848; Calvin Colton (ed.), *The Works of Henry Clay* (New York, 1857), III, 66; speech of R. M. T. Hunter in Senate, January 3, 1848, *Historical Pamphlets,* Durrett Collection, University of Chicago Library; Quaife, *Diary of Polk,* III, 226–27; George Dallas to Conley, January 25, 1848, *Niles' Register,* February 19, 1848.

26. *Cong. Globe,* 30 Cong., 1 Sess., Appendix, 2; *Cong. Globe,* 30 Cong., 1 Sess., 302.

27. John C. Calhoun to Duff Green, November 9, 1847, J. Franklin Jameson (ed.), *Correspondence of John C. Calhoun, Annual Report of the American Historical Association* (1899), II, 740; New York *Herald,* December 13, 1847.

28. *Niles' Register,* January 15, 1848; Daniel Webster, *The Works of Daniel Webster* (Boston, 1864), V, 266.

29. See John D. P. Fuller, "The Slavery Question and the Movement to Acquire Mexico, 1846–1848," *Mississippi Valley Historical Review,* XXI (June, 1934), 31–48.

30. See Edward Thornton to Trist, November 22, 24, 1847, Trist Papers.

31. Trist to Thornton, December 4, 1847, Trist to Buchanan, December 6, 1847, *ibid.* Historians have generally been critical of Trist's decision to remain in Mexico, although none has seen fit to condemn its results.

32. Notes, January, 1848, Trist Papers.

33. William de Drusina to Trist, April 11, 1848, Thornton to Trist, May 26, 1848, *ibid.*

34. Notes, January 3, 1848, Buchanan to Trist, October 25, 1847, Memorandum of Trist, January 4, 1848, *ibid.*

35. See Hunter Miller (ed.), *Treaties and Other International Acts of the United States of America* (Washington, 1937), V, 335–37, 362; Notes, January 4, 5, 7, 1848, Trist Papers.

36. Gideon J. Pillow to Polk, May 29, 1844, Polk Papers; Notes in Trist Papers, 1848; Washington *Union,* June 18, 1847; U. S. Grant, *Personal Memoirs of U. S. Grant* (New York, 1895), I, 94; Scott, *Memoirs,* II, 416–17.

37. Pillow to Trist, October 9, 1847, Notes, 1848, Trist Papers.

38. Washington *Union,* November 2, 1847; Quaife, *Diary of Polk,*

III, 246, 251, 253, 262–63; Polk to Pillow, December 19, 1847, Polk Letter Books. Pillow wrote to Polk on October 28, but this letter has never been found.

39. Marcy to Scott, January 13, 1848, Marcy Papers; Quaife, *Diary of Polk,* III, 266–67, 293; Crampton to Palmerston, January 27, 1848, Public Record Office, Foreign Office, America, Vol. 480 (Justin H. Smith Transcripts, Manuscripts Division, New York Public Library, Vol. III).

40. Quaife, *Diary of Polk,* III, 266–67, 283, 286, 300–301.

41. Washington *Union,* January 1, 1848; New York *Herald,* January 27, 1848.

42. Quaife, *Diary of Polk,* III, 312–17; Marcy to Butler, January 26, 1848, Marcy Papers.

43. Quaife, *Diary of Polk,* III, 345–46, 357–58; New York *Herald,* February 3, 1848; New Orleans *Picayune,* February 16, 1848; Washington *Union,* February 23, 1848.

44. Quaife, *Diary of Polk,* III, 365; Blair to Van Buren, March 3, 1848, Van Buren Papers.

45. Quaife, *Diary of Polk,* III, 365; Thomas Hart Benton, *Thirty Years' View* (New York, 1856), II, 710.

46. See Martin Van Buren, Jr., to Van Buren, February 3, 1848, in Van Buren Papers.

Chapter 11

1. New York *Herald,* March 31, December 11, 1844, July 4, August 9, September 17, 1845; "The Texas Question," *Democratic Review,* XV (1844), 252; F. Catron to Andrew Jackson, March 9, 1845, Jackson Papers (Manuscripts Division, Library of Congress); Charles Douglass to Gideon Welles, March 3, 1845, Welles Papers (Manuscripts Division, Library of Congress).

2. Charles Wilkes, *Narrative of the United States Exploring Expedition During the Years 1838, 1839, 1840, 1841, 1842* (Philadelphia, 1845), V, 182–83.

3. Charles Fletcher to James K. Polk, July 8, 1845, William Field to Polk, February 10, 1846, Polk Papers (Manuscripts Division, Library of Congress); St. Louis *Missourian,* April 17, 1846; St. Louis *Missouri Reporter,* September 1, 1845, February 12, 1846.

4. *Cong. Globe,* 29 Cong., 1 Sess., Appendix, 184.

5. Benton, quoted in *Niles' Register,* July 4, 1846.

6. Baltimore *American,* quoted in New Orleans *Picayune,* July 2, 1846; *Niles' Register,* July 4, 1846.

7. J. W. Boddam-Whetham, *Western Wanderings: A Record of Travel in the Evening Land* (London, 1874), 288.

8. See New York *Herald,* September 3, November 19, December 30, 1846; New York *Sun,* August 1, 1846; Washington *Union,* April 15, 1847.

9. New York *Journal of Commerce,* December 17, 1846.

10. Baltimore *American,* September 14, 1847, quoted in *Niles' Register,* September 18, 1847.

11. Corwin to Greene, March 16, 1848, L. Belle Hamlin (ed.), "Letters of Thomas Corwin to William Greene, 1841–1851," *Quarterly Publication of the Historical and Philosophical Society of Ohio,* XIII (1918), 27–28; New York *Herald,* February 25, 1848.

12. *Cong. Globe,* 30 Cong., 1 Sess., Appendix, 2–3.

13. *Cong. Globe,* 30 Cong., 1 Sess., 901, 990.

14. Lucien B. Chase, *History of the Polk Administration* (New York, 1850), 288–94.

15. Democratic Party, *The Democratic Party and Its Fruits* (Washington, 1848), 6.

16. Dillon to Minister, October 12, 1852, Abraham P. Nasatir (ed.), *French Activities in California: An Archival Calendar-Guide* (Stanford University, 1945), 96.

17. William M. Gwin to Lewis Cass, June 4, 1858, State Department Archives (Photostat in Gwin Papers, Bancroft Library, University of California).

BIBLIOGRAPHICAL ESSAY

This bibliographical essay is limited primarily to those sources which are essential for an understanding of the mercantile and political themes in American expansion to the Pacific. Such purpose, to be sure, narrows the field but imperceptibly, for all major sources on national policy in the forties illustrate the persistence of commercial motivation in the nation's westward extension and the importance of the Oregon and California issues in domestic policies. This book does not bring new materials to light, but endeavors rather to bring new significance to the old. For the convenience of the reader, a full citation is included for each item the first time it appears in every chapter.

MANUSCRIPTS. Manuscript collections of leading Americans fill a specific requirement in the study of American expansion. This was a national movement, and it could achieve its purpose through diplomacy alone. Its course, therefore, was determined largely by those who formulate and execute American foreign policy. Manuscripts comprise one key to the understanding of sectional and personal ambitions and the impact of these on national parties and policies.

Most of the manuscript collections cited in this work are located in the Library of Congress. The James K. Polk and the Nicholas P. Trist papers are important for policy formulation, but many other collections reveal the political aspects of the expansionist issue. Among these are the letters of Martin Van Buren, Gideon Welles, William L. Marcy, Robert Walker, William Allen, Andrew Jackson, Andrew Johnson, Andrew J. Donelson, Franklin Pierce, Richard Cralle, Duff Green, Francis P. Blair, Daniel Webster, Henry Clay, Salmon P. Chase, John J. Crittenden, and W. C. Rives. Of importance also are the photostats of British Foreign Office correspondence dating from the years of the Polk administration.

Collections scattered through a half dozen other libraries are of sufficient pertinence to be noted. The National Archives (Department of State) contain the correspondence between the Polk administration and American representatives in Mexico. This material, in fact, is essential to trace the formulation of American objectives along the Pacific of all the Presidents and Secretaries of State from the Jackson administration to that of Polk. Of some value in the political realm are the papers of Lewis Cass in the William L. Clements Library at Ann Arbor, the James Buchanan manuscripts at the Pennsylvania Historical Society, and the miscellaneous papers in the Chicago Historical Society. Revealing the close relationship between the Polk administration and New England merchants are the George Bancroft papers at the Massachusetts Historical Society. In the Bancroft Library, University of California, are the Thomas O. Larkin and William M. Gwin papers, as well as the Fremont collection. Of considerable value also are the Justin H. Smith transcripts of British Foreign Office manuscripts in the New York Public Library.

PUBLIC DOCUMENTS. Congressional opinion can have an enormous effect on the formulation of foreign policy, and this was especially true during the Polk administration. The *Congressional Globe* reveals in great detail both personal and sectional views toward the regions of Texas, Oregon, and California. House and Senate documents are good expressions of public sentiment and include much of the diplomatic correspondence, but much of this material is available also in private manuscript collections, such as the Trist papers, and in the National Archives.

MEMOIRS, DIARIES, AND COLLECTED PAPERS. Because of their great variety and quantity, printed sources are perhaps as essential as manuscripts. Polk's diary, edited by Milo Milton Quaife, is required for determining administration policy toward both Oregon and California. This is a curious diary, candid and complete, and it reveals unblushingly the inconsistencies to which political pressures drove Polk in his conduct of diplomacy.

Of special relevance for the study of politics and expansion are the numerous standard printed collections of letters and speeches of leading Americans of the forties. Three important compilations published by the American Historical Association are J. Franklin Jameson (ed.), *The Correspondence of John C. Calhoun, Annual Report of the American Historical Association* (1899); Chauncey S. Boucher and Robert P. Brooks (eds.), *Correspondence Addressed to John C. Calhoun 1837–1849, Annual Report* (1929); and Ulrich B. Phillips (ed.), *The Correspondence of Robert Toombs, Alexander H. Stephens, and Howell Cobb, Annual Report* (1911).

Of considerable importance also are other volumes of published correspondence: John Spencer Bassett (ed.), *Correspondence of Andrew Jackson,* VI (Washington, 1933); Morgan Dix (ed.), *Memoirs* of *John Adams Dix,* I (New York, 1883); R. H. Gillet (ed.), *The Life and Times of Silas Wright,* II (Albany, 1874); L. Belle Hamlin (ed.), "Letters of Thomas Corwin to William Greene, 1841–1851," *Quarterly Publication of the Historical and Philosophical Society of Ohio,* XIII (1918); Hamlin (ed.), "Selections from the Follett Papers," *ibid.,* IX (1914), X (1915), XIII (1918); Mrs. Chapman Coleman, *The Life of John J. Crittenden,* I (Philadelphia, 1871); John Bassett Moore (ed.), *The Works of James Buchanan,* VI (Philadelphia, 1909); William Wetmore Story, *Life and Letters of Joseph Story,* II (Boston, 1851); Lyon Gardiner Tyler, *Letters and Times of the Tylers,* II (Richmond, 1885); C. W. Van Tyne (ed.), *The Letters of Daniel Webster* (New York, 1902); and Fletcher Webster (ed.), *The Private Correspondence of Daniel Webster,* II (Boston, 1857).

Useful compilations of speeches include Joshua R. Giddings, *Speeches in Congress* (Boston, 1853); Calvin Colton (ed.), *The Works of Henry Clay,* III (New York, 1857); Richard K. Cralle (ed.), *Speeches of John C. Calhoun Delivered in the House of Representatives and the Senate of the United States,* IV (New York, 1854); John R. Dickinson (ed.), *Speeches, Correspondence, etc., of Daniel S. Dickinson* (New York, 1867); Stephen A. Douglas, *Life and Speeches of Stephen A. Douglas* (New York, 1860); Frank Moore (ed.), *Speeches of Andrew Johnson* (Boston, 1865); Josiah Morrow (ed.), *Life and Speeches of Thomas Corwin* (Cincinnati, 1896); and Robert C. Winthrop, *Addresses and Speeches on Various Occasions,* I (Boston, 1852).

Anyone concerned with European interests along the Pacific Coast must acknowledge a debt to Abraham P. Nasatir for his translating and editing of French diplomatic correspondence. This work can be found in Nasatir (ed.), *French Activities in California: An Archival Calendar-Guide* (Stanford, 1945) and in "The French Consulate in California, 1843–1856," *California Historical Society Quarterly,* XI (1932). For a survey of the British interest see Ephraim D. Adams, "English Interest in the Annexation of California," *American Historical Review,* XIV (July, 1909). Of great value is the volume of Hunter Miller (ed.), *Treaties and Other International Acts of the United States of America,* V (Washington, 1937).

TRAVELERS' ACCOUNTS. Many travelers who skirted the coasts of Oregon and California during the two decades prior to their acquisition by the United States have left accounts of their impressions. Since these numerous published adventures comprised the chief source of knowledge of those distant regions, they had a distinct impact on the formulation of attitudes toward the Pacific Coast throughout the

Atlantic states. These men came by way of the sea, and they measured the quality of the coastal regions in terms of their access to the sea. The objectives which these travelers, as a group, selected were those which the Polk Administration achieved. Their impressions were clear and astonishingly similar, and they were most graphic when they dealt with waterways.

Most significant of the accounts of American travelers are Captain Benjamin Morrell, *A Narrative of Four Voyages to the South Sea* (New York, 1832); W. S. W. Ruschenberger, *A Voyage Round the World in 1835, 1836, and 1837* (Philadelphia, 1838); Richard Henry Dana, *Two Years Before the Mast, a Personal Narrative of Life at Sea* (New York, 1840); Charles Wilkes, *Narrative of the United States Exploring Expedition During the Years 1838, 1839, 1840, 1841, 1842*, IV, V (Philadelphia, 1845); John C. Fremont, *Narrative of the Exploring Expedition to the Rocky Mountains in the Year 1842, and to Oregon and North California in the Years 1843–1844* (Washington, 1845); Thomas J. Farnham, *Travels in the Great Western Prairies, October 21–December 4, 1839*, in Reuben Gold Thwaites (ed.), *Early Western Travels 1748–1846*, XXIX (Cleveland, 1906); Farnham, *Life and Adventures in California* (New York, 1846); and Albert Gilliam, *Travels in Mexico, During the Years 1843 and 1844* (Aberdeen, 1847).

For two significant French accounts, see Eugène Duflot de Mofras, *Travels on the Pacific Coast*, translated by Marguerite Eyer Wilbur, 2 vols. (Santa Ana, 1937) and Charles Franklin Carter (ed.), "Duhault-Cilly's Account of California in the Years 1827–28," *California Historical Society Quarterly*, VIII (June, 1929). The noted British accounts are F. W. Beechey, *Narrative of a Voyage to the Pacific and Beering's Strait in the Years 1825, 26, 27, 28*, II (London, 1831); Sir Edward Belcher, *Narrative of a Voyage Round the World Performed in Her Majesty's Ship Sulphur during the Years 1836–1842*, I (London, 1843); Sir George Simpson, *Narrative of a Journey Round the World, During the Years 1841 and 1842*, I (London, 1847); and Simpson, *An Overland Journey Round the World, During the Years 1841 and 1842* (Philadelphia, 1847). Full citations to other accounts of less significance can be found in the notes for Chapters II, III, and IV. Three books not genuinely travelers' accounts but of similar nature and importance are Alexander Forbes, *California: A History of Upper and Lower California* (London, 1839); Robert Greenhow, *The History of Oregon and California* (Boston, 1844); and Lansford W. Hastings, *The Emigrant's Guide to Oregon and California* (Cincinnati, 1845).

NEWSPAPERS. Newspapers reflected well the motivation toward compromise on the Oregon question in 1846 and American attitudes toward California from the spring of 1845 until the Trist mission. Those newspapers which best reveal the expansionist mind are the New York *Herald,* the New York *Sun,* the New York *Journal of Commerce,* the Washington *Union* and the *Semi-Weekly Union, Niles' Register,* the St. Louis *Missourian,* the St. Louis *Missouri Reporter,* and the New Orleans *Picayune.* Of less importance but still useful are such papers as the Washington *National Intelligencer,* the New York *Tribune,* the Boston *Evening Transcript,* the Richmond *Enquirer,* the Charleston *Mercury,* the Columbus *Ohio State Journal,* the Cincinnati *Enquirer,* the *Maysville Eagle,* the Lexington *Observer and Reporter,* and the Springfield *Illinois State Register.* The London *Times* was amazingly acute in analyzing American expansionist sentiment.

PERIODICALS. Several periodicals of the forties contain significant articles regarding Oregon and California. These are the partisan *American Review* (Whig) and the *Democratic Review,* such commercial journals at *DeBow's Commercial Review* and *Hunt's Merchants' Magazine,* the *North American Review,* and the British *Edinburgh Review, Quarterly Review,* and *London Athenaeum.*

SECONDARY WORKS. Many writers have left an indelible impression on the historiography of American expansion to the Pacific. The files of the *Hispanic American Historical Review,* the *Pacific Historical Review,* the *California Historical Society Quarterly,* the *Oregon Historical Quarterly,* and the *Pacific Northwest Quarterly* contain many articles and collected papers that are essential to the study of the westward movement into Oregon and California. Of special significance is the work of Abraham P. Nasatir, Adele Ogden, and Charles Franklin Carter in the *CHSQ,* and of George Vern Blue in the *OHQ.*

General works dealing with the diplomacy of the Oregon and California questions are Jesse S. Reeves, *American Diplomacy under Tyler and Polk* (Baltimore, 1907); Eugene I. McCormac, *James K. Polk: A Political Biography* (Berkeley, 1922); and St. George L. Sioussat, "James Buchanan," in Samuel F. Bemis (ed.), *The American Secretaries of State and Their Diplomacy,* V (New York, 1928). On the theme of national expansionism are Albert K. Weinberg, *Manifest Destiny: A Study of Nationalist Expansionism in American History* (Baltimore, 1935) and Ephraim D. Adams, *The Power of Ideals in American History* (New Haven, 1913). Some observations on the role of the Pacific in American expansionism can be found in Robert

Glass Cleland, "Asiatic Trade and the American Occupation of the Pacific Coast," *Annual Report of the American Historical Association* (1914); H. Morse Stephens and Herbert E. Bolton (eds.), *The Pacific Ocean in History* (New York, 1917); and Foster Rhea Dulles, *America in the Pacific* (Boston, 1938).

Since the pioneering movement plays a minor role in the expansionist theme of this book, no bibliography on emigration into Oregon and California is included. Works which trace the growth of United States commercial interests along the Pacific Coast are Samuel Eliot Morison, *Maritime History of Massachusetts 1783–1860* (Boston, 1923); Alfred Robinson, *Life in California* (New York, 1846); Foster Rhea Dulles, *The Old China Trade* (Boston, 1930); Adele Ogden, *The California Sea Otter Trade, 1784–1848* (Berkeley, 1941); Ogden, "Boston Hide Droghers Along California Shores," *California Historical Society Quarterly*, VIII (December, 1929); and William Sturgis, "The Northwest Fur Trade, and the Indians of the Oregon Country, 1788–1830," *Old South Leaflet*, No. 219.

Writings on the 54-40 movement include Daniel W. Howe, "The Mississippi Valley in the Movement for Fifty-Four Forty or Fight," *Proceedings* of the Mississippi Valley Historical Association (1911–1912); Thomas Hart Benton, *Thirty Years' View*, II (New York, 1856); and Robert L. Schuyler, "Polk and the Oregon Compromise," *Political Science Quarterly*, XXVI (September, 1911); and stressing the problems confronting Polk because of pressures within the Democratic Party is Norman A. Graebner, "Polk, Politics, and Oregon," The East Tennessee Historical Society's *Publications*, XXIV (1952).

Most historians have accepted the view that England alone receded in the Oregon compromise. Their writings, therefore, are devoted largely to understanding the British position. A general survey of the British view is Joseph Schafer, "The British Attitude toward the Oregon Question, 1815–1846," *American Historical Review*, XVI (January, 1911). Analyses which attribute the British inclination to compromise to the American pioneers are Frederick Merk, "Oregon Pioneers and the Boundary Settlement," *American Historical Review*, XXIX (July, 1924); Melvin Jacobs, *Winning Oregon* (Caldwell, Idaho, 1938); Richard W. Van Alstyne, "International Rivalries in the Pacific Northwest," *Oregon Historical Quarterly*, XLVI (1945); and Leslie M. Scott, "Influence of American Settlement upon the Oregon Boundary Treaty of 1846," *Oregon Historical Quarterly*, XXIX (1928).

The free-trade thesis is developed by Thomas P. Martin, "Free Trade and the Oregon Question, 1842–1846," *Facts and Factors in Economic History: Articles by Former Students of Edwin Francis Gay*

(Cambridge, 1932) and is challenged in Frederick Merk, "The British Corn Crisis of 1845–46 and the Oregon Treaty," *Agricultural History*, VIII (1934). On Aberdeen's leadership and British opinion are Merk, "British Government Propaganda and the Oregon Treaty," *American Historical Review*, XL (October, 1934) and Merk, "British Party Politics and the Oregon Treaty," *American Historical Review*, XXXVII (July, 1932). That Polk favored compromise because of his fear of war is seen in Julius W. Pratt, "James K. Polk and John Bull," *The Canadian Historical Review*, XXIV (1943). For the importance of ports in Oregon diplomacy see Merk, *Albert Gallatin and the Oregon Problem: A Study in Anglo-American Diplomacy* (Cambridge, 1950) and Norman A. Graebner, "Maritime Factors in the Oregon Compromise," *Pacific Historical Review*, XX (November, 1951).

On American interest in California the basic survey is Robert Glass Cleland, *Early Sentiment for the Annexation of California 1835–1846* (Austin, 1915). For the British interest in California, see Ephraim D. Adams, "English Interest in the Annexation of California," *American Historical Review*, XIV (July, 1909) and Lester G. Engelson, "Proposals for the Colonization of California by England in Connection with the Mexican Debt to British Bondholders, 1837–1846," *California Historical Society Quarterly*, XVIII (1939). On the French interest are Rufus Kay Wyllys, "French Imperialists in California," *California Historical Society Quarterly*, VIII (June, 1929); of some value on this theme also is George Vern Blue, "France and the Oregon Question," *Oregon Historical Quarterly*, XXXIV (1933). An analysis of United States expansionist sentiment toward California in 1845 is found in Norman A. Graebner, "American Interest in California, 1845," *Pacific Historical Review*, XXII (February, 1953).

Polk's Mexican policy is traced in the writings of Jesse S. Reeves, Eugene I. McCormac, and St. George L. Sioussat which have been noted. Such standard works on the Mexican War as Justin H. Smith, *The War with Mexico*, 2 vols. (New York, 1919) and George Lockhart Rives, *The United States and Mexico, 1821–1848*, 2 vols. (New York, 1913) also contain material on Polk's diplomacy and the coming of the Mexican War. Since the military aspects of the Mexican War play a minor role in this work, the rather extensive bibliography on that subject is excluded. This book is more concerned with wartime territorial objectives and administration policy that secured those goals. On this theme is Norman A. Graebner, "James K. Polk's Wartime Expansionist Policy," *The East Tennessee Historical Society's Publications*, XXIII (1951).

General studies of the treaty of Guadalupe Hidalgo are Julius Klein, *The Making of the Treaty of Guadaloupe Hidalgo on February 2, 1848* (Berkeley, 1905) and Jesse S. Reeves, "The Treaty of Guadaloupe Hidalgo," *American Historical Review*, X (January, 1905). On attitudes toward Mexico are Edward G. Bourne, "The United States and Mexico, 1847–1848," *American Historical Review*, V (April, 1900) and John D. P. Fuller, *The Movement for the Acquisition of All Mexico, 1846–1848* (Baltimore, 1938).

Writings on Nicholas P. Trist have generally been quite critical. An effort to rehabilitate him is in Louis M. Sears, "Nicholas P. Trist, A Diplomat with Ideals," *Mississippi Valley Historical Review*, XI (June, 1924). Tracing Trist's relations with the Polk administration and his rejection for political reasons is Norman A. Graebner, "Party Politics and the Trist Mission," *Journal of Southern History*, XIX (May, 1953).

INDEX